FREEDOM'S PIONEER
John McGrath's Work in Theatre, Film and Television

'a gifted, passionate, dogged, sometimes intransigent, eloquent man, who, as well as making us sit up and listen, always wanted—as he so often said—to give us a good night out.'

'[McGrath's plays] combined high ideals, lack of pretension, artistic integrity, political sincerity and commercial success.'

from Richard Eyre's Foreword

Despite recognition of the central importance of John McGrath's work, very little has been written about him. This is the first full-length study of his work and collects together contributions from film and television directors, actors, designers, writers, university researchers and journalists, many of whom worked with McGrath.

Contributors and interviewees
John Bett • Ian Brown • John Bull • John Clifford • Stewart Conn • Robert Dawson Scott • Maria DiCenzo • Richard Eyre • Jack Gold • Stephen Greenhorn • Nadine Holdsworth • Pamela Howard • Troy Kennedy Martin • Stephen Lacey • Liz Lochhead • Tom McGrath • Elizabeth MacLennan • Ros Merkin • Robin Nelson • Bill Paterson • Randall Stevenson • Olga Taxidou • Peter Thomson • Jenny Tiramani

Also published by University of Exeter Press: *John McGrath—Plays for England* selected and introduced by Nadine Holdsworth.

David Bradby is Professor of Drama and Theatre Studies at Royal Holloway, University of London. **Susanna Capon** has worked as a director for the BBC and as an independent producer; she is now Senior Lecturer in Media Arts at Royal Holloway, University of London.

Cover image: John McGrath, by kind permission of Elizabeth MacLennan.

Exeter Performance Studies

Exeter Performance Studies aims to publish the best new scholarship from a variety of sources, presenting established authors alongside innovative work from new scholars. The list explores critically the relationship between theatre and history, relating performance studies to broader political, social and cultural contexts. It also includes titles which offer access to previously unavailable material.

Series editors: Peter Thomson, Professor of Drama at the University of Exeter; Graham Ley, Reader in Drama and Theory at the University of Exeter; Steve Nicholson, Reader in Twentieth-Century Drama at the University of Sheffield.

Also published by University of Exeter Press

Freedom's Pioneer

John McGrath's Work in Theatre, Film and Television

edited by

David Bradby and Susanna Capon

UNIVERSITY
of
EXETER
PRESS

First published 2005 by
University of Exeter Press
Reed Hall, Streatham Drive
Exeter EX4 4QR
UK
www.exeterpress.co.uk

British Library Cataloguing in Publication Data
A catalogue record for this book is available
from the British Library.

Hardback ISBN 0 85989 748 6
Paperback ISBN 0 85989 749 4

Typeset in 10pt Plantin Light by
Kestrel Data, Exeter, Devon

Printed in Great Britain by
Antony Rowe Ltd, Chippenham, Wiltshire

CONTENTS

Part Five—Working with John

ILLUSTRATIONS

NOTES ON CONTRIBUTORS

David Bradby is Professor of Drama and Theatre Studies at Royal Holloway, University of London. His books include *Modern French Drama 1940–1990, Beckett: Waiting for Godot, The Theater of Michel Vinaver* and (with Annie Sparks) *Mise en Scène: French Theatre Now*. He has translated Lecoq's *The Moving Body* and has translated and edited plays by Michel Vinaver and Bernard-Marie Koltès. With Maria M. Delgado, he edits the *Contemporary Theatre Review* and also co-edited *The Paris Jigsaw: Internationalism and the City's Stages*.

Ian Brown was Drama Director of the Arts Council of Great Britain (1986–94) and Professor of Drama (1995–2002), Head of the Department of Drama (1995–99) and Dean of Arts (1999–2002) at Queen Margaret University College, Edinburgh. He has been Chair of the Scottish Society of Playwrights on three occasions, is author of over twenty plays produced throughout the UK, and is also a freelance arts and educational consultant.

John Bull is Professor of Film and Drama at the University of Reading. He has published widely, mostly in the field of modern and contemporary theatre and drama, including *New British Political Dramatists, Stage Right: Crisis and Recovery in Contemporary British Mainstream Theatre*, and also in post-Restoration theatre, including *Vanbrugh and Farquhar*. He has edited a volume of Howard Brenton's early plays: *Howard Brenton: Three Plays: A Sky Blue Life, How Beautiful With Badges, Measure for Measure*, and is working on a six-volume project, *British and Irish Dramatists Since World War II*, the first two volumes of which have been published, with the third volume in press. The author of three produced plays, one a musical adaptation of Alfred Jarry's *Ubu* plays, he has also directed many contemporary and classic plays.

Susanna Capon, Senior Lecturer in Media Arts at Royal Holloway, University of London, is the Course Director for the MA in Producing Film and Television and has worked in academia since 1995. She was instrumental in setting up the Association of Media Practice Educators and chaired it for its first two years. She currently chairs the Executive Board of the Journal of Media Practice. She started her career as a director in the BBC before becoming an independent producer and has worked in documentaries and in drama. She is writing a biography of the writer David Mercer.

Robert Dawson Scott, writer on cultural affairs and theatre critic for *The Times* in Scotland, is founder of the Critics Awards for Theatre in Scotland, Scotland's national theatre awards. He was formerly arts editor of *The Scotsman* and has worked in arts journalism for fifteen years.

Maria DiCenzo, Associate Professor in the Department of English and Film Studies, Wilfrid Laurier University, Ontario, Canada, is author of *The Politics of Alternative Theatre in Britain, 1968–1990: The Case of 7:84 (Scotland)* and has published works on feminist theatre, Italian Canadian theatre and cultural funding. Currently she is working in the areas of media history and social movements on periodicals of the British suffrage movement.

Richard Eyre was Artistic Director of The Royal National Theatre from 1988 to 1997. He has directed numerous classics and new plays as well as directing the BAFTA award-winning BBC television drama *Tumbledown*. He has published *Utopia and Other Places*, *National Service* and, with Nicholas Wright, *Changing Stages: A View of British Theatre in the Twentieth Century*.

Nadine Holdsworth, Lecturer in Theatre and Performance in the School of Theatre Studies, University of Warwick, has written on 7:84, Theatre Workshop, Glasgow Unity and contemporary Scottish theatre. She edited John McGrath's collected writings on theatre, *Naked Thoughts That Roam About* and his *Plays for England* (University of Exeter Press, 2005). She is currently writing a book on Joan Littlewood.

Stephen Lacey is Principal Lecturer, Research and Graduate Studies, at Manchester Metropolitan University. His main research interests are post-war British drama/theatre and television drama. He is co-director of an AHRB-funded research project, 'Cultures of British Television Drama, 1960–82'. Publications include *British Realist Theatre: The New Wave in its Context 1956–65* (as joint editor), *British Television Drama: Past, Present and Future* and articles on Arnold Wesker, Augusto Boal, John McGrath and the relationship between theatre and television for the journal *New Theatre Quarterly*. He is currently working on a book about Tony Garnett.

Ros Merkin is Senior Lecturer in Drama at Liverpool John Moores University and has published work on popular and political theatre as well as on the work of Willy Russell and Alan Bleasdale. She is currently working on a digital catalogue of the Liverpool Everyman Theatre archives (with the help of a grant from the Arts and Humanities Research Board) and is compiling the theatre's *Fortieth Birthday Book*. This will be followed by a critical history of the Everyman and work on the state of our regional theatres.

Robin Nelson is Professor and Head of the Department of Contemporary Arts at Manchester Metropolitan University. He is currently working on a new book on British and American contemporary television cultures. Other recent publications about television include contributions to G. Creeber (ed.), *The Television Genre Book* and *Fifty Key Television Programmes*, whilst his own books include (with R. Millington) *Boys from the Blackstuff: The Making of TV Drama* and *TV Drama in Transition.*

Randall Stevenson is Reader in English Literature and Deputy Head of Department in the Department of English Literature, Edinburgh University. He reviews Scottish theatre regularly for the *Times Literary Supplement* and has edited (with Gavin Wallace) *Scottish Theatre since the Seventies* and (with Cairns Craig) *Twentieth-Century Scottish Drama: An Anthology*. Other publications include *Modernist Fiction* and the *Oxford English Literary History, vol. 12, 1960–2000: The Last of England?*

Olga Taxidou, Senior Lecturer in English Literature at Edinburgh University, teaches theatre history and performance theory. She works mainly in the areas of modernism and performance, gender and performance and on theories of tragedy. She is the author of *The Mask: A Periodical Performance by Edward Gordon Craig* and *Tragedy, Modernity and Mourning*. She has co-edited (with V. Kolocotroni and J. Goldman), *Modernism: An Anthology of Sources and Documents* and (with J. Orr) *Postwar Cinema and Modernity*. She also enjoys writing adaptations of classical Greek plays. Between 1992 and 1994 she collaborated with John McGrath on a production provisionally entitled 'Women and War', which drew on texts from Greek tragedies. (The project remained incomplete after two months of rehearsals with John Bett directing, because of funding problems.) At present, she is finishing a book entitled *Modernism and Performance: from Jarry to Brecht.*

Peter Thomson, Emeritus Professor of Drama at University of Exeter, has written books on Shakespeare, Brecht and, most recently, for University of Exeter Press, *On Actors and Acting*. He is a research associate of the New Dictionary of National Biography and general editor of *The Cambridge History of British Theatre.*

ACKNOWLEDGEMENTS

The conference on which this book was based was planned together with John McGrath and our greatest debt is to him. In his sad absence, we owe enormous thanks to Elizabeth MacLennan, his widow, who has helped us in every way possible at all stages of the planning and production of the book. The photographs throughout the book come from her private collection and we thank her enormously for all her help and kindness.

Many thanks too to Richard Eyre who interrupted a busy rehearsal schedule to give a keynote address at the conference which truly celebrated John. And to all of John's former colleagues who came to the conference to share memories of him and gave their time to be interviewed. We owe a debt of thanks to Christopher Hampton who provided the title of this book, through the poem he wrote for John's memorial evening, and allowed us to use it.

FOREWORD

Richard Eyre

It's probably a bleak admission of character defect to say that few of the important things in my life have happened on my own initiative, but it's true. I've always depended on the kindness of patrons—not financial patrons, but the more important kind, the ones who take an interest in you, the ones who form your taste, who change your way of looking at the world; the ones who sometimes save you from yourself. For some people this figure is a teacher; for some it's a parent; for me one of those people was John McGrath.

I met John, through Liz MacLennan[1], in 1966. What first attracted me to both of them—and it remained so over the years—was not only their commitment to theatre or to radical socialism; it was their glamour. They were both—to borrow the clichés of romantic fiction—dashing and handsome, and when I drove with John in his open-topped Chevrolet Corvette (or could it have been a Ford Mustang?) to Pinewood Studios to visit the giant set for *Doctor No*, it seemed bliss indeed to be alive in his company. At the time John was working for Harry Saltzman[2], writing a successor to *The Ipcress File*[3], and it seemed to me then—and I suppose must have seemed to him—possible to combine a career writing for Hollywood with one hand, while with the other writing provocative left-wing plays for the theatre. But I learned in time by his example that if you believe in a political ideal, it's not enough to state it, you have to live it.

In the first few years I knew John, I learned many of the most important things about the theatre: I learned to recognize what I liked and what I disliked and how to justify my opinion. I learned that theatre should be, as Brecht said, something more than an aid to digestion for the middle classes. I learned to question the Spartan pieties of the Royal Court and doubt the collegiate self-importance of the Royal Shakespeare Company. And I learned from John to turn instinct into conviction, believing that the most exciting work in London was Joan Littlewood's. In *Oh What a Lovely War*[4], which I'd only recently seen, she successfully brought together the traditions of popular entertainment with the aims of propaganda in a show

1. John McGrath at home in 1970.

that was skilful, vulgar, populist and unpatronising. This was political theatre that didn't try to reprimand or reform its audience: it sought to inform and to entertain, and it broke your heart in the process.

John infected me with an appetite for looking at and finding out about what went on in the world. From him I learned to read newspapers carefully. I learned to recognize the power of vested interests—whether they be economic or institutional. I learned to be sceptical of political positions that didn't account for the complexities and ambiguities of humanity, or ideologies that didn't recognize the merciful propensity of human beings to love as well as to hate each other.

Shortly after I met John, I saw his play *Events While Guarding the Bofors Gun*[5] at the Hampstead Theatre Club. It was a fine and timely play about conscription and the folly of nuclear defence, which dramatized the dilemma of the liberal conscience. A university-bound corporal on guard in West Germany is stretched on a rack of indecision, powerless and in pain. He fails to deal with a soldier under his command, who is goaded to mutiny and suicide by the debilitating futility of the Cold War. 'I refuse my consent', says the soldier's action, which spoke for a generation of anti-nuclear protesters. It also dramatized the frustrations of John's own position: politically engaged, yet commenting on the sidelines in plays presented to passive audiences in small metropolitan theatres.

I directed this play at the Lyceum Theatre in Edinburgh two years later and then encouraged John to write a play for the Edinburgh Festival. The play was called *Random Happenings in the Hebrides* and you could say, not entirely unfairly, that the title all too aptly resembled the structure of the play, but I was very fond of its rawness and imperfection. It stood clearly in a tradition of theatre with which I still haven't become impatient: a naturalistic play, threaded through with emotional nuance and political debate. It dramatized the tensions between a public world and a private one and its two protagonists embodied the dialectic in John's own person-ality between the pragmatist and the utopian. It's the utopian's words that I remember now—a drunken schoolmaster in a bar:

> All my life I've told myself I believe in *socialism*—but I don't believe in all this they *tell* me is socialism—the technological revolution, the five per cent growth rate and three per cent mortgage, the national plan and the old age increases—and I don't know what to do with it. I just want people to run their own lives and own their own land and to hell with capitalism. I don't believe in 'pragmatism'.

And increasingly John himself stopped believing in pragmatism. When we talked about another commission, a play about the Highland Clearances and the dissolution of the upper Clyde shipyards, it was clear that he wanted to change the *way* he made theatre as much as *where* he made theatre. He started to write—very fruitfully—for the Liverpool Everyman and then he married his political convictions with his aesthetic ones and founded the 7:84 Theatre Company. So John and Liz—both descendants of Irish and Scottish peasants, both socialists, both Oxford educated, the one a son of teachers from Birkenhead, the other the daughter of Glasgow doctors—abandoned their conventional careers, set up in Scotland and after years of living a deracinated London life, reclaimed a sense of belonging to somewhere. And the rest, as they say, is history.

I hope it's a history that won't suffer a fate similar to that accorded to the patron saint of 7:84, Joan Littlewood. The orthodox history of British theatre hasn't been generous to her work: it's elevated the ascetic air of the Royal Court and amply chronicled its self-proclaimed legend of a 'writers' theatre' against scant accounts of Littlewood's work. History favours those who write things down. Why are the theories of Brecht and Stanislavsky so remorselessly picked over? Answer: because their ideas were codified and can be studied and set for exams. Littlewood's productions—like the best of 7:84's—defied study: their legend lay in their spontaneity.

7:84's theatrical language was Littlewood's: the language of working-class entertainment—live, spontaneous, musical, highly regionalized, direct in address and in content—a language that is dissolved in the face of the juggernaut of television, special effects and virtual reality.

Like Littlewood's company, 7:84 was founded on these beliefs: that 'excellence' is not an objective conceit and that it doesn't reside exclusively in institutions such as the National Theatre or the Royal Shakespeare Company; that the theatre establishment has excluded the working-class audience and working-class culture; that all art (and all funding of art) is political; that art can change the world; and that Margaret Thatcher's dictum that there was no such thing as society was a heartless lie.

In their most successful shows, the aims of the company were utterly vindicated. They combined high ideals, lack of pretension, artistic integrity, political sincerity and commercial success. The company brought together a chaotic patchwork of styles, making a seamless unity without diminishing their individual colours.

Some people might suggest that John McGrath's work was marginal to the artistic and political life of this country. But I believe the opposite: it was at the core of a patchwork of artistic activity that was and still is dotted over the land like sunbursts, little islands of dissent. And 'it is in the archipelago of dissenting islands,' said E.P. Thompson, 'that the only forces are mustered which may at some time liberate the mainland.'

People say about all forms of political theatre that it is 'preaching to the converted'. But who else would you be likely to be addressing? No piece of theatre will change the mind of an Ariel Sharon or a Margaret Thatcher.

The people whose minds can be changed are the people who believe that society is transformable, even if there are wildly different views of how to go about it. I believe that people will continue, like John, to be excited by any theatre that speaks about how we should live our lives. Even Beckett's work gives you hope by saying life is hopeless, because the real hopelessness lies in being silent.

Philip Larkin said famously that 'What survives of us is love.' In that respect John will survive for a long time: you couldn't know him well and not love him well. What will also survive of him is the memory of a gifted, passionate, dogged, sometimes intransigent, eloquent man who, as well as making us sit up and listen, always wanted—as he so often said—to give us a good night out.

I was in New York when I heard about his death and was interviewed about him for a BBC TV programme. 'What will be the loss of John McGrath to the British theatre?' I was asked. 'I don't know if I can speak for the British theatre,' I said, 'but I can speak for myself: I've lost a very good friend. And for that matter so has the British theatre.' John and I didn't always agree over the years. He didn't share many of my enthusiasms and he didn't always approve of what I was doing; but he was never ungenerous in dispute and he was never inconstant in his friendship. I miss my friend, and I'm sad and angry that I can't see him again. But I'm so grateful that I knew him.

Notes

1. Elizabeth MacLennan, actress and writer, John McGrath's wife.
2. Harry Saltzman, Film Producer (1915–94). He founded Woodfall films with Tony Richardson and John Osborne and produced eight Ian Fleming 'James Bond' films with Cubby Broccoli, including *Doctor No*.
3. The Ipcress File (1965) was produced by Harry Saltzman and starred Michael Caine. John McGrath wrote *Billion Dollar Brain* in 1967, the third and last 'Harry Palmer' movie.
4. *Oh What a Lovely War* (Theatre Royal, Stratford East, 1963). Directed by Joan Littlewood.
5. *Events While Guarding the Bofors Gun* (Hampstead Theatre, 1966). Directed by Ronald Eyre.

INTRODUCTION

David Bradby and Susanna Capon

Injustice was the enemy
You ridiculed it without fear
And played the tunes of liberty
For you were freedom's pioneer
> (From *Laeti et Arrabundi. after Verlaine*
> *(For John)* by Christopher Hampton.[1])

This poem sums up well the achievement of an exemplary life, a life that this book sets out to celebrate as well as to interrogate. John McGrath's death in January 2002 provoked many people to record their memories of him, memories that were aptly summed up by Nadine Holdsworth, who wrote: 'McGrath and his collaborators in 7:84 took theatre by the scruff of the neck and signalled new ways of generating, executing and disseminating politicised theatre.'[2] This book collects together essays and interviews by a wide spectrum of people, from actors to scholars, all of whom have tried to distil something of his contribution to political thinking and performance in the late twentieth century. Part One begins by examining John McGrath's lifelong commitment to a search for radical alternatives to established cultural practices. His revolutionary socialist vision encompassed every aspect of life; it was not limited to politics understood as a narrow specialist concern, but was always concerned to see how the aspects of our daily lives are infused with and informed by the material conditions of our existence. Maria DiCenzo sets out John's own extremely influential thinking on cultural theory and politics, as expressed in his two books *A Good Night Out* and *The Bone Won't Break*, and points towards the uniquely interdisciplinary quality of John's very thinking, in which politics, culture, performance and image could not be separated, instead feeding back and forth into one another.

The writers of the remaining sections all aim to investigate aspects of John's work that raise questions or challenges. Part Two asks how important his early work for theatre was, work sometimes neglected by those who remember only the well-known highlights of *Z-Cars* and *The*

Cheviot. In addressing the early theatre work, Peter Thomson gives a very personal account of his experience of *Events While Guarding the Bofors Gun*. His essay demonstrates Proust's belief that it is by delving most deeply into the individual that the writer can hope to attain truths that are general, by showing how the struggle between Lance-Bombadier Evans and Private O'Rourke enacts an experience of social conflict and opposition to the cold war shared by a whole generation at the end of the 1950s. Ros Merkin shows the importance of John's contribution to the cultural revival of Liverpool at the end of the following decade, and Nadine Holdsworth reminds us of the variety, and the political force of the plays John wrote for 7:84 England which are often overlooked because of the better-known work of 7:84 Scotland.

The question of John's role in the revival of Scottish cultural traditions is addressed in Part Three by Randall Stevenson and Ian Brown. Both show, in their different ways, what an extraordinary catalytic role this non-Scot played in the development, not just of theatre, but also of political thought north of the border. Ian Brown's interviews with five Scottish writers add an important perspective by showing how the surprise and excitement of encountering John's work challenged them to develop original ideas and techniques of their own.

In Part Four, Stephen Lacey investigates the links between structures and meaning in John's work with special reference to *Blood Red Roses*, Robert Dawson Scott explores the power and originality of one of John's last works for television, *The Long Roads*, and Olga Taxidou analyses the remarkable political force packed into the one-woman plays that John wrote for Elizabeth MacLennan. Part Five, entitled 'Working with John', demonstrates John's gift for collaborative work in all three media: theatre, film and television. Troy Kennedy Martin discusses the making of *Z-Cars*, Jack Gold remembers some of John's work in film, the designers Pamela Howard and Jenny Tiramani write of John's remarkable visual imagination, and Bill Paterson and John Bett explain how he interacted with performers. The section concludes with a contribution by Elizabeth MacLennan, in which she meditates on all aspects of John's creative work, stressing the importance of music in every play or script he wrote or directed.

The origin of this book lies in a conference held at Royal Holloway, University of London, in Spring 2002, which set out to create a space for interdisciplinary work, and to attract writers or academics who would be interested in looking beyond their own specialisms in film or theatre or television, in order to learn something from those working in fields different from their own. It is impossible to escape the interdisciplinary dimension of John's work. Having begun in student theatre, he moved to television, then wrote the script for the *Billion Dollar Brain* at the same time as doing some of his most innovative work in theatre. Following this, he founded 7:84, a company whose extraordinary success with live audiences was followed by national and international recognition as a result of the successful transfer to television of *The Cheviot, the Stag and the Black, Black Oil*. In short, he never abandoned one form in favour of another, but moved with great ease across all the varied forms available to him, borrowing cinematic effects for live performances and vice versa. Whilst producing the feature film *Carrington*, for instance, he was still active in small-scale theatre, touring with shows such as *The Last of the MacEachans*.

Almost every one of the actors and other creative artists who worked with him commented on this ability to draw on all sorts of different ideas or techniques, and his gift for inspired lateral thinking. Many of the contributions to this book focus on John's gift for moving across different genres and weaving different materials into his creations. His gift for promoting interactions between designers, actors and writers is chronicled here in the two sets of interviews. Troy Kennedy Martin recalls his innovative approach to television drama, Pamela Howard remembers his 'cross-cutting' solution for how to present in the theatre a scene supposed to be taking place simultaneously inside and outside the Scottish parliament building, John Bull analyses his adaptation of a play by John Arden, and Robin Nelson examines the process involved in adapting *The Cheviot, the Stag and the Black, Black Oil* for television. The common thread that binds all these examples of cross-fertilization together is the underpinning political theory set out in John's own books and discussed by Maria DiCenzo in Part One.

One of the comments most frequently made about John was that he was a wonderful teacher. *A Good Night Out* and *The Bone Won't Break* both began life as lectures at Cambridge University and it is no surprise that in the last years of his life much of his time was spent organizing and teaching at Moonstone, the training organization for writers and directors that he founded and led. One of John's particular concerns at Moonstone was to open up opportunities for successful theatre directors to work in film, and the cross-disciplinary approach currently producing exciting work by directors such as Sam Mendes and Stephen Daldry coincides closely with his own ethos. The achievement of Moonstone was to bring together in a creative and productive way those who already had experience and could impart it to others (the teachers) and the aspiring practitioners themselves. This interaction between academia and practitioners remains relatively uncharted territory in the new discipline of media studies, and John McGrath remains its foremost champion in his work, both in professional contexts and in universities such as Cambridge and Royal Holloway, University of London.[3]

Notes

1. Written for the programme of the commemorative show *A Good Night Out*, 19 May 2002, in the Assembly Rooms, Edinburgh, and reproduced by kind permission of the author.
2. Nadine Holdsworth, 'Remembering John McGrath', *Contemporary Theatre Review*, vol. 13(1), 2003, p. 114.
3. John McGrath was the first Visiting Professor in Media Arts at Royal Holloway, University of London. He was a fount of wisdom in the early years of setting up a media practice course. In recognition of his service to British theatre, film and television, Royal Holloway conferred on him an honorary doctorate of the University of London in 2001.

PART ONE

Culture and the Socialist Vision

CHAPTER ONE

Theatre, Theory and Politics
The Contribution of John McGrath

Maria DiCenzo

It's always risky for writers to theorize about their work, and it's
especially dangerous to do so without benefit of hindsight. The reason
why I am embarking on this dangerous project is because I think we in
the arts are in the middle of a war which, whether we know it or like it
or not, is being fought in the language if not always on the actual terrain
of theory, and we've got to get in there and engage.
(David Edgar, *Festivals of the Oppressed*)[1]

But outside the university precincts another kind of knowledge-
production is going on all the time. I will agree that it is not always
rigorous. I am not careless of intellectual values nor unaware of the
difficulty of their attainment. But . . . knowledges have been and still
are formed outside the academic procedures. Nor have these been, in
the test of practice, negligible. They have assisted men and women to
till the fields, to construct houses, to support elaborate social
organisations, and even, on occasion, to challenge effectively the
conclusions of academic thought.
(E.P. Thompson, *The Poverty of Theory*)[2]

Randall Stevenson's motif of borders, in his essay for this book, highlights
the extent to which John McGrath was writing and producing across
borders of many kinds, notably those that exist within the categories
of nation, class, gender and media. Often acknowledged, but rarely
elaborated, have been McGrath's efforts to negotiate the border between
the artistic community and academe. He engaged on the 'terrain of theory'
throughout his career as he extrapolated from his own experiments and
those of his contemporaries in order to offer explanations, definitions and
general principles for a viable and effective socialist theatre. In revisiting
these writings, most notably *A Good Night Out* and *The Bone Won't Break*,

I would like to demonstrate why this body of work represents a significant retrospective account of pivotal developments in the arts in post-war Britain, and how it continues to serve as a point of reference informing ongoing debates about political theatre.[3] At the same time, I want to argue that in order to understand the scope of his contribution, it is necessary to situate his analyses of cultural forms and consumption historically and to consider how his hybrid use of genres and the controversial terms of his discourse complicated and limited the academic recognition and reception of this work.

The attempts by playwrights to theorize their own work have proven to be valuable resources in understanding the dynamic qualities of the medium, in part because these documents provide a record of the perceptions, judgements and artistic strategies of practitioners working in a given period. Perhaps the most widely acknowledged example is Bertolt Brecht, whose collected writings have come to represent a body of theory that is relevant to and cited by people who have never read or seen his plays. These writings have a value both because of their historical specificity (as accounts by a contemporary of the characteristics of theatre at a given time and in a given place) and because the artistic strategies he posited proved to be relevant to, and continued to be adapted by, playwrights in a variety of different contexts. It is not a coincidence that politically committed playwrights and directors in post-war Britain have made major contributions in this area.[4] If Brecht is the most obvious example, he is also an exception in so far as his theory has crossed disciplinary boundaries in academic scholarship. It is surprising, and unfortunate, that so much of what we recognize as theory in theatre studies is unknown to those outside the specific field in academe, let alone the larger sphere of social and political debate. The implications of these barriers and separation are particularly revealing when we consider the cultural issues McGrath was addressing in *A Good Night Out* at the end of the 1970s.

A Good Night Out Revisited

McGrath's 1977 article 'TV Drama: The Case Against Naturalism' is an important early example of his tendency to theorize and document his own work. It is based on a lecture he delivered as part of a retrospective look at the television work of James MacTaggart at the 1976 Edinburgh Festival. In it he deals with what it was like to work at the BBC in the early 1960s and provides a context for the experiments in these years, in particular his work with Troy Kennedy Martin, whom he quotes extensively. While he summarizes the issues they were debating at the time, he also formulates his own analysis of the problems of form in television and is adamant in his appeal to others to engage more actively in this process, concluding:

The answers to these questions [related to why television lags behind theatre and film in debates about form] lie partly in the hands of television executives, who create structures and impose their personalities. They lie mostly in the hands of the writers and directors, who need to acquire the habit of theoretical discussion before churning out yet another ten years of naturalism.[5]

As Jonathon Bignell noted, this essay has assumed an important status in the body of television theory. But in its style and tone, it also points to the more extensive treatment of the production of popular political theatre which McGrath tackled in his Cambridge lectures.

How central *A Good Night Out* has been to an understanding of McGrath's theatre work cannot be overestimated. In the field of theatre studies, the book has had a life of its own, independent of 7:84's work, and is cited or included on university course syllabi more regularly than any of his plays. But for all that analyses of McGrath's theatre practice draw on or take for granted the arguments in *A Good Night Out*, there have been very few attempts to classify or interrogate the book itself. Its value, as well as its peculiar position in the fields of theatre history and theory, stem from the diverse functions the book performs. Over twenty years on, any critical reconsideration of the book must situate it historically in order to understand why it was so groundbreaking and provocative at the time of its publication. But it is equally important to consider what it might mean to readers now, particularly students and young theatre practitioners.

A Good Night Out did after all begin life as a series of lectures to students and faculty at Cambridge University. In his 'Foreword' to the book, Raymond Williams stresses the value of what he terms 'contact between university and profession' while at the same time reinforcing the division and distance between the two spheres of activity. McGrath, on the other hand, complicates these boundaries by engaging in a variety of discourses over the course of the six chapters which make up the book.

In the interests of demonstrating that there are different—and equally legitimate—approaches to mediating reality in the theatre, the first chapter challenges prevailing assumptions about the 'universality' of theatre and its audiences. By offering a materialist analysis of theatre as a social event, McGrath reveals the ways in which the 'meaning, and value, of theatre can clearly change from . . . class to class' and how particular practices 'enshrine certain specific values and qualities of a play above others'.[6] He tries to show how the particular kind of theatre he associates with the Royal Court, the Royal Shakespeare Company and the National Theatre became 'equally respectable, conventional and pernicious', and locates the formative influences for these mainstream institutions in the decade between 1956 and 1966 at the Royal Court.[7] He focuses on the Royal

Court for the remainder of the chapter because, as a case in point, it illustrates why changing 'the content of *some* of what happens on the stage' is not enough to change the meaning or class orientation of theatre.[8] McGrath dispels what he sees as the claims of social significance made on behalf of the 'New Era' ushered in by John Osborne *et al.* in 1956 and argues that the Royal Court was not an expression of a new working class, but more about the embourgoisement of non-middle class young people and about 'an old middle class trying to renew itself'.[9]

This opening chapter of *A Good Night Out* presents a scathing account of the main attributes of bourgeois or dominant forms of theatre in order to pave the way for a discussion in Chapters 2 and 3 of the characteristics and functions of a working-class theatre—described as 'the most important kind of theatre politically, but also theatrically'.[10] Chapter 4 details the work of the English and Scottish 7:84 Theatre Companies in this context, while the final chapters take up more general issues related to the organizational aspects of theatre work and the political and creative choices writers face in theatre, as well as cinema and television. The whole of the book is informed by his own political position, which he articulates clearly in Chapter 2, and is based on a largely functionalist view of capitalist society in which social, cultural and political institutions exist to reproduce and protect bourgeois interests, while at the same time he maintains that this kind of functional closure can be disrupted by class struggle. He attributes to socialist theatre the role of helping to provide ideological alternatives that are crucial to the 'social, political and cultural development of the working class towards maturity and hegemony, leading to the possibility of a classless society at some time in the future'.[11]

The arguments, modes of analysis and the politics are important for a number of reasons. On one level, *A Good Night Out* is a revisionist account of post-war theatre history in Britain. It has become commonplace in recent years to re-evaluate the 'moment' of 1956 from a variety of perspectives, but McGrath is rarely credited for the insights he offers into the social and artistic dynamic of the period. On another level, documenting the experiments and evolving structure of the 7:84 companies also contributes to a body of theatre history. In fact this, along with his and Elizabeth MacLennan's other published writing, has ensured a life for 7:84's work, unlike other companies at the time whose work is now less well known. In spite of the emphasis on the working relations of theatre companies and the principles driving their creative practices, McGrath never wholly abandons the centrality of the 'author' and even praises (on a rather contradictory note) the literary skills that bourgeois education offers.[12] It is at this level that the book serves also as a memoir of McGrath's creative process as a writer working in different media. While these dimensions suggest his range as a commentator, they may also complicate the issue of genre and obscure some of the elements that distinguish *A Good Night Out*.

At the core of the book is his attempt to theorize the relationship between theatrical form and social class. I would argue that two of the most important passages are those involving the descriptions of a typical Sunday night production of a new play at the Royal Court in 1960 (a case study in cultural capital) and a night at a working-men's club in Chorlton-cum-Hardy *circa* 1963. Coupled with the attempt to identify the main differences between the demands of bourgeois and working-class audiences (namely, the elements of directness, comedy, music, emotion, variety, effect, immediacy and localism which characterize working-class forms of entertainment), these sections of the book form the basis of McGrath's contribution to a theory of cultural production and consumption. His questions and ideas about the ways in which certain practices and values come to constitute 'legitimate' culture and their specific distinguishing features in relation to social class bear striking similarities to those informing the work of a cultural theorist like Pierre Bourdieu. While I am not aware of any other attempts to draw links between these two figures, a brief consideration of the relationship between their work at a particular historical juncture and in different contexts serves to underscore the very pattern of the privileging of certain 'knowledges' over others.[13]

It is specifically Bourdieu's *Distinction: A Social Critique of the Judgement of Taste* that interests me here. It was originally published in 1979 (the year of the McGrath's Cambridge lectures) and while not translated in its entirety until 1984, the crucial chapter 'The Aristocracy of Culture' did appear in *Media, Culture and Society* in 1980 with an editorial by Raymond Williams and Nicholas Garnham. It may at first seem unusual to compare a work of this magnitude (in methodological and scholarly terms) to McGrath's personal observations and formal experiments, but they are ultimately interested in exploring the same phenomena, though they draw quite different conclusions and are invested in their projects in different ways. After all, Bourdieu tries to explain the principles on which the economy of cultural goods operates and he pays considerable attention to the distinctions between bourgeois aestheticism (the pure gaze/aesthetic) and a popular aesthetic or disposition, in the interests of demonstrating 'why art and cultural consumption are predisposed, consciously and deliberately or not, to fulfil a social function of legitimating social differences'.[14] Like McGrath, Bourdieu relates cultural preferences and responses to material necessity. Despite a 'scientific' approach to the collection and analysis of extensive data, Bourdieu is no less prone to generalized claims about the aesthetic predilections of particular classes, as we see for instance in his discussion of theatre:

> In the theatre as in the cinema, the popular audience delights in plots that proceed logically and chronologically towards a happy end, and 'identifies' better with simply drawn situations and characters than with ambiguous and symbolic figures and actions or enigmatic problems of the theatre of cruelty, not to mention the suspended animation of Beckettian heroes or the bland absurdities of Pinteresque dialogue. Their reluctance or refusal springs not just from lack of familiarity but from deep-rooted demand for participation, which formal experiment systematically disappoints . . .[15]

Similarly, he asserts that 'working-class people expect every image to explicitly perform a function, if only that of a sign, and their judgements make reference, often explicitly, to the norms of morality or agreeableness. Whether rejecting or praising, their appreciation always has an ethical basis'.[16]

I have quoted at length from Bourdieu in order to demonstrate how his emphasis on aesthetic distance versus immediacy/involvement, not to mention the educational and economic structures through which these tendencies are learned and obtained, has obvious parallels in McGrath's discussion of the differences between the demands of bourgeois and working-class audiences in the central chapter of *A Good Night Out*. Differences exist on a variety of levels, but as theorists of cultural forms, they part company most clearly on the issue of the political implications and potential of popular art. Bourdieu argues that:

> Those who believe in the existence of a 'popular culture', a paradoxical notion which imposes, willy-nilly, the dominant definition of culture, must expect to find—if they were to go and look—only the scattered fragments of an old erudite culture (such as folk medicine), selected and reinterpreted in terms of the fundamental principles of the class habitus and integrated into the unitary world view it engenders, and not the counter-culture they call for, a culture truly raised in opposition to the dominant culture and consciously claimed as a symbol of status or a declaration of separate existence.[17]

The claim is reminiscent of the debate between David Edgar and McGrath concerning popular cultural forms in the UK and which McGrath refutes in *A Good Night Out*.[18] In countering the dismissal of these forms as obsolete or reactive, but never proactive, McGrath draws on Gramsci's concept of popular culture as 'the site of political struggle' as his model. Not only would McGrath have disagreed with Bourdieu about the potential of popular art to serve as a counter-cultural force, but he devoted most of his career to his belief in the idea of 'the working class as the only social force capable of transforming society in a progressive manner'.[19]

These schematic comparisons are intended to serve two main functions. First, by establishing this larger frame of reference, my aim is to reassert what was and continues to be so valuable about McGrath's contribution in *A Good Night Out*. His thinking was at the cutting edge of broader tendencies in the arts and in disciplines such as history, anthropology and sociology involved in documenting and theorizing working-class culture in the late 1970s and early 1980s.[20] But the impact of his theoretical writing remained largely confined to the theatre world and to theatre studies. Outside drama departments and theatre journals, theatre intersected with the sphere of political activism; however, it was less likely to be acknowledged by academics in other fields, especially as the conflicts between empirical and more abstract, theoretical discourses became more pronounced. Given the scope of socialist theatre produced throughout the 1970s, it is surprising that we find so few direct references in the work of historians and social scientists.[21] The growing interest in 'media' rarely included theatre. Most striking perhaps is the fact that figures like McGrath and Bourdieu were engaged by and actively theorizing similar phenomena, but McGrath's sphere of influence has remained limited, while Bourdieu's work, in spite of being highly problematic, has achieved major status across many disciplines in the academic world.

Even Raymond Williams, who straddled these worlds more effectively than most, sees the connections, but treats their articulation as separate. In his Foreword to *A Good Night Out* he notes: 'What interests me is the connection with the quite different work I and some others have been doing about the "audience" . . . I have worked on this in history and theory . . .'.[22] If that 'quite different work' is in fact represented by the 1980 issue of *Media, Culture and Society* (referred to above), it becomes clearer why the two worlds seem to have little to do with one another. While Williams and Garnham elaborate the ways in which Bourdieu's work represents a major contribution to the field of British media and cultural studies, they seem obliged at the end of the paper to raise 'the question of Bourdieu's politics'; while they dismiss charges of 'relativistic pessimism' as nothing more than Bourdieu's tendency to be 'as objective as possible', they do concede 'it has to be said that there seems to us . . . to be a functionalist/determinist residue in Bourdieu's concept of reproduction which leads him to place less emphasis on the possibilities of real change and innovation than either his theory or his empirical research makes necessary'.[23] The fact that the 'politics' are not always clear is not insignificant. In the other key article included in the issue, Philip Corrigan and Paul Willis offer a critique of discourse theory from their positions as 'historian and ethnographer of working class culture'. In virtually impenetrable prose, they posit some very tentative claims in order to defend the very simple idea that 'the possibility that working class cultural forms *do* generate "knowledges"' and argue for, among other things, 'a recognition of the complex system of codes and genres in how meanings are made by working class people, that they are not "dumb" passive audiences'.[24] There is a certain irony inherent in the relationship between the political/ activist imperative and the exclusionary language that characterizes a large part of this work. It purports to analyse and express concern on behalf of the working class from a remote and privileged position—discursively and institutionally.[25] In spite of some of the political contradictions that plagued his writing, at least McGrath was out there taking risks at the level of theatrical practice, rather than exploring the arguments on a purely discursive level. His theorizing came from working with audiences, not just talking about them, and he was able to realize his ideas in concrete ways, going where most theorists never could.

This takes me to the second reason for situating McGrath's writing in the larger theoretical/academic context of the late 1970s. *A Good Night Out* was significant as part of a body of writing on working-class history and culture emerging in these years and the institutionalization of left-wing discourses more generally. At the same time, these general comparisons point to how his approach and language may have undermined the potential impact of the book. McGrath never practises such academic 'distance' and his 'politics' are never in question. Rather than distanced and abstract, his observations are couched in personal and polemical terms. He even warns in the opening chapter that 'This process can become autobiographical, egocentric, even at times megalomaniac, but if you wish a more measured, "objective" approach, I cannot oblige.'[26] His most ardent admirers have to admit his tendency towards overstatement (however provocative) as he describes his 'overwhelming sensation of nausea' in the presence of so-called 'political' plays that are expressed in the language of high cultural theatre or his characterization of twentieth-century theatre as 'stunted, childish, retarded'.[27] The dichotomy between bourgeois and working-class forms of theatre—including the repeated and total dismissal of the former in favour of the latter—may have been effective for the sake of argument (and deliberately antagonistic at Cambridge), but ultimately too schematic. His rigid use of the categories of class would prove increasingly problematic in the 1980s.

Changing Vocabularies and The Bone Won't Break

A Good Night Out remains a more significant work than the second set of Cambridge lectures, published as *The Bone Won't Break*. The circumstances and dates of their composition—McGrath addresses the same audience roughly ten years later—demand that they be considered in relation to one another. *The Bone Won't Break* functions as a sequel insofar

as it provides an account of the 7:84 Theatre Companies in the intervening years and places their fates in the context of the shifting world of
cultural production—and the vagaries of arts funding bodies—in the UK.
Especially compelling in this book is the discussion of the 'values' and
'standards' on which artistic work is judged and supported, and what he
refers to as 'the danger of cultural standardisation in a post-industrial
mass-media-dominated Britain'.[28] If McGrath's tone changed, it was
perhaps more personal and apologetic. He admits to 'a touch of
paternalism' and explains:

> I am beating my breast in this way because I think the developments
> in 7:84 (Scotland) cannot be attributed solely to the workings of a
> consciously malign political force: many of them were . . . but for the
> record, it must be said that this need for an atmosphere of trust and
> familiarity to work in, when denied or frustrated, has led me into many
> of the miseries and negative feelings that have marked the last five years,
> and have been my personal contribution to the downfall of 7:84
> (Scotland).[29]

But his reasons for documenting these experiences were far from personal
and his analysis is intended to shed light on the developments in the
theatre more generally. In responding to the invitation to return to Cambridge he recalls: 'I was, of course, keen to chart my own shatteringly
archetypal adventures in some hopefully illuminating detail, as a modest
contribution to the social history of British theatre in the 80s'.[30]

McGrath's more cautious and self-conscious use of language in *The
Bone Won't Break* signals some of the problems he confronted in continuing to create 'socialist theatre' for 'working-class audiences' at a time
when these terms seemed dated, even obsolete. He explains:

> One of the main planks of the work was the need for 'class-
> consciousness' in the working class, that is, knowledge of, solidarity with
> those with common interests and roles in society. Through the 60s and
> 70s this concept of 'class-consciousness' raised no problems: people
> knew what it meant, and knew it existed, and could chart its growth.
> Now, ten years later, the concept is unfamiliar, a word for something
> that no longer exists, something that failed.[31]

The first chapter deals largely with accounting for this phenomenon
(describing the changes the working class underwent in that time) and
redefining the subject and audience for his work as 'The Resistance'. For
all that he tries to repackage the message, McGrath never abandons the
concept of a ruling-class/working-class binary as the central organizing
principle for his analysis of social and cultural problems, as well as the

possible solutions to them. The language repeatedly slips back into identifying oppressed groups or the audiences that matter as 'working class' or in similarly monolithic terms, and his attempts to account for diversity in terms of issues and audiences, however genuine, often appear in summaries and remain peripheral. At times, he seems unaware of the implications of his own categories. Recounting the impact of 7:84's production of Barrie Keefe's *Sus*, he claims: 'We took it to black communities as well as our regular audiences, and shocked both.'[32] The use of an asymmetrical distinction, between 'black' and 'regular', to describe these audiences begs many questions.

These problematic aspects of McGrath's writing matter for a variety of reasons. He argued more convincingly than most that form and language are crucial to reaching, and communicating with, an audience. This must hold true for the readerships addressed by published work, as well as for theatre audiences. His socialist analysis, centred chiefly on the concept of the 'the working class' (or even 'the working classes'), was too limited to speak to more broadly based and diverse social groupings, inside and outside university settings. Not because gender, race, sexual orientation and ethnicity/regional identity became more important—even though for many, including huge numbers of young people, they were—but because, all of these categories can no longer usefully describe or capture the complexities of the ways in which people actually live their lives and form solidarities. New social movements are a case in point. As I have noted elsewhere, the traditional image of a 'working class' employed in skilled/ semi-skilled manual labour, rooted in stable and homogeneous households and communities, united by ties of family, union and culture, has largely disappeared.[33] For these reasons even trade unions face significant challenges in their attempts to organize solidarity between members and groups in order to be effective.[34] This is not to say that inequalities, hardships and exploitation of the powerless by the powerful have disappeared as well. But how people understand and experience these inequalities and translate them into social and political action has changed.

The question becomes where can activists and artists turn for social/ political analysis and models that reflect these changing circumstances and can serve them in practical ways. A recent thought-provoking attempt to address these changes can be seen in the work of Ulrich Beck, who argues that while class retains its objectivity, it seems to be losing its subjectivity. In their analysis of the process of individualization, Beck and Beck-Gernsheim try to account for the fact that there has been no significant change in the relations of inequality between major groups in society, and yet public political debate suggests that the explanations for inequality are not considered in terms of class questions.[35] Beck is interested in how changes in the labour market have affected people, both at the level of identity and consciousness, and in terms of how the patterns of their lives have changed.[36] He argues that entry into the labour market, rather than serving to reinforce the traditional ties we associate with social class, actually 'release[s] people from fixed ties of family, neighbourhood and occupation, as well as from ties to a particular regional culture and landscape'.[37] This is linked to the larger process of individualization in which the individual becomes 'the basic unit of social reproduction'.[38] He uses the example of how the 'household', as a geographic, economic and social unit central to the construction of classes, has become so difficult to define and indicates the fluid and contradictory ways in which people have to make choices about where, how and with whom they live. Beck is by no means pessimistic about the formation of new and empowering social groupings as people confront social problems. However, he admits that these alliances are often pragmatic and temporary, given the ways in which people combine multiple loyalties and identities in their lives. Much of his work involves constructive attempts to redefine redundant concepts and categories—always grounded in the empirical world—in the interests of finding more effective ways of understanding and addressing the increasingly complex and contradictory demands people face in the 'risk society' and the devastating effects of growing social inequalities.[39]

I cannot do justice to Beck's work in this short space, but I use it as an example of a compelling social critique which forces us to re-examine our terms of reference and helps to elucidate current problems that are crucial to mobilizing people politically. It also offers an explanation of why previous, chiefly Marxist, models cannot usefully account for recent social and economic developments. It might also provide a broader context for thinking about McGrath's own shift towards an emphasis on 'citizens' and the 'rights and responsibilities of the individual' in authentic democracies in his 1999 essay, 'Theatre and Democracy'.[40] More importantly, the spirit of Beck's critique is animated by the same need to struggle against social inequality that was at the core of McGrath's art and life. The need to question the terms of McGrath's discourse is not to deny the underlying concerns of his work, but rather to point ahead to more relevant and effective strategies for using theatre as a tool for social and political action. These formulations have serious implications for ongoing debates in political theatre, namely how practitioners understand, appeal to and engage their audiences. In his typically direct way, McGrath warned authors and creators 'never [to] fall in the trap of trying to make mechanical theatre, with lumps of ideological Meccano'.[41]

John McGrath's Legacy

In celebrating the work of John McGrath, it seemed necessary to reflect on his valuable contribution, but also to point to some of the controversies his writing has generated. My goal has been to document critically in order to affirm the work's continuing significance. This may be particularly important for students who encounter his writings in the future. As a result of his forays into the academic sphere, McGrath's theories for the production of socialist theatre, like Brecht's theoretical writings, will continue to be mined and adapted by both those who make theatre and those who study and teach theatre. *A Good Night Out* and *The Bone Won't Break* constitute some of the most significant and influential attempts to theorize popular political theatre in the post-war period. But they tell only part of the story. If the language and analytical framework (specifically in the case of the second book) became increasingly problematic in the 1980s and 1990s, his playwriting actually pointed to a process of change and the exploration of new and diverse forms, ranging from solo pieces to the large-scale promenade productions for the Tramway Theatre, not to mention the variety of work for television and film. This collection of essays will help to offer that broader perspective on McGrath's long and varied career.

His contribution to the debates surrounding political theatre and his determination to sustain them cannot be overestimated. In the end, it is impossible to ignore the fact that his uncompromising nature was one of his greatest strengths. Even the anger in his writing was a result of how much he invested and expected of himself in what he was doing; theatre and politics were not just an academic exercise. John McGrath never lost the courage of his convictions about the critical and challenging function theatre could play in society. He remained committed to creating, as well as encouraging and facilitating, the expression of alternative and oppositional views, to combat the larger tendency towards the homogenization of culture and cultural forms, but mainly to make the world a better place.

PART TWO

Early Work

CHAPTER TWO

Get Out and Get On

Events While Guarding the Bofors Gun

Peter Thomson

John McGrath did his national service in the Royal Artillery (1953–55): I did mine in the Royal Air Force (1956–58). For any recent school-leaver, those two years were a perilous gash between sixth form and university. The survival of a recognizable self was put at hazard by the sheer irrationality of the demands made during square-bashing: sweep the floor with a toothbrush; cut the grass with nail-scissors; paint the coal white and the coal buckets black; dig the rubbish out from under one hut and carry it across camp to deposit it under another. And please God, don't let the corporal notice me. There was constant fear in the pit of the stomach and the choices were never yours, always somebody else's. On one side of me in the billet was a bespectacled classicist, bound for King's College, Cambridge. On the other was a light-heavyweight boxer from Blackpool. The classicist, arhythmic and uncoordinated, was a natural victim on the parade ground. For him, the eight weeks of square-bashing were an unbroken nightmare. The boxer, never more than half aware that scape-goats have their uses, treated him with contempt and it was a tiny Scottish bus driver—by some years the oldest man in the billet—who tried hardest to protect him. (Within the social world of the billet, whatever attempts I made were always liable to be counter-productive.) The most intimidating figure was a massive lorry driver from Preston, given to lashing out in uncontrollable bouts of fury. When I watched *Events While Guarding the Bofors Gun* at the Manchester Library Theatre in June 1967, I knew the territory.

Bofors Gun stands before and outside the work for which John McGrath is best remembered, but its engagement in the politics of choice looks forward to the Liverpool Everyman and 7:84. To be sure, the watershed of 1968 was ahead of him, but the whole conduct of this comparatively conventional play is indicative of a disposition to be 'changed', whose roots lie in the experience of national service. A brief detour into Arnold Wesker's *Chips with Everything* may sharpen the point.

Unlike *Bofors Gun*, *Chips with Everything* is outwardly a play about square-bashing. What is more, its setting is an RAF camp and its timespan is the *eight* weeks (not six, as in the army at that time) set aside for knocking the new recruits into shape. Having read a few reviews, I went to the Royal Court in 1962 expecting to see national service as I had known it. The different camps set aside for basic training, as we learned during the preliminary week at RAF Cardington (nothing to do there except get kitted out and have your hair cut once a day), had separately sinister reputations, but Padgate held the record for suicides: if yours was the Thursday train from Cardington, you went there. Mine was the Tuesday train and I ended up at Bridgnorth (there was only one successful suicide while I was there and two thwarted attempts). Where did Wesker go in 1950? His lucky bunch are allowed time in the Naafi on their first evening, have a drill instructor who socializes with them in the billet ('Come off it, Corp', says Ginger Richardson at one point[1]—an utter impossibility in Flight 28 at Bridgnorth, where either Corporal Pottinger or Lance-Corporal Holmes would have had Ginger charged and back-flighted) and get away with talking back, not only to the NCOs but even to the commissioned officers. This is square-bashing in Cloud Cuckoo Land. Even the victimization of Smiler Washington is mild compared with that of the King's College classicist (and others, of whom I was occasionally one) at Bridgnorth. It can fairly be argued, though it seems not to have been by reviewers, that it was never Wesker's intention to give a realistic account of service life. His target is the British class system and his unlikely 'hero' a general's son perversely set on life at the bottom. The breaking of Pip Thompson's resolve is so easily accomplished that it hardly merits the name of 'resolve'. His is a character wholly in thrall to Wesker's thesis—that power is self-perpetuating and inescapable by those born to it. Pip is among the least attractive figures ever to stand in the place of a hero and his transparency (he's a snob, he boasts, but not a prig)[2] blunts the force of the drama. Quite early in the play, Andrew McClure's outburst is effectively prophetic: 'I've known a lot of people like you, Pip. They come drinking in the pub and talk to us as though we were the salt of the earth, and then, one day, for no reason any of us can see, they go off, drop us as though that was another game they were tired of.'[3] When he wrote the play, Wesker had not entirely severed his ties with Centre 42—he donated the profits to the Roundhouse—and the informing vision of that aborted project is captured in Chas Wingate's hunger for the kind of cultural food that Pip supplies him. Like Beatie Bryant in *Roots*, Chas is ensnared by words, but he can never make them his own after Pip rejects him. Still, he comes to a recognition of a sort: 'Your bleedin' stuffed grandfathers kept us stupid all this time, and now you come along with your pretty words and tell us to fend for ourselves.[4] It was never my experience that you could impress fellow-recruits by 'talking posh' and, however Wesker may have protested, Pip Thompson would have had a rough time at Bridgnorth. If the lorry driver hadn't flattened him, the boxer would have done.

Events While Guarding the Bofors Gun exhibits an awareness of the almost unbearable aloneness of the national serviceman that *Chips with Everything* engages with only in Smiler Washington's monologue (Act 2 Scene 10). A decade after the play was first staged at the Hampstead Theatre Club (12 April 1966), McGrath told Cathy Itzin that '[t]he real conflict in *Bofors Gun* was between the way I felt then, in 1966, and the way I felt when I was in Germany, in the army in 1953 or 1954—a kind of polarisation'.[5] In context, and despite a following sentence that purports to explain it, the statement is enigmatic. I choose to believe that he was referring to the felt disjunction between his adolescent, miltary self and his adult, civilian self. It is clearly in the character of Lance-Bombardier Evans that McGrath configures himself. The character-description[6] tells us things about Evans that the play doesn't:

> [He is] a nice boy, trying hard to be liked, and not really succeeding: he lacks a basic level of humanity. He is a Grammar School boy from the suburbs of Manchester, who has won a scholarship in mathematics to Cambridge. This is his first week as an N.C.O. and he is very unhappy about it but manages a kind of nervous sense of humour about his situation. He is eighteen and a half.

That wry self-portrait—'a nice boy, trying hard to be liked'—might have been painted by so many of us, still wet behind the school ears, but much of the rest is a mirror image of McGrath. A grammar school in the suburbs of Manchester instead of North Wales, but with a Welsh tang in the surname: a mathematics scholarship at Cambridge rather than an English scholarship at Oxford. This is the author in 1965–66 looking back at the person he was in 1953–54 and conscious that, unsurprisingly, he lacked 'a basic level of humanity'. One way or another, we rise on stepping stones of our dead selves[7] and it is an uncomfortable business to identify one's own corpse. In *Bofors Gun*, McGrath has set his eighteen-year-old dead self a dilemma, more extreme than, but not different in kind from, dilemmas faced by the living self a dozen years earlier.

At the risk of carrying out my own version of 'pulling rank', I have to say that Evans's dilemma cannot be fully appreciated by anyone who has no experience of the peculiar isolation of the national serviceman. The comforting assumption that our intelligence always provides us with a choice gets in the way of understanding. On the Theatre-in-Education circuit during the 1980s, there was a participatory text called *No Heroes, No Cowards* in which the audience 'became' soldiers. Confronted with an ethical dilemma, we were invited to choose whether we would or would not obey orders, fight, kill etc. As the performance progressed, I found myself in a minority of one. Alone in the room, I would 'opt' to obey orders and I would do so because the very notion of 'option' was alien to my experience of national service. There is no choice where survival is the motive. Like Evans, I was once, and only once, a guard commander. We were guarding the totally unthreatened Joint Services School for Linguists in Crail on the east coast of Fife and my job was to allocate to a disgruntled group of six servicemen the sequence of two-hour watches. They had only one advantage over me: they could sleep when not on watch; I had to stay awake all night. We all knew that the exercise was pointless and that a certain amount of cheating (two-by-two trips to the Naafi) was traditional, but the guard would be called out for inspection at some time during the night and my head would be on the block if there were any absentees. I was luckier than Evans in that I had only national servicemen to deal with and we were all much the same age. Evans has two national servicemen and four regulars, two of them nearly twice his age; and there is almost as much distance between a regular and a national serviceman as there is between a national serviceman and a civilian. The single stripe that signifies Lance-Bombardier Evans's outranking of the Gunners is, in the circumstance, a flimsy symbol of authority, but it marks him out as peculiarly vulnerable in the event of discovered indiscipline. The action of *Bofors Gun* is, in effect, determined variously by the decisions Evans makes and by his indecisiveness. It is a play that subjects the idea of choice to a scrutiny that is inherently political. It is also a play that charts the progress of the John McGrath we have probably forgotten towards the John McGrath we know.

The position is this. After seven months of his mandatory two years, Evans has climbed a single step to lance-bombardier, but it has been noticed that he has o.l.q. (officer-like qualities) and he is scheduled *tomorrow* for a return from Germany to England to attend a selection board:

> If I go now, and pass the Board, in five months' time I'll be an officer: right—right, that means a year to push; fair enough—but if I don't go now, there'll not be another place on the Board for three months, right, even assuming they still thought me suitable. Then, if I pass, another five months, then a spot of leave and a bit of waiting around and I'll be practically out of the army before they start to get their moneysworth.

They'll never bother. And here I'll be, for another year and a half. I think
I'd go mad.[8]

There is surely some autobiography here—the (guilty) recollection of a
progress from Gunner to Lance-Bombardier to Second Lieutenant that
carried the 'dead' McGrath to the relative comfort of the officers' mess. It
was a discomforting discovery of national service—discomforting, anyway,
for a young man inclined to socialism—that 'our boys', the gallant soldiers
who make safe the streets of Belfast, Bosnia and Basra, are not much fun
to be with. None of the Gunners under Evans's charge, not even Flynn,
offers anything secure in the way of companionship and O'Rourke and
Featherstone are the extreme equivalents of the Bridgnorth lorry driver
and boxer. In the temporary totality of the guardroom, Evans is desert-
islanded with a hostile group of subordinates. What choice does he have?
He *could* refuse to allow any of them to go to the Naafi, but they might go
anyway—O'Rourke certainly and Featherstone probably would—and he's
'a nice boy, trying hard to be liked'. Allowing the Naafi-trips is his only
way of maintaining even a semblance of command. And when O'Rourke
puts everything at risk by getting roaring drunk, throwing himself out of a
window and failing to return for his sentry detail, Evans *could* report him.
But that would be to expose his own dereliction of duty—and let's not
forget that he's 'a nice boy' who doesn't want to be responsible for
condemning O'Rourke to the horrors of a military prison. In his retro-
spect, McGrath has only modified compassion for Evans: 'It was all about
the difference between Evans, who is climbing out of a working-class
mentality into a middle-class one, with everything that that entails, and the
total, life-destructive fanaticism of his desire to get out, get on'.[9] This
distinction between the 'real' Evans and the fanaticism that possesses him
in his life as a national serviceman is an unexpected one. It speaks of a
remembered alienation from the self that is/was the experience of enforced
service. The whole impulse of the national serviceman is to escape,
but there is no escape until the seemingly interminable two years have
passed—and '[d]o you not find time the most alarming thing of all?' asks
Flynn.[10] Evans's wish to be an officer is primarily a wish to escape from
what he is, a perhaps illusory quest for purpose as an alternative to the
purposelessness vividly represented by the ritual protection of two bofors
guns that nobody is threatening and that have been obsolete for twelve
years anyway.

National service was my first conscious encounter with what Marx
identified as the condition of the proletariat under capitalism. I believe it
was John McGrath's too. It was an amorphous oppression that had us
labouring, under often humiliating conditions, for no tangible return other
than the capacity to survive. Without the embodied experience of it, I

might have reacted with less visceral fury to Norman Tebbit's counter-
unemployment slogan, 'Get on your bikes', to which the Beckettean stage
direction, '*There is no bike*', was an availably military riposte. In place of
choice, in the army, is hierarchy: a pervasive pecking order rendered
visible by stripes, pips, rings on uniforms. Every rise in rank earns a
new privilege. The callow Evans has been sufficiently indoctrinated to
conclude, in a telling exchange with Flynn,[11] that 'somebody has got to be
an officer, and carry the can'. Flynn's response may be that of a man who
has made a choice, or it may be that of a man who chose once (he is a
regular soldier) and knows that he can never choose again: 'Don't let it be
me, that's all I ask. Never be on the side of the judges.' In *Bofors Gun*, we
meet only one person who carries the Queen's commission, to which
Evans aspires. McGrath's special scorn for Second Lieutenant Pickering is
compressed into a stage direction.[12] He is 'an eighteen-year-old National
Service Subaltern from an ecclesiastical public school' and he has 'a high
voice and clear, high sense of duty'. This is the man/boy who, at the end of
the play, stands over the dead body of O'Rourke while Evans marks time
(how do we mark time? Isn't it time that marks us?) and salutes. Pickering
is 'on the side of the judges'. What choice did he have? And who chose
him?

In a lecture, probably dating from the late 1980s but unpublished until
2002, McGrath includes 'choice' among the keywords of the Thatcher
period. It meant 'a sound reason for transferring a monopoly from state to
private ownership—the real reason for the sell-off being the need to raise
cash for the Exchequer, i.e. to further reduce taxes. The "choice" being, if
anything, narrowed'.[13] Choice has no meaning without the prior existence
of a chooser, but we choose within the constraints of those who have
chosen for us. Once the passenger services have been privatized, I cannot
choose to travel by British Rail. People do not choose to live below the
poverty line, but if that is where they live their choices are narrowed.
'Evans' did not, McGrath did not, I did not choose to undergo two years
of national service during which the basis of choice had to be reassessed. It
cannot, for example, be seriously argued that Evans is ever in a position to
select the good and reject the bad of two options. It's not even clear to me
that the choice is between the bad and the worse. In dramatizing Evans's
dilemma, McGrath is adumbrating the recognitions on which a radical
theatre practice must be based. It cannot take for granted the good will of
the populace or the beneficence of the authorities. O'Rourke, whose
unarticulated experience of futility finds expression in acts of violence and
in eventual self-destruction, is part of the populace, and Pickering is
the messenger boy of the authorities. A campaign that aims to reduce the
distance between O'Rourke and Pickering has to be carefully planned.

John McGrath, throughout the thirty years of our sporadic meeting, had always something of a patrician air about him. He carried it very casually and I'm fairly sure he would have liked to divest himself of it, except when it was politically useful. But he had too many 'officer-like qualities' to remain a Gunner in the status-conscious world of the Royal Artillery. I suspect, in the subtext of *Bofors Gun*, an attempt to reconstitute history in the name of class solidarity by 'decommissioning' himself. At the play's end, when Evans's dreams of becoming an officer are in tatters, John McGrath announces his own return to the ranks. If this had been consciously a declaration, he would probably have said so to Catherine Itzin. Instead, he focuses in that interview on an aspect of *Bofors Gun* that I had overlooked: Evans's homesickness, openly avowed in one of his confessional dialogues with Flynn:

> I dream all day about home, but the laugh is, when I'm there I can't stand the place. I don't know what I'm doing here, nor why, nor who for, not even where I am on the map at all accurately. All I know is that I have to go home. I will even offer myself as a jumped-up eighteen-year-old joke of a Second Lieutenant for just one chance to get home.[14]

In a significant modification of his previous description of 'the life-destructive fanaticism' of Evans's 'desire to get out, get on', McGrath connected this ambition to homesickness:

> It's very interesting, this homesickness thing, because very few people believe it or understand it, but in fact I think that homesickness is an emotion, an overwhelming, over-powering emotion—something you find in Anglo-Saxon poems, 'The Wanderer' or 'The Seafarer'. And nearly all Celtic literature has this really strong feeling, too.

When Catherine Itzin suggests that 'home' may refer to anything from family to culture to nation, McGrath goes on:

> Yes, but particularly as it's experienced in exile. And I find it quite interesting [he is still talking about *Bofors Gun*] that not many people today—or then—understood that. They thought it was just a trivial element in the whole show [that's certainly true of me]. But it's very much part of Evans's relationship with reality, his disorientation, the feeling of exile. And that's something that I found totally sympathetic.

The disorientation—a sense of parenthetical presence—is at the heart of my own experience of national service. The effort of substituting a persona for the person I was on the way to becoming, and the even greater effort of trying to sustain that persona, whether through silence or bravado, brought about a feeling that McGrath has now persuaded me to associate with exile. But I have no clear recall of anything that I could honestly describe as homesickness.

There are at least three reasons to explain this difference in McGrath's and my experience of national service, the first two being merely circumstantial. Unlike him, I had spent the past ten years as a boarder (at Kingswood School in Bath), miles from my parents' successive homes in Sheffield, Warwick and Colchester. As the Dorset-born son of a Dorset mother and a father whose family was dyed-in-the-wool Glaswegian, I had no square mile that I could call my own. He, by contrast, must have known the territory from Buckley to Mold with the kind of intimacy that is the preserve of childhood. And then, my two years of national service were divided between Crail and Cambridge, while his took him to Germany, Egypt, Jordan, Malta, Libya and Italy. *Bofors Gun* is set in 'the corner of a gun-park in the British Zone of Germany, in February 1954', where McGrath might, after all, have met 'Evans' before 'becoming' him. The military presence, I am fairly sure, is even more marginalized abroad than it is at home. To be there, yet scarcely there, in Egypt, Jordan, Malta, Libya, would have produced a profounder disorientation than any imposed on me by geography. Those, as I have said, are circumstantial differences. Much more significant, as a leitmotiv in McGrath's theatrical career, is his unquenchable urge to localize his creativity, and that may properly be read as an artistic response to the homesickness he experienced in the army.

Events While Guarding the Bofors Gun may not be a great play, but it is an uncommonly good one. At the Library Theatre in Manchester, there was a toweringly dangerous performance of O'Rourke by a little-known (then) actor called Warren Clark. I don't remember who played Evans (it was James Bolam in Hampstead), but the notes I made the next day suggest that he made 'reluctance to lead' the keynote of his performance. The text provides ample justification for that and I find it poignant that John McGrath, who seemed from the outside a natural leader, should have, when projecting his remembered self into a fictional world, presented that self from the inside as a reluctant one. There may even be a significant footnote to the subsequent history of the two 7:84 companies here. If anyone is looking for evidence of that kind, it's there in *Bofors Gun*.

CHAPTER THREE

A Life Outside 7:84
John McGrath and the
Everyman Theatre, Liverpool

Ros Merkin

> During 1971 and 1972 I worked a lot at the Liverpool Everyman. I
> was excited at what Alan Dossor and the company were trying to do,
> and wanted to help them build up the working-class audience they
> now have. Besides I was born on Merseyside and wanted to write
> for the people I knew.[1]

How many times have we heard or used McGrath's words 'I'd rather
have a bad night in Bootle' (than write a play for the National Theatre)?
Yet, in writing the history (or histories) of John McGrath's life and work,
we tend to skate over the work he did for and about the people of Bootle.
Plugged in to History was one of a series of short plays originally called
Unruly Elements and written for the Everyman Theatre in March 1971.[2]
It was the first in a series of collaborations between McGrath and the
theatre in his home town[3] in the early 1970s, a series of collaborations
which included *Soft or a Girl?*, *Fish in the Sea* and versions of Brecht's
Caucasian Chalk Circle and Peter Terson's *Prisoners of War* as well as
visiting performances by the newly formed 7:84 company—the formation
of the company coinciding with his work at the Everyman. It was also the
first in a series of collaborations with Alan Dossor, at the time newly
in place as artistic director of the theatre. It is a series of connections
which, it could be argued, offers us more than some 'lost' plays; it is a
connection that may also help us to understand the development of a style,
a method of working that we have come to identify with McGrath, a style
influenced and informed by the work which was taking place at the
Everyman under the guidance of Dossor. What follows is some of that
history in an attempt to fill some of the blank space with a focus on the

two plays not (currently) readily available in print: *Unruly Elements* and *Soft or a Girl?*.

The Everyman

> If 'rep' tends to be associated in the public mind with the conventional,
> with a predictable programme of 'safe' classics and recent West End
> successes spiced with the occasional 'risk', then the Everyman might
> seem to require a whole new category. 'Alternative rep' might be one.
> From its very beginning it was conceived as something different, and
> the taking of risks came to be its *sine qua non*.[4]

The Everyman Theatre started life in 1964, the work of three university graduates: Martin Jenkins; Terry Hands and Peter James. At first its focus was very much on educational work and producing a mixture of classics and newer plays which would not otherwise have been seen in the city. At the same time it was trying to develop a 'house style' and an ensemble company on a very small budget. The style consisted of 'a bold way with the classics' (Rosalind in dungarees or Malaprop in drag) that still 'respected the basic meaning of the texts' but it was through new work, most notably work with a local flavour, that the theatre really developed its 'house style' and Stephen Fagan's *The Mersey Funnel* (1967) serves as a good example. Written to commemorate the opening of the Roman Catholic cathedral it was:

> . . . the essence of community theatre; a play on a topic under actual and
> sometimes heated discussion in pub and supermarket. It was a naive
> enough affair, childish compared to the later documentary musicals, but
> honest enough to capture the preoccupations of the city. It was the first
> sketch of a form that was to play a major part in the theatre's eventual
> success . . . A serious theme given a comic twist; it was musical; it was
> uniquely Scouse, and it was the company's own work, devised and
> carried out as a collective effort. All these elements, or most of them,
> would be included in the theatre's greatest successes, and in some of the
> most interesting near misses as well.[5]

It was a style that was to be developed by the artistic director appointed in 1970, Alan Dossor, a man who had an immense admiration for Joan Littlewood and who had worked previously with Peter Cheeseman at Stoke: 'He had assembled a company of excellent young actors who worked in the inventive, confident, audience-grabbing way of Theatre Workshop . . . in subject, style and attack, Alan was going somewhere positive.'[6] He felt 'that the work of the theatre should be directly con-cerned with Liverpool . . . that any sort of theatre that we were going to make work in Liverpool would have to contain the sort of elements contained in Joan Littlewood's work: music, jokes, vulgarity and colour. I also knew it would have to be very clearly based in the city and its class history.'[7]

The Braddocks Time

> The Everyman's programme of new work is more
> exciting than most of the West End shows.[8]

In October 1970, for his second production, Dossor directed *The Braddocks Time* by Stephen Fagan, a musical documentary about the MP Bessie Braddock, 'the Amazon of St Anne's'. Not so much a play, this was more of a contest; a fifteen-round boxing match which rendered all political activity in terms of violent contest in the ring paying tribute not just to Bessie Braddock's battling spirit but also to the fact that she was honorary president of the Professional Boxers' Association. With a company of twelve playing forty characters, this was a musical comedy in broad cartoon style complete with pantomime-style red-nosed Tories:

> . . . a hectic, tight-knit kaleidoscope of satirical cameos . . . giants in a
> cartoon world of buffoons, bobbies and bloated capitalists, they breast
> through the turbulent years of Poor Law reform, unemployment, the
> General Strike and housing shortages. Historical fact is never far away.
> The play borrows its conscience from its subjects and in its stylised way,
> echoes their caustic Left-wing evangelism.[9]

The *Daily Telegraph* reviewer continued by complaining that all the attempts to brighten a dull subject had given birth to a 'surfeit of red nosed corn, zany patter and gimmicks', but the young Michael Billington (originally a junior reporter in Liverpool and by then writing reviews for *The Times*) was more encouraging, suggesting that Fagan had created 'a first rate piece of local theatre' which outlined the social factors that made Bessie and her husband embattled campaigners and demonstrated 'how compassion can be as much a motive force in politics as personal ambition or power lust'. He was also quick to point out that the show, both in content and staging, owed a great deal to *Oh What a Lovely War!* and the whole school of repertory documentary.[10] Another of the audience members might have drawn the connections with Joan Littlewood too; persuaded against his better judgement to revisit the Everyman after an unhappy experience there two years earlier watching 'a highly pretentious piece of avant-garde whimsy, the hero of which was a pair of Siamese twins dressed in green and purple satin' was John McGrath.[11] Following a meeting with Dossor, he decided to try and work with him to fill the theatre (despite its local appeal *The Braddocks Time* was playing to 30% capacity) and to write a show for the Everyman.

Unruly Elements

> Unruly elements change people—unruly elements change things—ruly changements. I wrote a set of short plays, mostly set in Liverpool . . . that began to break new ground for me in style, and that began to open up whole areas of my life that I had been wanting to write about for years.[12]

That show was in fact a comedy called *Unruly Elements*, five plays linked together by a common theme—people faced with change.[13] They were plays for and about the working class and all 'show characters who are split apart by the bewilderment of unconsciously forsaking their identities to the commercially oriented media world and its welter of images destructive to the basic dignity of man'.[14] As such, the plays have a curiously contemporary feel. Set amidst piles of furniture and grotesquely inflated consumer goods (including a six-foot toothbrush, ten-foot coke bottle and a giant packet of detergent) and against a background of geometric shapes of contemporary life in bright colours where coloured lights flash on and off, they offered a nightmare image of grasping commerce. Their concerns, as well as being about the media, are also of lost ideals, defeat, uncertainty, anti-capitalism and multinationals. *They're Knocking Down the Pie Shop* shows a family faced with the prospect of their local pie shop (founded 150 years ago) being knocked down and replaced by an American Inter-Continental Hotel. In the ensuing debate, generations come into conflict. On the one hand there is the father who has fought all his life but who is now tired and defeated, unsure if they can win or even if they should. He relates to the world from a distance (news of the hotel reaches him through the local evening paper), tells stories about the defeat of the working class and how people no longer stick up for each other and starts to think about getting an allotment for the long evenings and letting history take its course: 'It's not paid much attention to my exertions so far, anyway: why should it ever?'[15] Ranged against him is his seventeen-year-old daughter Jenny who slopes off to political meetings after school and who is determined to fight:

> Listen, the buggers who are knocking down the pie-shop are burning whole villages in Cambodia, napalming children in Laos, cutting Vietnamese women in half because they look like enemy. The men who build 20 storey hotels in Liverpool are building rocket-silos in

Greenland, to protect themselves, and dropping bombs on Asian villages, to secure their interests. How can you just *give* up? There's a war on.[16]

Both of them are deftly undercut by the arrival of Mrs Malden bearing the last of Pelissier's pork pies for tea and dreaming of a 'soft job' in the new hotel.

Generations (and men and women) come into conflict again in *Angel of the Morning*. Mr Lodwick, awaiting his daughter's late-night return, is visited instead by Tralee Clausewitz, second commando of the Fazakerley Tuperamos. Her job is to distract him whilst her accomplices go upstairs to tie up his wife and steal his life savings. In the process, and by way of some sexual banter, he discovers that his daughter is also an 'urban liberator' and he is persuaded into admitting he too thinks the world could be a better place. At the heart of his dilemma is his perception of the young, who they are and what they deserve. A part of him wants to think of them as 'intelligent, well-educated', trying to live their lives in ways 'they might have read about or dreamed about, pushing onwards to something better'. Yet, as Tralee's mission unfolds, faced with the reality of what those dreams might be and how they might be achieved, he changes his mind proclaiming them to be parasites 'holding the country up to ransom':

> Who are these hoodlums bashing old women over the head—they're free milk—free meals—free-assistance-money kids . . . molesting old age pensioners for three and sixpence, harassing bus-conductors on late night buses, kicking each other's heads in, knifing, knuckle dusters, bicycle chains, acid-guns, sawn-off shotguns, air-pistols, Lugers—it's like Chicago—Liverpool the Windy City of England . . .[17]

The role of the media and its impact on our humanity comes under scrutiny in *Out of Sight* where Nat, the professional hippie, is so hooked on the media that he cannot even begin to connect to his girlfriend until she starts the camera rolling. But it is *Plugged in to History* which is most damning of the media. On the surface it is a dialogue between Kay, a young middle-aged, middle-class mother teetering on the edge, and Derek, a man looking for somewhere to stay. But dialogue is the wrong way to describe a piece in which little or no communication takes place between the two people sat side-by-side on the bench; they don't meet 'at any edge'. Both are too wrapped up in their own obsessions. Derek has just split up with his student girlfriend in Leeds—or more correctly has been thrown out by her for beating her up—and has come back to Liverpool in search of her. He is rootless and jobless, the latter out of choice, for he loses 'enthusiasm for work after four hours'. He longs for a romantic, idealized life of leisure where he can walk along canals 'hitting myself over the head for the sheer bloody joy of a sunny day'. Kay's method of cutting herself off from the world, on the other hand, is to submerge herself in stories from the news. She reads and then recites stories from the newspaper she carries—stories of mining disasters, of luxury cruise liners running aground, of black militants, of the terror bombings of statues in Portsmouth and of juicier show business gossip. Her speeches are as fragmented and disconnected as a news programme. When Derek attempts to break through these recitals and engage with Kay in a real dialogue, she retorts: 'Don't you dare come between me and my illness. My sanity depends on it.' Hiding behind the stories is her way of escape, her way of fending off the insanity in a world in which people aren't able 'to all fit on together', as she tries to explain:

> When I read my papers, I feel plugged in to history. I feel the course of events coursing through my veins. I feel taken over, crushed by many, many men. I feel occupied, a house, squatted in, defiled. I feel like a deserted ball-room being defecated in by a halted army. I feel like South America after the Yankees have finished with it, like Dresden after the bombing. I feel like a shed full of cats. I feel like a midnight zoo. I feel like a clump of trees outside a barracks, full of soldiers in rough khaki having under-age village tarts. I feel like Pompeii the next morning. I become a human news-tape, mile after mile of me, torn out, ripped off, abandoned. Do you know why? Do you begin to? It's because I feel everything, all the way through me.[18]

The final image of the play is Kay, alone again, the sounds and shadows of people walking past all around. With 'a sickening, compulsive gulp' she looks, 'almost bites, down at the paper in front of her, plugging herself in to history'. Yet being 'plugged in' doesn't make her happy—the language of her speech is the language of being dirty and defiled. She might be plugged in to the world outside, but she is not plugged in to her own history, so she is as disconnected as Derek. However, she has some moments of insight. Moments when she attacks Derek for not hearing 'the deafening crunch of millions of small animals, eating each other' or 'the thundering echoes of women's tears' as he walks beside the canal. Moments when she attacks Derek for beating up his girlfriend, for wanting to crush her for 'all men are crushers'. Moments when she rebels against being a woman stifled in a box, complying. Even if those moments don't allow her to escape from the newspaper, they show that not all life has been squeezed out of her.

The five plays are held together and introduced by a number of bizarre

2.   Elizabeth MacLennan and Robert Hamilton in *Plugged in to History*. 1974
(Photo: Julian Sheppard)

cosmopolitan characters, a series of myopic little men in the Liverpool streets, mouthing well worn clichés in a curious new language that merges Irish, Polish, West Indian and Pakistani with James Joyce, John Lennon and Roger McGough. They lead us through a semi-comprehensible urban jungle bemoaning the state of society today, and in the words of the park-keeper who introduces *They're Knocking Down the Pie Shop*, looking nostalgically to the past, to the:

> . . . dole days, when a good dole King George da vee an da good dung King George da sick was raining, da commun people wass in a sty of pigality. Dey digged what dey was tolled an dey obeyed when dey was paid. Dey had luvly ickle ousses, an dey keptum goodan clean. Dey was nice, da commun people and dey noed der stay-shun, and der dey shunnted, steaming an glad, gladda da hand-out, so sweet an so neat.

Now, they point to the ills of society, to the 'unksters' who are 'dingrateful' and 'ageetaters', to the 'pig-men' who 'make-a piles a doe', to those who 'doan do ennuff irk' and to the whole 'irking clas' who are 'da hole trouble wit da cuntry'. They are the people who are 'truly unreally, dey'm really unruly' and they need to be given 'da big stick': 'You seeum: das wass wrong mit da nay'shun. Shuck 'em in clink; da hole lot ovum.'[19]

The 'narrators' fall for every anti-working-class cliché they have been fed; they certainly do not offer us an image of the romantic working-class hero, nor do they signpost a way forward. And throughout the plays, easy answers are hard to find. Neil, the son in *They're Knocking Down the Pie Shop*, is a figure who recurs in McGrath's later plays—the son who very firmly turns his back on his father's ideals, wanting to be a civil engineer, to make money and not to be washed in the blood of Joe Stalin or Mao Tse Tung or Fidel Castro. Confusions and splits in the left are also reflected in Jenny's description of the meetings she attends: the Maoists want to go all out for burning down the hotel; the anarchists want to burn down the pie shop and the Spartacus League want to burn them both down. Political uncertainty is also present in *Angel of the Morning*. The guerrilla consciousness of Tralee and the Fazakerly Tuperamos is not presented as an easy answer (her dreams of 'wonderland' are never convincingly fleshed out) and even she believes that people don't really know what they want: '. . . deep down they're covering up an awful monster that . . . feeds on what they think, gobbles up every idea, crams every experience into its big fat mouth; the terrible monster called, Don't Know, lurking somewhere between your stomach and your back-side, growling at everything.'[20] When she leaves Mr Lodwick, he doesn't immediately rush upstairs to rescue his wife or telephone the police. Instead he sits, pulled in two conflicting directions. Partly inspired by the possibilities Tralee offers, he wants to get out, work on construction, apply himself in some meaningful way before he is stifled by the world. In part he rants against everything Tralee stands for:

> They can't do this to normal, civilised people! My family demands the full protection of the law! They ought to stop these things before they begin, grapple with them before they gnaw away at the very foundation of our society! . . .
>
> These wild unfettered imps of darkness on the rampage through the night must be given a good seeing to, hammered, smashed, wiped out, removed, *exterminated* from England's green and pleasant land.
>
> Yes, exterminated. *Exterminated!*[21]

In the end, he sits, doing nothing, representative of the silent majority confused about what is to happen: 'I wonder how this is going to turn out?' It's a question no one in the plays can answer; faced with change they are all but paralysed and, collectively, the plays stand as an uncertain search for signposts for the next decade, both in terms of ideas and theatrical style.

Experiments in attracting audiences

> The Everyman believes that in a city of this size there must be a few thousand people who would like to see good new plays— particularly ones with local interest.[22]

McGrath claimed that when *Unruly Elements* was playing audience figures went up to 75%, the audience responding to the jokes, the presence of recognizable local people and problems and the style of the pieces:

> The plays, and the actors and director, created a sense of excitement about the theatre in the community; and encouraged by a determined publicity campaign, by the price of the tickets, by the informality, lack of middle-class bullshit about the theatre, and by the fact you could get a decent pint of ale before, during and after the show, some young working-class blokes came with their wives for a night out. They enjoyed themselves and sent their friends . . . The way was open to a new kind of theatre.[23]

But a series of articles in the press from the same month suggest the picture was far less rosy. Audiences for new work were in fact reaching dangerously low levels and Alan Dossor threatened that if more interest was not shown by Liverpool audiences in the new plays at the theatre, opportunities for seeing new work might disappear altogether. And the

figures bear this out; whilst Charles Wood's *Welfare* had barely reached the
13% mark and *Unruly Elements* more than doubled that to 35%, it was in
fact *Waiting for Godot* that had saved the day by attracting houses in excess
of 73%. All that was to change in the near future however, although not
before a small experiment in new writing later in May when six writers
were asked to read Brecht's *The Private Life of the Master Race* and to write
a short contemporary equivalent. McGrath produced *Hover Through the
Fog*, 'an excruciatingly accurate cameo of a university lefty on a Government wage arbitration panel. Firmly convinced of whatever the last person
she spoke to has told her, Gillian Hanna gives a delicious impersonation of
Barbara Castle . . .'.[24] Overall, the evening provided a varied programme
in a jumble of styles, and it was a useful experiment as they 'could see
what was working with the audience and guess why. But all the time I was
quite sure that the thing to do was to fill the theatre, and I knew that then
we could really move and take the audience with us.'[25]

Soft or a Girl?

> . . . a Liverpool play with loads of songs and lots of comedy, lots of
> local involvement and a serious theme.[26]

> He hopes that it reflects, among other things, his concern about
> the destruction of living communities which are not replaced by new
> ones and what he sees as a distortion of human relationships by
> false ideas of economic competition.[27]

McGrath's clear response to this experiment and to the challenge of filling
the theatre was to turn to a different form of popular entertainment, a
form of popular entertainment which had resonated through Liverpool in
the 1960s:

> The rock concert is one form of entertainment that has fascinated me,
> partly because I like a lot of that kind of music, partly because the
> Beatles, Loving Spoonful and the folk-rock groups had developed lyrics
> which were literate and worth listening to, and partly because the UFO
> groups like Pink Floyd had established a whole rather twee performance
> or acting level during and between their numbers.[28]

The format was used to tell the story of two families, starting from two
soldiers (Mr Hurley and Mr Martin), two 'very ordinary people . . . my pal
and me' on fire-watching duty during the Blitz at the top of St George's
Tower, defending their city in order to be able to build a new and beautiful
way of living. Suddenly they find themselves catapulted into the bright
new future that is the 1970s, watching the lives of their children. Central to

the story is Mick, Mr Hurley's son, and his sexual exploits as he moves from Jenny to Mr Martin's daughter Ella. He is also the focus for the title song, accused by both fathers of having no punch or drive:

> What can be
> The matter with him
> His hair's so long
> His waist's so slim
> He sings sweet songs
> His clothes fit tight
> He talks so quietly
> And he won't fight—
>
> The lad's
> Gone mad
> What's happened to the world
> He's round the bend
> Is he soft or a girl?

The changing sexual politics that ensue from this make up one of the themes of the play and, even within the context of the song, the older generation are not allowed to get away with their ideas unchallenged. Verses follow from the youngsters in which they tell the 'old men' that they do not care what they say but will live lives in their own way:

> So screw your collars
> And screw your ties
> Screw your suits
> 'Cos they're all lies
> Screw your razors
> Let it grow
> Screw your haircuts
> Let it all flow
>
> We don't care
> If we're plain or purl
> We don't care
> If we're soft or a girl.[29]

But not all the youngsters can live their life by new ideas. The reason Mick stops seeing Jenny is because she becomes too political, too sharp; she is 'trying to be a feller . . . all this about fighting and accusing and judging—it sounds a bit, well, awkward coming from a girl.'[30] Caught up in this is Mick's own sense of lack of worth (he's left school at sixteen while Jenny is planning to go to university) and sections of the play deal with questions of self-worth and identity, including a moment where Mick contemplates suicide and wishes he'd been born rich so he had con- fidence, poise, ability, courage, defiance and savoir-faire. Despite the teasing, Jenny is not to be put off and argues her corner throughout, becoming the political heart of the play—from telling Mick his song might be nice but singing isn't going to change anything—to reminding Mr Hurley that being sociable with your enemies is the whole story of the English working class and making him realize in the end that Mr Martin is not his friend but his class enemy. For alongside sex and sexual politics, the theme of class is never far away and the real thrust of the play is the move from Mr Hurley believing in the wartime ethos of all being in it together to the final scene when he remembers (with Jenny's help) that Mr Martin is the enemy. Caught up with this is his shame that he's not brought his son up to see it more clearly but left him chasing after Ella, like a two-year-old with his face glued to a toy-shop window looking at a big beautiful doll 'panting for what you can't have', grovelling 'for the favour of them up there, lusting after their daughter because she's all I've taught him to long for'. Ironically, the final lines go to Mr Martin, reminding Mr Hurley that he's not on his own—'there's millions more of you than there is of us—what are you waiting for? Are you soft or a girl?'[31]

This time success was unquestionable: 'The working class, young and old, flocked to the Everyman. We played to 109 per cent of capacity . . . for the three weeks scheduled and then came back for another three weeks and could have gone on for another three.'[32] The policy of the theatre had not changed, yet this was to mark a turning point, but one that had been built towards in the preceding years.

Make it local: rewriting plays

> One borrows the spittle of history, spits at a historical corpse and
> nevertheless has the satisfying feeling of having today spat in the right
> direction.[33]

McGrath's next work for the Everyman was a reworking of Brecht's *The Caucasian Chalk Circle*—one with a distinctly Liverpool feel and one with a distinctly 1970s' feel. Set on a building site, the play opens, not with an argument about land, but with an accident on the site. A piece of scaffolding collapses and a building worker is taken to hospital badly injured. His fellow workers down tools and stage a sit-in during which they are entertained by a troupe of not quite prepared actors who have turned up to see if they can come back and perform a play in three weeks' time. Instead, like 'Joan Littlewood's Theatre Workshop at its best' they find themselves persuaded to put on the show there and then, the whole ending with a reworded conclusion in which the promise 'what there is shall go to those who are good for it' is now included:

> and the building to the builders
> and those who will live in it: That
> it shall be built for living in, not dying on
> for people—not for profit.[34]

A few months later, Peter Terson's *Prisoners of War* received the same localizing treatment. Translated from Geordie to Scouse by McGrath (and including back projections of Liverpool), the play is ostensibly a series of anti-war sketches held together by a narrator, but it is as much a play about being prisoners today living in the wake of war's cruelties and absurdities as it is about the soldiers and families they left behind in the Second World War. There is some debate about how much rewriting McGrath actually did, or how much he added to the text. The *Daily Post*'s Doreen Tanner suspected that he had added the extended post-war episodes 'with their raw theatrically undigested message of political gloom' and the series of familiar comments on Liverpool (including references to demolition and vacant office blocks), but until scripts for both the original and McGrath's version turn up, we can only conjecture.

A Conclusion and *Fish in the Sea*

> I think just gradually Liverpool people are beginning to look on the Everyman as part of their lives. This process has got to continue . . . So the Everyman will continue to hold up the mirror to a Liverpool torn apart, as John McGrath put it, and stuck out on the East Lancashire Road.[35]

> If Liverpool had had this sort of culture when I was a youngster maybe my whole future would have been different.[36]

There is certainly far less conjecture over McGrath's final contribution to the Everyman which has gone on to become far better known and far more written about than his previous contributions. Using a form developed from *Soft or a Girl?* and still focusing on a family (this time the Maconochies), *Fish in the Sea* was an almost inevitable follow-on from the success of the former: '. . . it's a very ambitious play, and I would not have believed it would work if I hadn't learnt a great deal from the Everyman audience'.[37] In part the argument here is about filling in a piece of history, looking at the overlapping period when McGrath was involved in setting up 7:84 and at the same time was writing for the Everyman, trying out and developing ideas, a style, an approach that were to become familiar in the following years—localism, use of music and popular forms and working with an ensemble company and for an audience. But there is something more than that too. The chance he had to try out and develop those ideas came because a theatre like the Everyman existed and was trying to do similar work. McGrath (alongside a host of other actors and directors) 'cut their teeth' at the Everyman, and it is an honourable roll call even when looked at simply at the moment McGrath had the chance to work there. Richard Eyre directed *Prisoners of War* and McGrath worked with actors who included Jonathan Pryce, Anthony Sher, Alison Steadman, Gavin Richards and Gillian Hanna (the latter two leaving with him to work with 7:84). And in the process of experimenting with creating a theatre that celebrated the values and views of the people in the city, they developed a theatre that local audiences came to:

> The audience did stay. Alan [Dossor], as director, found ways to present Shakespeare and other new writers, and Brecht, and kept faith with that audience's expectations . . . In 1972 I was in the Fisher-Bendix factory while it was being occupied by the workforce. Almost every worker there that I spoke to had been to the Everyman and was going to keep on going. And the work at the Everyman as getting better, livelier and more like real theatre than anything I had seen at the Royal Court or the Old Vic.[38]

CHAPTER FOUR

'Serjeant Musgrave Dances to a Different Tune'

John McGrath's Adaptation of John Arden's
Serjeant Musgrave's Dance

John Bull

In May 1968, John McGrath travelled to Paris to witness the student protests. 'He was very involved with the students at the Beaux Arts and with Jean Jacques Lebel, instigator of street "happenings".'[1] He was working on a new play at the time and his experiences of the French Spring were to influence both that play and his developing theatrical strategies.

> I started to write . . . and in May 68 things started happening in Paris. And I went over and spent some time there . . . And the importance of the thinking around that whole time, the excitement of that whole complex set of attitudes to life which that para-revolutionary situation threw up was incredible—the thinking about ordinary life, the urgency and the beauty of the ideas was amazing. *But* what didn't happen was the organisation . . . In the middle of all that you have this absolute contradiction. I came back and left the play, actually for about six months to a year, and then I finished it. But it was changed by that whole experience.[2]

The play was *Random Happenings in the Hebrides*, to which when he returned he added a sub-title, *The Social Democrat and the Stormy Sea*. What he had learnt in Paris was twofold: the need for direct action, outside the discourse of conventional 'parliamentary' politics; and as he stresses strongly, the need for organization. These two themes are reflected in the play as it was finally completed: the 'interaction between spontaneous and unorganised left activity and the attempts of a newly elected Scottish

3. 7:84 poster for *Serjeant Musgrave Dances On.* 1974

Labour MP to work for change within the parliamentary system'.[3] Elizabeth MacLennan has described the play as 'a bridge between the kind of writing in *The Bofors Gun* and the later McGrath 7:84 plays',[4] and if we pursue this image we see on one side of the bridge a play, *Events While Guarding the Bofors Gun* (1966), concerned with soldiers and a gun, and on the other side a very different play, also concerned with soldiers and a gun, which helps in the construction of a new bridge that takes McGrath into the work of 7:84 Scotland.

From August to November 1972, the 7:84 Theatre Company toured with a production of *Serjeant Musgrave Dances On*, an adaptation by John McGrath of the John Arden play, *Serjeant Musgrave's Dance* (1959). The company's initial production had been McGrath's *Trees in the Wind* at the Edinburgh Festival in 1971 and in between there had been six other productions: two of plays by Trevor Griffiths (*Apricots and Thermidor* and *Occupations*); three by McGrath (*Plugged in to History*, *Out of Sight* and *Underneath*); and one by Arden and Margaretta D'Arcy (*The Ballygombeen Bequest*). *Serjeant Musgrave Dances On* was to be the final production of the single 7:84 company before the formation of 7:84 England and 7:84 Scotland in 1973, and for this fact alone it deserves memorializing. However, it occupies a very particular place in the development of McGrath's and 7:84's work in other ways, ways that have never been really considered, largely I suspect because the adapted text has yet to be published.

For a start, it is far more than simply an adaptation of Arden's original: it contains within itself a dialogue with the 1959 play, and reaches conclusions that at that time at least Arden felt personally unwilling, or perhaps historically unable, to approach. Not the least reason for the particular significance that can be claimed for this production is that it toured with another play by Arden (and D'Arcy), *The Ballygombeen Bequest*—and was not a hands-off adaptation—and thus must also be considered as offering a dialogue between the political and theatrical strategies not only of Arden and McGrath but, in addition, of the younger and the older Arden. In short, a comparison between the two 'texts' will shed much light on what had happened in the intervening years, as well as on what was to come.

McGrath and D'Arcy and Arden had known each other for fifteen years at the time of the production, and he had been 'asking John and Margaretta for some time for the play'. He saw *The Ballygombeen Bequest* as a logical progression of the previous work of 7:84, enlarging the company and strengthening the importance of music:

> There were a lot more songs, a lot more direct stuff for the audiences, it
> was a more kind of free and easy structure although obviously it had a

tremendous logic underneath it theatrically; the musical involvement of
the actors in not only singing but in playing was much greater and the
style, the connection between the actor and audience, was beginning to
be even more direct than it had been previously.[5]

The fact that Arden and D'Arcy's play was about Ireland—was indeed the
first of their Irish plays—was also not without significance and Arden's
suggestion that McGrath adapt his own *Serjeant Musgrave's Dance* must be
seen, therefore, not only as the fruit of their discussions 'about companies
and things . . . they were keen to get their own company together',[6] but as
evidence of the way in which Arden and D'Arcy's play and McGrath's
adaptation touring in tandem can be seen almost as a manifesto of intent,
both theatrically and politically. After its first year of activity, McGrath
was ambitious both to expand activity and reformulate the way in which
7:84 would organize this activity:

> I considered it quite politically seriously that in the first year if the
> thing was to continue it had to have a push and an organisation, a
> centralisation. But from the beginning we wanted to evolve power as
> much as possible, as soon as the first year was over, as soon as we were
> in the position I have just described, this I tried to do by creating a
> collective machinery where discussions took place on all major decisions,
> where the power to take other decisions was delegated by the collective
> to individuals who were responsible to the collective for what they did,
> where the collective decided what plays they wanted to do, what subjects
> they thought we ought to do, how we ought to do them, who ought to
> direct them, what kind of directing there ought to be, and who ought to
> join and so on. I think that was the right moment to do it and with the
> next shows . . . *The Ballygombeen Bequest* and *Serjeant Musgrave Dances
> On* we put this into process.[7]

To this end, the direction of *The Ballygombeen Bequest* passed to Gavin
Richards,[8] and it is apparent that the introduction of this collective
consciousness at the time of these two productions was the necessary
foundation for 7:84 Scotland's first production, the seminal *The Cheviot,
the Stag and the Black, Black Oil* (1973).

The immediate theatrical context for Arden's *Musgrave* had been the
development of the English Stage Company under George Devine at
London's Royal Court Theatre; this caused considerable problems for its
initial production. It had been surrounded by a number of new plays that,
rightly or wrongly, were perceived to be offering a progressive perspective
and, in the case of Arnold Wesker in particular, even a radical socialist
stance. *Musgrave* failed initially because it baffled audiences who failed to
find a consistent authorial voice that was either properly progressive or

radical, discovering instead a view of existence as 'senseless, absurd, useless'.[9] Arden tried to come to terms with this bafflement in his 'Introduction' to the published play in 1960. He claimed that it was 'not a nihilistic play . . . nor does it advocate bloody revolution'. He continued:

> I have endeavoured to write about the violence that is so evident in the world, and to do so through a story that is partly one of wish fulfilment. I think that many of us must at some time have felt an overpowering urge to match some particularly outrageous piece of violence with an even greater and more outrageous retaliation. Musgrave tries to do this: and the fact that the sympathies of the play are clearly with him in his original horror, and then turn against him and his intended remedy, seems to have bewildered many people.[10]

His play was concerned with the arrival of Serjeant Musgrave and three other soldiers at a colliery village in the midst of what is alternately described as a strike (by the mine-owner) and a lockout (by the colliers). Intent on pursuing his own agenda of seeking reparation for the death of an ex-collier, Billy Hicks, enlisted from the town, and the related retribution on the population of the 'sort of Protectorate, but British' where his regiment has been serving, Musgrave and the other deserters apparently go along with the Mayor's plan to recruit dissident colliers into the army in order to diffuse the situation. All is set up for a final confrontation, only briefly interrupted by the accidental killing of one of their number, Sparky, when—five having been killed for the one soldier—twenty-five of the townspeople are to be mown down. An articulated skeleton, dressed as a soldier and representing Billy, is hung from a lamp-post and, after performing his dance of death, Musgrave prepares to take revenge. At the last moment one of the soldiers, Attercliffe, refuses to follow the plan through and the townspeople are rescued, Hollywood Western fashion, by the arrival of the Dragoons. In his 'Introduction', Arden suggested that 'a study of the roles of the women, and of Private Attercliffe, should be sufficient to remove any doubts as to where the "moral" of the plays lies', and concluded that, 'Complete pacifism is a very hard doctrine: and if this play appears to advocate it, it is probably because I am naturally a timid man—and also because I know that if I am hit I very easily hit back: and I do not care to preach too confidently what I am not sure I can practice.'[11]

This pointer to a possible 'moral' that is immediately undercut caused problems for early audiences and these were compounded by the historical location of the events in the play. 'The exact date of the play is deliberately not given,' Arden stated. 'In the London production, the details of costume covered approximately the years between 1860 and 1880.'[12] The

actual historical context for *Musgrave* is the British intervention into
Cyprus and the effect of the time displacement—Arden described the play
in a sub-title as 'An un-historical parable'—is such as to make the political
content of the play even more ambiguous. Curiously, however, it is largely
this sense of ambiguity of commitment, as well as the very real qualities of
a quite remarkable play, that has resulted in its becoming, as Arden
ruefully acknowledged in 1977, a 'modern classic',[13] and latterly a familiar
text for study on English Literature examined courses: it was seen to
discuss political agendas without ever positing a real threat to the status
quo. To argue in this way is to do a real disservice to both play and
playwright, but it is not difficult to see how this situation has arisen.

Actually, Arden's play contains two quite distinct, though related,
thematic elements: the business of Musgrave and his men, outlined above,
and the struggle between the colliers and the forces of law and order,
represented by the Constable, the Parson and the Mayor (also the mine-
owner). If there is ambiguity about the first, there certainly is not about the
second. There is not a unanimity of intent amongst the colliers, many of
whom are only too easily bought off with the promise of free drinks and an
apparently generous offer to enlist; but in Walsh, 'an earnest collier',
Arden has created a committed Union member, well aware of the way in
which his less politically sophisticated workmates might be fooled by the
tricks of the ruling class. 'This town lives by collieries. That's coal-owners
and it's pitmen—aye, and they battle, and the pitmen'll win. But not wi' no
soldier-boys to order our fight for us. Remember their trade: you give 'em
one smell of a broken town, you'll never get 'em out!' With the arrival of
the dragoons and the re-establishment of 'law and order', however, Walsh
is left only with anger, and with no answer to the Bargee's riposte:

> WALSH: (*With great bitterness*) The community's been saved. Peace and
>   prosperity rules. We're all friends and neighbours for the rest of
>   today. We're all sorted out. We're back where we were. So what
>   do we do?
> BARGEE: Free beer. It's still here.

It is when we consider the behaviour and the language of, in particular, the
Parson and the Mayor, that the situation becomes clearer: the colliers may
lack a fully formulated programme of action but their 'betters' do not. In
Act 1, Scene 2 the Mayor makes an anxious visit to the inn where the
soldiers are billeted, offering additional money to encourage the trouble-
makers to enlist: 'constable, perhaps you might let in the serjeant on a few
likely names for his list, eh? Could you pick him some passable strong-set
men, could you?' The Parson, whose first thought on hearing about
the arrival of the soldiers is that they have been sent to deal with the

impending unrest, gives a public performance at the beginning of the 'recruiting scene' that could have come straight out of the mouth of the Minister in McGrath's *The Cheviot, the Stag and the Black, Black Oil* (1973). After a sanctimonious appeal to abandon 'petty differences and grievances—but all united under a common flag', he concludes: 'The Empire calls! Greatness is at hand! Serjeant Musgrave will take down the names of any men willing, if you'll file on to the platform in an orderly fashion, in the name of the Father, the Son and mumble mumble . . .'. This sort of deconstruction of the ideology of ruling-class rhetoric was to become a staple of British agit-prop theatre of the 1970s.[14]

In adapting the play, McGrath made several alterations to the *dramatis personae*. His 'earnest collier' Walsh becomes Jacky, a more constructededly militant counterpart. The bargee—a strange mocking character, part chorus and part active participant, his presence adding an almost mythical dimension to Arden's play—is removed entirely and the Constable is up-ranked to an 'inexperienced' Inspector Williams, the better able to liase between strikers, soldiers and the authorities. The Parson and the Mayor (and mine-owner) also disappear. In their place is Burrell, the pit-manager. He is an example of the betrayal of class solidarity in the play. In our first meeting with him, he is grateful for the presence of the troops and talks of 'some class of violent revolution in the air . . . stirred up by half-a-dozen hot-heads, not even locals'. He is a man with the same roots as the miners, but has climbed the ladder a little. 'Of course, I am a Labour man myself, a working class feller, same as you.' It's not the ordinary pit-men who are responsible, he claims, 'it's a bunch of extremists out to wreck the country'.

Burrell borrows from the dialogue of Arden's bargee, parson and mayor, as appropriate, as well as being provided with fresh material of his own. His importance is, then, that he is seen as the link between the miners and the Coal Board and Government: his incorporation of the voices of all these figures of authority[15] places greater stress on his particular role in the struggle—as a betrayer of his own kind and not a figure from outside the mining community—and interestingly, in view of the greater stress on agit-prop methodology in McGrath's version, makes him less of a two-dimensional character than the Mayor and the Parson had been. That is to say that there is some attempt made for an audience to understand what goes into the creation of such a middle-management figure, rather than simply a use of him to exemplify abstract authority.

When adapting Arden's play, McGrath kept the dual-plot element, but brought the two strands together in a very different manner. That he would do so is apparent from the very beginning of *Musgrave Dances On*. Where the original had started with the soldiers preparing to be ferried across the canal to the town by the bargee, McGrath opens with a

direct sung address to the audience by Jacky. He fills in the background to the strike, emphasising that we are no longer somewhere in a
nineteenth-century past but, as the stage directions indicate, in a 'Yorkshire mining village' on 'a cold night in February '72, during the miners'
strike'.

> They sacked all the owners in brave forty-six
> And now for the Coal Board we're swinging our picks:
> Those same proud coal-owners are still doing well—
> Are we any richer? Are we bloody hell—
> And everybody reckons that's normal,
> The way it has to be—natural.

Jacky is joined by another strike picket, Ted, who brings news that a scab
lorry has tried to break through the line, injuring a colleague in the
process. They talk about the way in which the media lie about what
happens and McGrath effectively sets up the voices of the strikers as the
only reliable source of communication. So, by opening with the miners, we
know the context of events from the outset and are not reliant on learning
through the soldiers' own coming to knowledge. This importantly re-
defines the audience perspective—foregrounding the narrative of the
strike, which is more incidental in Arden's play.

The opening also points to a key difference in contextualization between
the two texts. Although a certain amount of Arden's period flavour is
retained, McGrath is intent on asserting the direct contemporaneity of the
events. When Hurst, Sparky and Attercliffe eventually arrive in this first
scene they further underscore events: 'Disturbances. Miners. Picketing'.
In June 1970, Harold Wilson's Labour Government had somewhat un-
expectedly lost a General Election and the Conservatives under Edward
Heath had taken power. Heath immediately set about lessening the power
of the Trade Unions, which he saw as a hindrance to a revival of the
country's economic welfare. He did so aware of the combined efforts of
those unions to cause an abandonment of Wilson's proposed 'reform' of
them in 1969. By August 1971, a new Industrial Relations Bill received the
Royal Assent and in June 1972, the 'Pentonville Five' were imprisoned for
defying the new bill's strictures on picketing, though subsequently released
after trade-union agitation. In January of that year, with the unemployment figures running at over a million, the National Union of Miners took
on the Government, with 280,000 miners on strike. The effects on
industrial output were immense and by February the strike ended with a
union victory. In December 1973 the Government would declare a 'state
of emergency' and the introduction of a 'three-day week' to conserve
energy supplies during the second Miners' Strike. In February 1974 Heath

was to use the state of emergency to call a General Election, which his party lost narrowly to the Labour Party under Wilson. These would be lessons well learnt by Margaret Thatcher in her preparation for the rerun of the confrontation with the miners in 1984–5.

McGrath is thus writing within a period of considerable working-class militancy and *Musgrave Dances On* contains many elements of direct agit-prop theatre, including frequent direct addresses to the audience, something that is notably absent from *Serjeant Musgrave's Dance.* The piece was created with the specific intention of touring, by now a central platform of 7:84's programme, and, in particular, of visiting mining areas in the immediate aftermath of the strike victory. The restructuring of the play demonstrates well the difference between the conventional theatre performance that *Musgrave* had received at the Royal Court Theatre and subsequently and the more limited conditions of a touring production. McGrath's play is still divided into essentially the same three acts as Arden's, but the scenic divisions within each are more fluid. Usually a character addresses the audience while the new set is put minimally in place: so that Act 1, Scene 1, for instance is bridged by Annie speaking to 'a drum rhythm', and when finished 'she turns, the pub room is set behind her'. There is no need for complicated sets and, indeed, often an interior location in Arden is converted into a continuous exterior in McGrath. Similar devices are used throughout although, significantly, it is almost always the voices of the strikers that are heard, again preventing the audience's engagement with the emerging philosophy of Musgrave and the soldiers.

The point can be reinforced. It is not just that McGrath had in mind a touring production when he worked on the play: consistent with 7:84's stated aims, he had a different kind of audience in mind, one not necessarily familiar with a theatre as a venue for performance. Act 3 has the following introductory stage directions: 'The theatre is transformed into the local Town Hall, dressed ready for a recruiting session.[16] The walls of the theatre are now covered with recruiting posters which have been let down during the interval, and Union Jacks, and red, white and blue bunting is spread around the place.' What the audience is confronted with on their return is not a set that they can look at as theatrical voyeurs, but an uninterrupted space in which they are present as active spectators in the drama that is about to unfold. Three of the major characters are located 'amongst the audience', and the 'Inspector is in evidence amongst the audience; when the speeches begin he moves down and stands at the front near the stage'. This disruption of conventional theatrical expectancy is stressed by a further stage direction, 'the house lights don't go down': the audience is reconfigured as both part of the action and as, in essence, the critical jury who are to be encouraged to make a judgement on the various arguments presented to them.

The blurring between theatrical performance and social reality, already obvious in the contemporary reference to the desired audience's own lives and experience, is suddenly and importantly reversed towards the end of the play. Musgrave's protest having failed, Burrell is anxious to stress to the audience that what they have been watching is *only* a play. Stepping out of his role, he grabs a microphone and assumes a part that is both the Chair of a political meeting and the Master of Ceremonies in a working-men's club:

> Well, I suppose as your Chairman, I should round off the meeting with a note of thanks for the speakers. Most illuminating I must say. I'm sorry if any of you of a nervous disposition have been upset or terrorised in any way by the proceedings, all most unusual. But there's nothing to worry about. The crisis is over. Let normal life begin again. Let's have some music, shall we?

It is left to Attercliffe to cry, 'No, by God, we'll have no music', before Jacky has the final words of the play

> And that's the end of Sergeant Musgrave. Court martial. Fifteen years in an Army prison . . . At least he tried to make people see what they're doing, even if it had sent him round the bend first. It's one way of doing it. *But it was a piece of theatre.* What we're doing—the pit-men, the dockers, the builders, the shipyard men—*that's to do with real life.*[17] And you haven't heard the end of us. Good night.

Here, theatre becomes associated with falsity: reality being the continuing political struggle that has been presented. As we will see, this point has further ramifications with reference to the other strand of the play's narrative.

There is the need for further contextualization. Not only does Arden's appropriation of a mining village on strike fit well with McGrath's relocation of the action to the present, but 1972 was also a key year in the long history of English colonial adventure that is central to Musgrave and the soldiers' plan in the original play. Where Sparky talks of fighting in the Crimea and Sebastopol at the beginning of *Musgrave*, his counterpart in *Musgrave Dances On* is silent: we are at first given no hint of where it is that they have deserted from. It is not until the 'recruiting scene' (Act 3, Scene 1) that the audience gradually and terrifyingly are brought to realize just how small a journey the deserters have made. The first part of the scene proceeds much as it had in Arden, with Burrell offering an updated version of the inducements to enlist put originally in the mouth of the mayor. The machine-gun loaded and turned on the audience—all the audience—Musgrave now offers a more contemporary list of engagements than he had in 1960, when it had been 'we've beat the Russians in Crimea, there's no war with France . . . and Germany's our friend, who do we have to fight? . . . We belong to a regiment which is a few thousand miles from here, in a little country without much importance except from the point of view that there's a Union Jack flies over it, and the people of that country can write British Subject after their names'. Now, it is updated to include Germany, Cyprus, Kenya, Borneo and Aden, with Russia and China as potential new adversaries.

As the soldiers explain what happened after the killing of Billy Hicks, images begin to take on the familiarity of television news pictures:

HURST: We were out on patrol, through this scruffy estate, and all the kids and the women, blowing whistles, battering dustbins, raising a hullabaloo like the end of the world.

ATTERCLIFFE: And we came round this corner, and forty or fifty of them, youths, if you follow me—attacking us, half-bricks, petrol-bombs, nail-bombs, screaming like nutters.

HURST: And this woman put her head over the wall, to have a look for her husband, or maybe her son.

ATTERCLIFFE: And I shot her: dead. Just behind the ear-hole.

British troops had been sent into Northern Ireland in August 1969, following the build-up of agitation following the beginnings of the Civil Rights movement and the reanimation of IRA activity. Just two years later came the introduction of internment without trial in Northern Ireland. It is a situation only too familiar to McGrath's soldiers:

ATTERCLIFFE: And then there was the camps. We never worked in the camps, but we know them as did, we know what occurred in them. Hoods over heads, boots in the balls, standing and standing for day after day, compressors and sleeplessness, till they wished they was dead . . . And the raids and the searches, kicking the doors down, bash on the skull, boys, chuck 'em in the wagons, the toddlers are staring, the mothers gone balmy—the killers all gone, miles off, sporting away over the border, hid in some field.

Exasperated at their failure to get to the exact point, Musgrave finally interrupts: 'So I'll tell you quietly exactly what happened. They wanted their march, you see, a Sunday or two back. Twenty odd thousand, to stop the internment.' Suddenly, we can date almost exactly the arrival of the soldiers. In January 1972, as the Miners' Strike continued, British soldiers in Derry broke up a march protesting against internment. Thirteen people were killed in what became known as the 'Bloody Sunday Massacre'. Arden's soldiers have been pulled out of their nineteenth-century 'parable' context to take part in the massacre. The pace now quickens, with the soldiers interrupting each other to describe the events of that day, until finally we reach the roll call of the dead:

HURST: There were ten thousand in the square, after their marching; and lads, behind a little barricade, defying us.

MUSGRAVE: So out like a flood, into the back of ten thousand, and flats all round, windows, roofs, balconies, could be from anywhere, what we were frightened of.

HURST: But live rounds up the spout, and the orders, shoot to kill, and lads throwing stones.

MUSGRAVE: We took aim at the priests, tending the dying, we shot at the fathers, weeping over their sons.

ATTERCLIFFE: Jack Duddy, aged 17. Kevin McEthinney, aged 16. Patsy Doherty, just 21. Bernard McGuigan, 41, shot in the head running to help a young lad:

MUSGRAVE: I tell you it makes us proud—

ATTERCLIFFE: Hugh Gilmore, aged 17, William Nash, 19, William McDaid, 17, John Young, 17, shot in the chest crawling out to his mate,

MUSGRAVE: Proud! I tell you it makes us proud!

ATTERCLIFFE: Michael Kelly, 17 years, Jim Wray, 23 years. Gerry Donaghy, 17 years, and Gerald McKinney, 35 and William McKinney, 27— not one of them armed, not one a gunman—

MUSGRAVE: Not so very many. Confusing conditions. A natural surge of rage—

Musgrave's bitterly sardonic praise of the army's action on Bloody Sunday is counterparted by the calm listing of the names of the victims. It is a moment carefully prepared for by McGrath, for it is the third act of Arden's play that received the greatest amount of reworking. To this point the audience's sense of the contemporaneity of the events has been confined to the Miners' Strike. Not only is this sudden swoop into contemporary Ireland deliberately disturbing in itself, but it brings together the two strands of the narrative with its insistent threat that, if British troops can be deployed in Ireland to 'keep the peace', then so might they be on the mainland. It is what Burrell ('Did the Inspector send for you?') and the Inspector ('I had hoped that maybe—unofficially, of course—. . . I mean, we know there are troops standing by all over in case of, well, unforeseen events') thought the soldiers were doing there initially, after all.

Despite Jacky's attempts to intervene with an analysis of the soldiers' role ('You go for a soldier, you find yourself in someone else's country, you deserve all you get'), Musgrave insists on giving his promised dance. The body of Billy Hicks is pulled from its box, but it is no longer the symbolic skeleton of Arden's play. It presents itself as a real body, of a real soldier, freshly killed:

> ATTERCLIFFE *opens up a big box and tips it forward, the body of a young Private tips out onto the floor. His face is black and unrecognisable, there is blood staining the back of his uniform.* HURST *and* ATTERCLIFFE *lift the body and lay it out on the table. They strap the body under the arms to the table and by the legs and then tip the table up so that the body is facing the audience upright hanging from the top of the table. The people draw back in horror. Musgrave begins to dance, his face contorted with demoniac fury.*

The dramatic effect is quite different from that sought at the equivalent point in Arden's play: stage representation is replaced by stage reality, especially since the revelation now follows the account of the massacre. Instead of the twenty-five corpses demanded by Arden's Musgrave, now he demands just thirteen, one for each of the Irishmen killed. Attercliffe turns Musgrave over to the Inspector and that effectively is it for the narrative, with no final scene allowing the audience to re-engage with Musgrave's situation as there had been in the original. The final moments of the play are dominated by the militant, Jacky. He addresses first Musgrave and then the miners:

> Sergeant Musgrave, we know what you're saying. We know what you and your mates in Ireland are doing. No more than a practice for what they're going to do to us, when we stand up demanding our rights. We've some of us ignored it and some gone along with the television and the newspapers and let ourselves think it was all for the good of the country, and all for keeping the peace. But these last few years, we've been fighting our own battles against the men you're talking about, and we have our own methods that you know nothing about. When we move it's not like one man standing up on his own waving a gun, it's thousands, millions of us altogether . . . We're fighting for power for the working masses, and that's what we'll settle for; not a few bloody corpses. We don't want killing, we want living, for everybody, not just a few. (*To colliers*) And if you lot fall for those individualistic, adventurist uncoordinated tactics, I've been wasting my time talking to you.

The ambiguity about the actions of the original Musgrave is now removed at a stroke. The early 1970s had seen an escalation of urban guerrilla warfare across Europe and America as the radical optimism of the 1960s gave way to a despair about the possibility of change. In England, the contemporary context was the activities of the Angry Brigade which had targeted a number of political and corporate targets (many of which went deliberately unreported at the time), including the home of Robert Carr, Secretary of State for Employment, which had been bombed in January 1971. At the end of 1972 eight members of the Brigade received prolonged prison sentences after the longest criminal trial in British history. What McGrath has done is to ally Musgrave's desire for revenge with a political programme that ignores the supremacy of class solidarity as the way forward. Musgrave is reconstructed as an individual terrorist, independent of any larger movement: his planned revenge is politically of no value to the larger cause. There is an interesting parallel with another play of 1972.

Howard Brenton also went to Paris in May 1968. He too was working on a play, *Magnificence*: 'May 68 was crucial. It was a great watershed. A lot of the ideas in *Magnificence* came straight out of the writing of that time in Paris . . . But . . . it failed. It was defeated. A generation dreaming of a beautiful utopia was kicked—kicked awake and not dead. I've got to believe not kicked dead. May 68 gave me a desperation I still have.'[18] *Magnificence* is a hybrid play: largely fuelled by situationist ideas, it ends with just such a piece of individualistic, adventurist uncoordinated tactics that Jacky condemns at the of *Musgrave Dances On*. A meaningless act of violence destroys both the target, presented as totally peripheral to the contemporary struggle anyway, and the perpetrator, Jed. Earlier, his friend Cliff, a political activist in the mould of Jacky, has attacked his strategy: 'There's only one way, time was you knew it, Jed. Work, corny work, with and for the people. Politicising them and learning from them, everyone of them. Millions. O.K. O.K. come a time you'll have to go out there. (*Sharp gesture, his fingers as a gun*) But only with the people, as a people's army, borne along by them.' Now Cliff ends the play deploring 'the waste of your anger'.

Although not entirely sharing the same sense of working with and for the people, the ending of both plays captures the mood on the left in 1972. The utopian dreams of the 1960s long since faded, there was a revival of traditional class politics evidenced all around and the terrible nightmares of Ireland beginning all over again. McGrath's particular achievement—and Arden's too—is to find a way of linking the two areas of contention. A small coda is in order.

McGrath was not the only playwright whose thoughts had turned to the link at this time. *The Ballygombeen Bequest* itself, which had started life as a commission to write a play about Ulster, presented an argument for Ireland as a socialist republic, the actualization of which was being actively prevented by the British army. One of the most disturbing scenes in the play, the torture of a member of the IRA by British troops, had indeed prompted two letters of complaint to the Arts Council of Great Britain as 7:84 toured. One was from General Tuzo, the British

Commander-in-Chief of the occupying army in Northern Ireland, who had thoughtfully taken the precaution of not seeing the play before he wrote.[19] In 1971, Howard Brenton was commissioned to write a radio play by the BBC. Although completed in 1972, it was never produced on radio, although later produced in a stage version at the Aarhus Theatre in Amsterdam. The script that Brenton submitted was entitled *Government Property* and it was set in a political concentration camp. His intentions were quite clear: 'it was in part an attempt to write about Ireland, and it was written in the shadow of the Industrial unrest of that year, the miners' strike, the three-day week, and the very strong possibility of anti-Trade Union legislation'.[20] It would eventually find form as part of *The Churchill Play* (1974), also set in a camp for detainees in 1984, where the Sergeant is quite explicit on the connection between the industrial and the political struggles: 'Ten years down Ulster then English streets. Then the late seventies and the laws against industrial unrest. Soldier boy at the picket line, working men 'is own kind comin' at 'im yellin' Scab Scab. I went down a mine, a corporal then, in the strike o' nineteen eighty. The miners o' that pit tried t'kill us, y'know that? . . . The British Army's got politicised, y'see.' But already, in 1972, Brenton was intent on making much the same connection as McGrath. In *Government Property*, an Irish detainee, Convery, is beaten up, an incident only reported in *The Churchill Play*, and Brenton is adamant about the connection between the introduction of internment in Ireland and on the mainland: 'If you want to stop troublesome trade unionists, disorderly pickets, hooligans, the drug crazed, why "do unto them as is done in Ireland". Set up a bit of wire round an old airfield and shove the scum behind it . . .' It made its point by giving the listener the sound of what was being done in Northern Ireland and its gaols, but with English voices.'[21] The play ends with the mortally injured Convery escaping and arriving at the home of Dan and Doris Archer (representative ordinary English people from the radio serial). Unable to speak because of his injuries, he is enjoined to write:

> DORIS: I'm sorry. Look we . . . Don't really know what goes on. Over there. And this is England. (*Urgently*) Look . . . Write down who put you in there? Maybe I can help you, if you tell me that . . . (*Pause*) What have you written? (*Pause*) You . . . did. (*Softly*.) I did?
> *Silence*
> *End Play*

The conclusion offers the same analysis of ultimate blame as that of McGrath's Musgrave ('You sent us the order, you people here today—or maybe no, maybe it was sent on your behalf, maybe you didn't know about it—but it was your Army, your representatives', he tells the theatre audience in respect of the events on Bloody Sunday); and it is in keeping with the liberal Doctor Thomson's realization in *The Churchill Play* that the cosy 'house, lawn, plants under the roof' of England's Home Counties is 'all built' on the 'mud, these men' of the detention camp.

1972 was also the year of *England's Ireland*, the collaborative piece with which Portable Theatre unsuccessfully attempted to tour. Like *Government Property* it contained a savage account of torture by the British army.[22] It drew on material from eyewitness reports, of the Civil Rights March on Derry, and accounts of internment, for instance, and mixes these with sinisterly comic routines, such as the soldier dressed as the 'Yellow Card' telling the others when to fire. Although it played at the Mickery Theatre, Amsterdam, in September 1972, English theatres refused it a performance, afraid of what it had to say about the situation in Ireland or what its audiences would make of it: 'fifty-odd theatres refused to take it. Many lied directly. We knew they'd lied'.[23] In the event, this proved the final straw for Portable Theatre, and it collapsed. It would be a further nine years before one of the collaborators, Howard Brenton, would bring his play about the colonization of Ireland, *The Romans in Britain* (1980), to the National Theatre in London.

Now, bearing in mind the reluctance of the BBC and theatres to touch anything in the least controversial about contemporary Ireland, it makes 7:84's double-handed tour the more significant; although, of course, *The Ballygombeen Bequest* was itself forced off the road by its involvement in a libel case.[24] That playwrights and companies should even make the attempt might tell us something about the need for a theatre that is able to respond quickly to changing political events. Through their long histories, the 7:84 companies sought to do just that, not (in Jacky's words) going along with 'the television and the newspapers and let[ting] ourselves think it was all for the good of the country, and all for keeping the peace'. Two decades on from *Serjeant Musgrave Dances On* it is worth recording the effort, particularly when it is realized that it was not until 2002, the thirtieth anniversary of Bloody Sunday, that two films were finally allowed to try to document the events of that day on television.

CHAPTER FIVE

Finding the Right Places, Finding the Right Audiences
Topicality and Entertainment in the Work of 7:84 England

Nadine Holdsworth

Tributes to and celebrations of John McGrath's life and work have understandably focused on the significant role he and 7:84 Scotland played in transforming Scottish theatre with performance events exploring Scottish history, politics and cultural identity. Amidst this body of work it is easy to forget that McGrath also produced plays for the English arm of 7:84; as Randall Stevenson argues, 'Scottish commentators and audiences are likely to forget this simply because his work was so import-ant within Scotland—so influential on Scottish theatre; so clearly shaped by it, too.'[1] Frequently relegated to a footnote of theatre history, 7:84 England has suffered an interesting reversal of the cultural imperialism that often leaves Scottish theatre overshadowed by its English counterpart. Nonetheless, McGrath's work with 7:84 England deserves recognition and, in this chapter, I hope to reinsert a small piece of that history into the narrative of McGrath's contribution to the British theatrical landscape. In particular, I want to focus on the company's output during 1975, a year McGrath described as 'the peak of 7:84 activities in England'[2], and Elizabeth MacLennan called 'the English company's most outstanding and consistent year'.[3]

During 1975, 7:84 England toured an updated version of McGrath's *Fish in the Sea* (1972) directed by Pam Brighton, followed by *Lay Off* and *Yobbo Nowt*, written and directed by McGrath. These three productions significantly developed 7:84 England's reputation for providing socially committed entertainment aligned to the Labour Movement. These pieces are also interesting for the varied formal strategies they employ and their responsiveness to topical issues and contemporary political, industrial and ideological campaigns.

7:84 England—The Beginning

After its formation in 1971, 7:84 produced several works by McGrath including *Trees in the Wind* (1971), *Underneath* (1972) and *Serjeant Musgrave Dances On* (1972). This was an adaptation of John Arden's political parable *Serjeant Musgrave's Dance* (1959), which toured with *The Ballygombeen Bequest*, written by Arden and Margaretta D'Arcy. The company toured England, Scotland, Ireland and Wales on Arts Council project funding and money secured from McGrath's work in film and television. The Arts Council of England indicated that an annual subsidy would be available to the company from 1973, but this was thwarted by the political and legal controversy over 7:84's treatment of the Northern Ireland situation in *Serjeant Musgrave's Dances On* and *The Ballygombeen Bequest*. Forced to remain on project funding, discussions took place about the company's future as company members dispersed at the end of 1972. It was decided that Gavin Richards would leave 7:84 to establish Belt and Braces; McGrath, Elizabeth MacLennan and David MacLennan would go to Scotland to start a Scottish company and those remaining would produce *Man Friday* (1973) by Adrian Mitchell. As 7:84 Scotland emerged, the English branch followed *Man Friday* with a collectively produced piece called *The Reign of Terror and the Great Money Trick* (1973) and ceased to produce work in 1974. Nevertheless, when McGrath returned from his success in Scotland, the Arts Council awarded 7:84 England an annual subsidy from April 1975, an important development that enabled McGrath to assemble a permanent company. Performers including Harriet Walter, Colum Meaney, Hilton McRae and Chrissie Cotterill joined, Sandy Craig returned to administrate the company and McGrath began a long-standing collaboration with the musical director Mark Brown and the musicians, Chas Ambler, Mike Barton and Mike O'Neill.

Locating an Audience

McGrath and Craig realized that a network of local supporters, and the venues in which 7:84 England were booked to play, were both critical in fulfilling their ideological impetus to communicate a socialist agenda to working-class audiences and throughout 1975 they worked tirelessly to promote the company with alternative venues, funding bodies, trades unions, Trades Councils, Labour Movement activists and audiences. For instance, during June, McGrath spent a week travelling around the Welsh

Valleys to make contacts in local clubs and community centres. On his return to London, McGrath immediately followed up leads, as a letter sent to the Double Diamond Club in Caerphilly illustrates: '. . . I enjoyed meeting you and seeing your club last week, and hope very much that we can arrange to visit with our show at some stage. It certainly would be a splendid venue', praise that accompanied the offer of two tickets for *Lay Off* at the Unity Theatre in London and the opportunity to have a further chat after the show.[4] McGrath's persistence paid off with a booking for *Yobbo Nowt* during the autumn tour. Equally, McGrath and Craig fostered on-going relationships with promoters by acknowledging any assistance received. Typical is a letter from McGrath to Alan Tweedie, a Community Development Officer in Cleator Moor, Cumbria: 'Thanks anyway for the great efforts you made to get the right places and the right audiences. I cannot tell you how much we appreciate that kind of work. We all realize how dependent we are on people like yourself and we are really grateful when clearly enthusiasm is applied in a practical way.'[5] Craig also sought financial aid to support 7:84 England's particular remit; for example, he charged differential rates for arts centres and work-based clubs and successfully lobbied Merseyside Arts for subsidy to facilitate a five-night mini-tour of *Fish in the Sea*. Support from Merseyside Arts enabled access to audiences in non-traditional Liverpool venues including Titsfield Street Community Centre, Tate and Lyle Social Club, Kirby Labour Club and the Fisher-Bendix factory.

Fish in the Sea

Arguably, the decision to revive *Fish in the Sea* relied on the reputation the play secured during its successful run at the Liverpool Everyman a few years earlier as part of Alan Dossor's promotion of localized entertainment about and for working-class audiences. The large-scale nature of the production was also important, as the press release makes clear: '*Fish in the Sea* is the largest production ever mounted by 7:84: it includes a cast of ten and band of five in a total production staff of 24.'[6] 7:84 England wanted to re-announce itself in style and to insist that, although it was targeting many small non-theatre venues, it would not compromise on production values. The company signalled its desire for a high profile return to English touring by approaching Joan Littlewood to guest direct. Littlewood declined 7:84's invitation claiming, 'As a visiting director I would be a dead loss', but she welcomed the company's return: 'I would very much like to see 7:84 in action on the old hunting grounds.'[7] Littlewood's stylistic influence is clearly present in *Fish in the Sea*, which utilizes popular, social realist and Brechtian epic traditions. More specifically, it further develops the Liverpool-based domestic drama in a rock concert format with which McGrath experimented in *Soft or a Girl?* (1971). *Fish in the Sea* successfully combines emotive drama, romance, comedy and direct address with varied musical styles to drive the narrative, illuminate character and offer political commentary; an eclectic approach reviewers variously described as 'political pantomime', 'soap opera', 'dramatised documentary' and 'multi-layered chronicle'. Joanna Mack found the play '. . . extremely funny, but [it] is much more than just good entertainment. It raises a mass of questions at both an intellectual and personal level'[8]: questions primarily centred on McGrath's interrogation of the distractions, contradictions and prejudices evident in working-class culture. In the preface to the published edition, McGrath writes

> The main elements I wanted to set in some form of dialectical motion were—the need for militant organisation by the working class; the anarchistic, anti-organisational violence of the frustrated working-class individual in search of self-fulfilment here and now; the backwardness of some elements of working-class living: attitudes to women, to socialist theory, to sexual oppression, poetry, myth, etc.; the connections between this backwardness and Christianity; the shallow optimism of the demagogic left, self-appointed leaders of the working class; and the intimate realities of growing up and living in a working-class home on Merseyside.[9]

In the play, McGrath stresses the presence and power of working-class agency and calls for 'more maturity, and more determination from the working class, its allies, and the socialist movement in Britain'.[10] As such, McGrath directly challenges post-war perceptions that increasing prosperity, individualism and commodity-consciousness threatened collective working-class identification and rigidly demarcated class divisions as the working class adopted the culture, lifestyle and voting patterns of the middle classes. Sociologists similarly argued that the growth of 'privatised' workers, characterized by low job involvement, weak kin links and individualistic socio-political proclivities, had the potential to erode the rationale behind Labour Movement activism. In *Fish in the Sea*, McGrath acknowledges these social and economic shifts, but he offers an alternative vision of the individual worker, nuclear family and community as the Maconochie family undertake domestic chores, forge new relationships, socialize, marry, fight, work and strike.

We All Have Choices

McGrath uses the Maconochies and their associates to explore various pathways available to the working class during this period. The patriarch,

Mr Maconochie, represents the old-school proletarian worker tradition. He views the media and police as hegemonic forces and believes in securing a 'better world' through class struggle, even though he has little faith in the post-war generation he perceives as apathetic and seduced by consumer culture. His fears are realized through the humourless son Derek. A beneficiary of post-war prosperity and the white-collar opportunities available to the working class, Derek pursues self-advancement in the 'affluent worker' tradition and dismisses his father's working-class identification. His opposition to his father's belief systems is epitomized by his decision to join the police cadets, his rejection of trades unionism and his unquestioning acceptance of his deferential worker role: 'I just carry out orders. I don't question them. If I carry them out to the best of my ability, I get looked after, that's the way it is in this life.'[11]

At the other end of the spectrum from Derek's compliance with the status quo, McGrath presents Andy, an intense, psychologically complex and dangerously unstable character, who channels his considerable energies away from class politics into anarchic nihilism and macho posturing. His aggression is dissipated into acts of self-destruction: heavy drinking; picking fights and paramilitary activity in the Ulster Defence Association as he chases risk and commits atrocities to avoid the culture of complacency he despises. Willy, who works with Mr Maconochie at Robertson's factory and is engaged to Sandra, one of Mr Maconochie's three daughters, provides a more progressive image of the new generation. Initially presented as a shoplifting 'scally', through the play Willy matures into a committed campaigner for workers' rights, culminating in his strike action at and subsequent occupation of Robertson's factory.

Distanced from the other characters by his middle-class origins and Reverend father's retreat from the community he serves, Yorry embodies McGrath's concern with 'the political education and growing to socialist consciousness of the individual'.[12] Initially McGrath parodies Yorry's enthusiastic rhetoric on the theoretical tracts of Marx, Luxembourg and Gramsci, but he also allows him a degree of critical self-reflection when he acknowledges that, '. . . the more I said, the more powerful I became as a champion of the workers, the further I got away from them'.[13] Moreover, Yorry demonstrates his capacity to learn and change when he relinquishes his university career and gets involved in industrial action alongside Willy and Mr Maconochie. At this point, McGrath proposes 'how the intelligentsia can be of actual practical use in political struggle'.[14] Yorry uses his skills to provide a daily newsletter for the workers and community, printing speeches ignored by conventional press coverage and brief treatises by Gramsci, Marx and Engels. More importantly, he includes worker profiles detailing 'their lives, families, interests',[15] signalling his growing appreciation of the relationship between lived experience and political action. As the play closes, Yorry decides to relinquish ownership of his dead father's house to live communally with Sandra, Willy and their baby. As Janelle Reinelt concludes: 'the sense of extended family, of communal struggle, is what the strike action produces. It unites the two families—one could even say across class lines—and provides a way of living, if not tidy closure'.[16] Solidarity and the triumph of a common socialist cause over diverse perspectives provides McGrath's core message, but he also stresses the need for the working class to accommodate the increasing ideological presence of identity politics. For instance, McGrath undermines the homophobia that greets a donation to the strike fund from the Gay Liberation Front and he raises issues about the roles available to working-class women through the juxtaposition of Mrs Maconochie's life with the rebellious independence of her three daughters who recoil from the domestic drudgery that defines their mother's existence.

Industrial Action and the Labour Movement

For the strike and occupation that forms the central political narrative of *Fish in the Sea*, McGrath received inspiration from the widespread industrial campaigns involving sit-ins, work-ins and workers' co-operatives taking place across Britain during the 'politics of confrontation' era. As the programme for *Fish in the Sea* documents: 'There have been at least 22 wholly or partially successful factory occupants [sic] in England, Scotland and Wales since Upper Clyde Shipbuilders. . . All were effective to some degree in preventing redundancies.'[17] The ongoing work-in at International Property Development (formerly Fisher-Bendix) in Kirby, Liverpool, proved particularly relevant for the 1975 tour, as McGrath based several of the industrial scenes in *Fish in the Sea* on this dispute. During the tour, 7:84 England performed at the former Fisher-Bendix factory and parts of the performance were included in a film made for the British Film Institute about the occupation. As with Fisher-Bendix, the industrial action McGrath depicts is acrimonious and fraught with difficulties. Although McGrath promotes trades union activism as the best way to fight exploitative practices within capitalist structures, he offers a searing critique of the Labour Movement's willingness to capitulate in pursuit of reformist, rather than revolutionary, politics. Indeed, McGrath's theatrical treatment demonstrates his frustration with what Anthony Crosland and Ralph Dahrendorf were theorizing as the 'institutionalisation of dissent', which involved the increasing use of non-confrontational conflict management and conciliation by trades unions and the Labour Party during industrial disputes; a shift consolidated in 1975 when the Employment Protection Act provided statutory recognition to the

Advisory, Conciliation and Arbitration Service. The failure of the Labour Movement to support workers' interests fully is made horribly apparent in *Fish in the Sea* when the settlement reached between union leaders and bosses is rendered useless because it coincides with a government-ordered wage freeze. Moreover, the unions fail to negotiate long-term workers' rights, Mr Maconochie and Willy face redundancy and operations are set to move to Germany, indicating new threats by multinational corporations and a globalization of the market place. As Yorry asks at the end of the play: 'Capitalism was changing: the question was: were we going to change with it— fast enough, big enough and well enough organised to catch up with it?'[18] It is to this shift, from the individual boss of the small business to the all-consuming power of multinational corporations such as ITT, IBM, GEC and General Motors, that McGrath turned for 7:84 England's next play for 1975, *Lay Off*.

Lay Off

Based on extensive research, *Lay Off* explores a range of topical economic, political and social issues that were influencing people in Britain and overseas. It interrogates how an international workforce can be exploited by inter-connecting factors including: scientific advancements; new technologies; increased mechanization; changing labour relations; the failures of the TUC; the capitulation of governments to big business and the formation of worldwide multinationals. In particular, McGrath scrutinizes how company take-overs, buy-outs and mergers were affecting workers, an apposite theme given their increasingly prominent place in the global economic landscape. As McGrath declares in *Lay Off*, 'In two years, 1967 and 1968, 5,000 British firms were taken over or eaten alive by the bigger fish.'[19] Many of these 'bigger fish' were international corporations and, in many ways, *Lay Off* resonates with recent political commentary and activism around anti-globalisation and the all-pervasive influence of corporatism, documented in Naomi Klein's *No Logo*.[20] Certainly, nearly thirty years after *Lay Off* was written, McGrath's recognition of the erosion of national borders as capitalism's ultimate utopia appears alarmingly prophetic in the context of a world dominated more and more by American economic interest and the World Trade Organization:

> Utopia for an international corporation would be world government. A world without frontiers. Absolute freedom of movement of people, goods, ideas, services and money to and from anywhere . . . A single global system of patents and trademarks, of buildings and safety codes, of food and drug regulations. A single, global currency. A single central bank.[21]

During the mid-1970s, the British economy became erratic, inflation accelerated out of control, unemployment grew and an unstable balance of payments prevailed. Increasingly attention focused on multinationals because of their power over export drives, the value of their tax contributions and their ability to influence inflation and deflation by moving profits from one country to another. McGrath explores these factors alongside concerns that this economic power enabled multinationals to exert ideological pressure on governments to act in their interests. For instance, in *Lay Off*, McGrath quotes Harold Wilson's 1974 pre-election pledge to oppose the excessive profits multinationals were raising from North Sea oil: 'Our North Sea oil is vital to the nation, and we cannot see the profits from our oil, and the control over the production of it, going outside this country. We must nationalise it.'[22] However, McGrath also reveals Wilson's blatant capitulation to the multinationals when, in February 1975, despite setting up a new British National Oil Corporation, Wilson reneged on his promise to nationalize the industry and instead levied a 45 per cent petroleum revenue tax, which maintained a 20 per cent profit margin for oil companies. Taking an international outlook, McGrath also includes a bitter attack on governments using their powers to quell countries that proved resistant to the exploitation of their people for capitalist profit. Using Chile as his primary example, McGrath provides a lengthy exposition of the brutal events following Salvador Allende's election as President in 1970 after promising a 'transition to socialism'. After a recital of Allende's moving election speech, McGrath details how, in the interests of American business and particularly that of ITT, Richard Nixon and Henry Kissinger put Allende under severe economic pressure. America withdrew aid, encouraged right-wing insurrection, employed the CIA to cause trouble and supported the 1973 military coup under General Pinochet, when Allende was murdered. By listing other incidences in the post-war period ranging, from a CIA financed coup in Persia during 1951 to the use of the SAS to protect Shell Oil's interests in the Middle East during the 1960s, *Lay Off* stresses the pervasive nature of political and economic engineering as a response to plans for renationalization or an increased socialist agenda.

From Retreat to Activism

In an echo of *Fish in the Sea*, McGrath repeats his concern that the post-war consumer boom, expanding leisure industry and increasing prevalence of popular culture potentially diminishes workers' activism. Theatrically, this issue is highlighted by giant soap-powder boxes, songs about cars, white goods and jokes about lounging in a 'polyvinyl space-craft-shaped inflatable armchair, with your feet up on the brushed-nylon latex-foam filled beer-barrel-shaped pouf'.[23] As an antidote to this retreat into the myth of 'you've never had it so good', McGrath provides a model of how the working class can build on its capacity to organize and cooperate internationally to resist and undermine the divisive practices of multinationals. At the end of the play, *Lay Off* documents four strikes at Standard Telephones and Cables, a subsidiary of ITT, in East Kilbride between 1961 and February 1975. McGrath reveals how, after a series of defeats by ITT, union activists made unofficial links with ITT workers across Europe. This contact meant that when workers in East Kilbride came out on strike over a pay dispute in 1975 they were able to call on other factories to 'black' parts made in other plants so that ITT's previous trick of moving production to another country became redundant and the workers could claim a hard-fought victory. The immediacy of this event, which took place a few of months before *Lay Off* started touring, was crucial to the form, content and success of the piece.

A Didactic Cabaret

Stylistically, *Lay Off* marked a radical departure from *Fish in the Sea*'s emphasis on how politics is embedded and embodied in the daily lives and relationships of subtle and idiosyncratic characters; instead it consists of a Workers' Theatre Movement style agit-prop script divided between named 7:84 England members. It relies on the transferral of information through topical, didactic cabaret-style sketches, interspersed with songs, comic interludes, captions and information. Presented 'out front' through chatty direct address, *Lay Off*'s variety format and performance strategies shield the didacticism of the piece from becoming too hectoring. For instance, it makes extensive use of use of high-energy songs and first-person narratives that personalize the broad depiction of class struggle through stories of under-nourished children, police brutality and premature death caused by stress, exhaustion and working with toxic chemicals. Countering this emotive dimension is the use of documentary evidence such as quotations and statistics to substantiate the play's political analysis. It is worth quoting McGrath at length to illustrate the rationale behind this formal organization:

> . . . the rather complicated history of rationalization of industry with government support in the late 60s may not sound too promising for a joke-routine. But by the time, in 7:84 England's show *Lay Off*, a large Irish actor had finished explaining, as Arnold Weinstock, just how beneficial to the country, or at least to GEC, this process was, and we had brought the news to the audience of how many people had been laid off, and where, to allow GEC to amalgamate, take over, rationalize and

prosper, not only were the audience highly entertained by the manic and comic manoeuvres of Weinstock, but also they had grasped how this process affected their lives—in terms of jobs, and the products they can buy—and something of how structural unemployment is created by capitalist solutions to working-class problems. So when the show zoomed in on one individual who had been laid off, feeling upset in a launderette, and mucking about in the garden, that individual was seen as part of a major social process of change with technological, industrial and political determinations, rather than just as a poor unfortunate layabout as he might be presented in a sentimental bourgeois drama. And the audience had grasped the essentials of the theoretical and historical ideas relevant to his—and possibly their—position.[24]

Lay Off toured throughout Lancashire, Merseyside, Wales, Cumbria, the Midlands and Scotland and the subject matter and style of the show, combined with the well-known political affiliations of 7:84 England, ensured that trades unionists actively sought performances for work-based organizations. Typical is a request from Roger Hands from Dudley: 'On behalf of the Cannon Industries Shop Stewards Committees (AUEW & TASS) I would like to enquire about the possibility of booking your theatre group for a union concert. I feel that the play *Lay Off* is of particular relevance to us working in the GEC frontline.'[25] Critics and political activists alike recognized that *Lay Off* had something urgent to say and audience letters, coupled with reviews, suggest that spectators were hugely appreciative, whether in more obviously receptive environments, such as occupied factories, or traditional venues. For example, the reviewer for the *Sunday Times,* who saw the production at Cardiff Arts Centre, confirms, 'I was informed, stimulated and vastly entertained'[26] and *Time Out* reviewer Anne McFerran reports a performance at Ruskin College, Oxford when: '. . . the audience enjoyed themselves so much they wouldn't go home. "More, more," they cried, though it was past closing time and we'd been there since 7.30'.[27] On this occasion, 7:84 England met demands for an encore by giving a second outing to songs from the show. Composed by Brown, with lyrics by McGrath, songs were a vital component of *Lay Off* as they contributed to the variety format, conveyed information and kept the show lively and entertaining. Indeed, the music was so popular that 7:84 England released an LP of songs from *Lay Off.*

Yobbo Nowt

7:84 England's last show in 1975, *Yobbo Nowt,* while designed to 'be a contrast to *Lay Off*,'[28] built extensively on the use of song to create a musical comedy. Of this experimentation, McGrath declared, 'With Mark Brown, who composed the music, I set out to explore several ways of relating music to speech and story-telling: the sung narrative, straight-forward character- and situation-songs, plus scenes in which the characters cut from speech to song, and scenes completely set to music.'[29] This development, Michael Billington found, 'acts not as an anodyne diversion but as a pungent melodic commentary'.[30] Overall, the form of *Yobbo Nowt* combines elements of *Fish in the Sea*'s domestic comic drama and rock musical with direct address to the audience, popular cultural references and an extensive use of Brechtian-style narrators whose poetry and song comment on the action. In a shift from the collectivism of *Lay Off*, *Yobbo Nowt* centres on the personal narrative of Marie to examine the mutually reinforcing structures of patriarchy and capitalism. Although abandoning the polemical didacticism of *Lay Off*, political processes are central to *Yobbo Nowt* as it engages with the women's liberation movement and specific ideological campaigns fought by women to secure rights in the personal, social, work-based, institutional and legal arenas during the mid-1970s.

Yobbo Nowt toured during the year when the 1970 Equal Pay Act was supposed to be fully implemented, the Sex Discrimination Act was passed, the Equal Opportunities Commission was established and the TUC adopted the Working Women's Charter. Therefore, the play intersected with various projects to tackle discriminatory practices against women, including the Labour Movement's campaign to confront the male bias of trades union discourse and activity. The decision to produce *Yobbo Nowt* similarly responded to pressure exerted within 7:84 for the company to address its own gender bias in the issues it tackled and the represen-tations it offered. As Harriet Walter, a member of the company throughout 1975, states, 'the socialist theatre in general was notoriously guilty of marginalizing women quite as much as the establishment theatre'.[31] Even McGrath confessed that one of the reasons for doing *Yobbo Nowt* was to address 'complaints that in *Lay Off* the women hadn't had enough to do',[32] a view supported by such hot-beds of radicalism as the *Whitehaven News* which reported, 'Chrissie Cotterill and Vari Sylvester had "bit" parts, when their talents could clearly have been used to greater advantage in more important roles. After all, it is supposed to be Inter-national Women's Year!'[33]

She's Just a 'Yobbo Nowt'

Yobbo Nowt deconstructs the traditional (male-defined and constructed) representation and perception of women as on the margins of activity by placing them in the focal, central position of subject defined not solely by private (sexual and familial) identity, but also in relation to a public (economic) role. The play reverses the historical 'absence' of women, by foregrounding a female presence involved in a dialectical battle with patriarchy and capitalism. Alongside other plays of the period, such as Red Ladder's *Strike While the Iron is Hot* (1974), *Yobbo Nowt* took inspiration from Brecht's adaptation of Gorki's *The Mother*, the story of a working-class woman's rise to political consciousness and militancy. *The Mother* was performed a number of times during the early 1970s; in 1972 Steve Gooch's adaptation was shown at the Half Moon Theatre in London and Belt and Braces Theatre Company toured a version in 1975. McGrath was 'interested in telling a similar story'[34] and in *Yobbo Nowt*, he takes *The Mother* as a structural and thematic model to trace a woman's journey into feminist and class-consciousness in England during the 1970s. Importantly, this model enabled McGrath to represent women as many of them were at this time: in a process of transformation informed by a growing consciousness that 'the personal is political'.

Act 1 predominately explores women's inequality with men in the home and the state. With references to domestic violence, the sexual division of domestic labour, equal pay, single-parent families, payment for house-work, sexual objectification, contraception, sexual fulfilment and societal pressure on women to define themselves in relation to men, the play is firmly located within the agenda of women's liberation. Specifically, McGrath presents a socialist feminist analysis of Marie's condition by stressing the interdependence of her class, low economic status and role of nurturer within the domestic arena. The initial sequence charts Marie's awakening to her subordinate position within the classic nuclear family and lack of power against Jack, her errant, sexually abusive and violent husband. She has internalized the lack of value afforded her role in society and appraises herself as 'lethargic, and dull, and pathetic',[35] a position juxtaposed with Jack, who is able to embark on sustained personal and professional development: 'I'm nobody. Yobbo nowt. All the rest of them seem to be up to something. Growing. Learning. Flirting. Mending fuses, making electricity hum. That's Jack—he started off as a boilerman but he's doing night-classes and now he's going to be an electrical fitter in a plastics factory.'[36] Marie is in stasis, numbed by her mundane domestic existence that revolves around satisfying others' needs. The character talks directly to the audience about her desire for a job, independent status and Jack's refusal to appreciate the validity of her request; hence when Marie kicks him out, McGrath has firmly established this as a triumphant moment for his character. For the first time, Marie takes an active role in the decision-making process that determines her life and that of her two teenage children, Valerie and Stephen.

By focusing on Marie's transferral from private patriarchy to the patriarchal control of the state, McGrath insists that Marie's subordinate position extends beyond the home environment. *Yobbo Nowt* emphasizes

Marie's lack of autonomy and economic dependence on men as defined by the Government. According to the social security officer, Jack owes Marie: 'He *is* your husband. In the eyes of the law he owes you a living . . . Until such time as you take up with another man—then *he* owes you a living',[37] information that also stresses the divisions inherent between women, as clearly it is far easier for a woman of independent means to leave her husband. In the Labour Exchange, Marie explains that she wants a job producing goods, a request that attempts to invert her previous role as consumer, but she is offered part-time, low-paid jobs tied to the domestic realm: cleaning; laundry; or school meal service. It is not only Marie's gender that stands against her, but also her age and working-class roots, illustrated by the reception she receives from Marks and Spencers: '. . . this woman looked at me like I'd been dragged in by the cat. "We want girls, smart young girls, to set off on the first rung of our ladder," she said. "I don't think you'd fit in to our scheme of things." "No," I said, "I'm not the climbing type".'[38]

After months on social security, Marie secures a job in an electronics factory, setting up the focus in Act 2 on women's subjugation within the workplace and as workers within capitalism. Marie's journey to an industrial-based, political consciousness begins when she learns about exploitative practices such as training rates and piecework, revelations that initiate discussions around women's apathy towards unions. McGrath tackles the problematic sexual politics in union organization and activity through George, the union representative. Instead of negotiating a settlement on a guaranteed wage, he concentrates on jokes and sexual innuendo, highlighting how the primacy of sexual oppression could circumvent legislation such as the Equal Pay Act. When Marie threatens strike action, his loyalties are revealed, 'Strike? But these parts are needed —you go on strike and there's men with families, out of work.'[39]

Defined by a Male Framework?

A central tenet of 1970s feminism was for women to find a voice without the necessity of male intervention; hence McGrath's decision to write a pro-feminist text raises difficult issues, including accusations of appropriation and concern that women-centred discourse is dissipated when refracted through male agendas, structures and dialogue. Michelene Wandor argues that McGrath subordinates gender issues to a male-defined, traditional economic class struggle and that Marie discovers nothing about sexism, feminism or sexuality.[40] She also suggests women-centred experience is negated by the fact that Marie has to enter the 'male' public sphere, before becoming politically motivated. Whilst McGrath does portray the battling individual woman, which ignores the collective power of the women's movement, and he fails to consider specific women-centred industrial issues such as flexible hours, workplace nurseries, maternity leave and sexual harassment, Wandor's assessment is harsh as it denies the socio-political issues McGrath does confront. In addition, accepting Wandor's claim that *Yobbo Nowt* is counter-productive because it deals with the political and public realm suggests a dangerous adherence to gender stereotyping that restricts women's experience to the private domain. The strength of *Yobbo Nowt* is that Marie's quest for knowledge drives the action forward in both private and public arenas and that McGrath depicts her growing political consciousness in the home and the workplace. As McGrath stated, 'Marie . . . is shown in the oppressed, passive state of many women. She is then shown in the process of self-assertion, self-realisation, active participation in life and articulate, positive militancy.'[41] Significantly, McGrath avoids presenting industrial militancy as his ultimate goal by, in the final scene, returning to the domestic sphere and Jack's attempt to resume his dominant position. To close the play, McGrath stresses Marie's autonomy and feminist consciousness when she rejects Jack, making it clear that, 'things have changed—attitudes, ways of looking at things'.[42] As further proof of this process of development, McGrath depicts Stephen rejecting his father's chauvinistic stance by contributing, through domestic chores, to the home environment.

Above all, it is important to assess the impact of *Yobbo Nowt* in relation to the venues and audiences reached by 7:84 England and by taking into account the contemporary climate in which women's inequality was coming under increasing scrutiny. Alongside arts centres and traditional theatres, *Yobbo Nowt* toured trades union organizations, working-men's clubs and Miners' Institutes in places such as Caerphilly and Maerdy in Wales; venues associated with the working-class, male-centred industrial base critiqued in the play. Hence, *Yobbo Nowt* was a potential consciousness-raiser for women in the audience to confront their position within the home, workplace and to take advantage of new legislation; but also, for men to address their own gender advantage and the male bias and culture of the Labour Movement. However, once again, this social agenda did not negate 7:84's desire to entertain, with Billington enthusing that 'this exuberant musical nails the old myth that left-wing theatre must necessarily be grey as a plate of cold porridge and just about as digestible . . . this is political theatre with guts and gaiety'.[43] Similarly, Desmond Pratt of the *Yorkshire Post* called it 'a remarkable production, full of rhythm, humour and pathos, all revealing the human condition'.[44] The success of *Yobbo Nowt*, together with *Fish in the Sea* and *Lay Off*, should be judged, not only by positive reviews, but also by the substantial number of letters written by ordinary audience members to demonstrate appreciation of the work, request further information or to offer practical assistance setting up future touring dates. All letters received a personal response inviting people to join a network of 'contacts/helpers around the country who will see that local publicity is done, that unions, trades councils, movement groups are contacted before we arrive, spread the word, etc'.[45] For 1975, and the years that followed, this practical and personal engagement with audiences, community groups and socialist activists ensured that 7:84 England could command large audiences for its particular brand of topical, accessible, socially committed and politically informed popular entertainment. Even if McGrath's creative activism became increasingly located in Scotland, and this sustained period of critical appreciation and popular success proved hard to repeat, the output produced during this year illuminates the political impetus, practical strategies and theatrical experimentation that defined 7:84 England's work through the following decade.

PART THREE

John McGrath and Scotland

CHAPTER SIX

Border Warranty
John McGrath and Scotland

Randall Stevenson

An invitation to discuss John McGrath's work in the Scottish theatre seems at first—to any Scottish critic, anyway—exceptionally generous and unconstraining: like being asked at a conference on Shakespeare to talk *only* about the dramatic works; or, at a conference on icebergs, to concentrate on the bits underwater. It only takes a moment, of course, to recall how far McGrath's career extended beyond Scotland, and indeed beyond the theatre. Scottish commentators and audiences are likely to forget this simply because his work was so important within Scotland—so influential on Scottish theatre and so clearly shaped by it too. This is a perspective which may well be less accessible outside Scotland: in any case, it is worth beginning by outlining its principal components.

From one point of view, now rather an old-fashioned one, McGrath's high standing in the history of Scottish drama might simply be attributed to the poverty of the competition. Notoriously, G. Gregory Smith's 1919 study of Scottish literature considered dramatic writing as scarce as the 'owls and snakes of Iceland'. At mid-century, the playwright George Munro continued to find only 'deserts and wild beasts' on Scotland's 'Theatre Chart'. Two decades later, Christopher Small, editor of the *Glasgow Herald*, was still ready to refer to 'Snakes in the History of Iceland' as a metaphor for the scarcity of contemporary plays.[1] Such views are almost as clichéd as assumptions that the English theatre barely existed before *Look Back in Anger*, in 1956, and have been much amended in the last twenty years or so, with the general conclusion that Scottish drama went through a strong revival, beginning in the 1970s, which quickly took it well beyond the chilly deserts of earlier years. In looking harder at those earlier years, too, Bill Findlay's recent *History of Scottish Theatre* (1998) showed that however attenuated play-*writing* may have been in Scotland, the country never really lacked a *theatrical* tradition—one especially strong in popular performance modes, with pantomime and music-hall enjoying particular success in the late nineteenth century and for much of the twentieth. Commentators such as Femi Folorunso and Frank Bruce have argued recently that 'probably no other cultural form has exerted as much imaginative influence on the popular mind in Scotland as the music hall and its confederates', and that 'Scotland's most consistent theatrical tradition is its popular theatre'.[2] In a way, this tradition might even be retraced to Scotland's first great dramatic success, Sir David Lindsay's *Ane Satyre of the Thrie Estaitis* in 1554, which included song, knockabout action, broad comedy and a rich humour latent in vernacular Scots to develop solidarity with its audience and to direct satire on contemporary poverty, social conditions generally, and the deficiencies of the Catholic clergy in particular. Ironically, Lindsay's attention to this last subject helped to move Scotland towards the Reformation, and hence towards forms of Christianity far less tolerant of the theatre. As Findlay's *History* shows, suspicion, persecution or sometimes physical assault by churchmen regularly added to the difficulties of theatre companies over the next 300 years. Problems were further compounded by the removal of the Court in 1603, and by a diminished sense of national confidence and identity after the Union of the Parliaments in 1707.

The revival in Scottish dramatic writing in the 1970s—maybe even in England's, in the 1950s—could perhaps be related to the Church's decline, and to a corresponding return of the Dionysiac to national life. In Scotland's case, there is even an argument that ministers offered their congregations such riveting, weekly versions of fire and brimstone, battles between the Beast and the Lord, as to have made other forms of drama almost superfluous. More plausibly, the growing hold of the theatre on Scottish imagination in the 1970s can be shown to have had political and ultimately economic causes. Scottish nationalism had begun to be a political force even in the 1960s: by the start of the next decade, it was much fuelled by the discovery of the resources under the North Sea and the ubiquitous Scottish National Party claim that 'It's Scotland's Oil'. It was a claim directly reflected in contemporary drama. The mercenary soldier in Stewart Conn's *Play Donkey* (1977), for example, ponders 'fighting for wur freedom, after all these centuries', significantly adding that there 'might even be a chance of . . . getting paid for it, now there's all that oil'. Tom Gallacher set an adaptation of *The Tempest*, *The Sea Change* (1976), on an oil rig, commenting that 'the burgeoning riches of oil off the Scottish coast accomplished a sea change in the Arts as well . . . Scottishness was an asset, not a liability'.[3] Renewed self-interest in the 'asset' of Scottishness appeared at several other levels in the dramatic revival of the time, encouraging playwrights to explore further—as Hugh

MacDiarmid had recommended as long ago as 1926 that they should —specific *differentia* of Scottish outlook and experience.[4] Scots language played an especially significant part in this. Throughout the 1970s, playwrights such as Donald Campbell, Roddy McMillan and Bill Bryden contributed to a rediscovery of the dramatic power of Scots speech in creating solidarities and immediacies of communication between stage and audience. With most other media still dominated by standard English, this helped to make the theatre a unique public space at the time—one encouraging national interests to speak in their own voice, national identity to be particularly accented and collective outlooks to coalesce. In these ways, and to an extent probably not yet fully recognized, it was the theatre which actually led the wider, much-vaunted, Scottish literary revival usually supposed to have occurred after, and as compensation for, the failure of the Devolution Bill in 1979.

John McGrath's work made significant contributions in this area. His use of Gaelic in *The Cheviot, the Stag and the Black, Black Oil* (1973) was still more emotive—a still greater lever on the sympathies of Highland audiences, who might never have encountered it in live theatre performance—than the use of Scots at that time for Lowland audiences. For the latter, too, McGrath soon showed himself, in plays such as *Out of Our Heads* (1976) and *Blood Red Roses* (1980), thoroughly adept in the gallus colloquialism of the West of Scotland; also, in *Joe's Drum* (1979), in the different tones of the East. Yet his key contribution to the 1970s dramatic revival was in another area of contemporary rediscovery: of the imaginative and theatrical potentials of Scottish history. Several playwrights had begun to use history in an essentially Yeatsian way, reconsidering, or reshaping, heroic episodes in Scotland's past which could empower nationalist consciousness in the present, consolidating ideas of 'fighting for wur freedom after all these centuries'. Possibly the best example appeared earlier, in Sidney Goodsir Smith's rousing dramatic pageant *The Wallace*, in 1960. A prototype *Braveheart*, its Edinburgh Festival revival in the mid-1980s led to SNP factions 'spontaneously' raising banners in the auditorium at the end of each performance and demanding Scotland's freedom. Playwrights in the 1970s had continued to work in this vein and with similar implications. Characters in Hector MacMillan's *The Rising*, for example, persecuted for their wish to 'set up a Scottish Assembly, or Parliament, in Edinburgh', could obviously 'appeal wi confidence tae posterity' if the posterity concerned was a Scottish theatre audience in 1973.[5]

History, in McGrath's writing, was put to rather different uses—more Brechtian, more analytic as well as being emotive in more structured ways. In concentrating on the Highland clearances in the *Cheviot*, McGrath could hardly have fixed on a more emotive phase of Scottish history, yet the play's radical shifts between epochs and alienated performance style ensured that the emotions concerned could not be indulged only for their own sake, or as part of what McGrath called the 'lament syndrome' so often associated with the Highland past. Instead, they directed and heightened audiences' awareness of 'why the tragedies of the past happened', of the capitalist machinations which threatened to reduplicate them in the present, and of the need 'to fight and agitate for the alternative'. The sentimental nationalism of the song the audience join at the beginning, 'These are my mountains . . .', develops in this way into recognition that they are not their mountains at all, but belonged first to some sheep, then to Queen Victoria and eventually to Texas Jim. A consequent recognition, once memorably delivered to a Scottish National Party conference, is that 'Nationalism is not enough. The enemy of the Scottish people is Scottish capital, as much as the foreign exploiter'.[6] The prescience of this warning—that unless the population was very careful, the slogan 'It's Scotland's Oil' might as well be rewritten as 'It's the Oil Companies' Scotland'—became widely apparent even before the Piper Alpha oil rig disaster killed scores of workers in 1988.

Similar warnings were delivered by McGrath's work later in the 1970s. Concentrating on different phases of history from most other authors at the time, he continued to highlight the limits of contemporary nationalism and the need for socialist alternatives, in plays such as *The Game's a Bogey* (1974) and *Little Red Hen* (1975), portraying the 'Red Clydeside' agitation, following the First World War, led by the legendary Glasgow Marxist, John MacLean. Similar priorities remained more or less in evidence, and were sometimes further clarified, over the next two decades. In 'From Cheviots to Silver Darlings', his interview with Olga Taxidou in *Scottish Theatre since the Seventies*, McGrath outlined complex relations to nationalism, certainly never straightforwardly antipathetic, and praised Tom Nairn's version of 'Civic Nationalism' as a 'fruitful movement, a fruitful communal emotion' increasingly important within a globalized culture and the growing political centralism of modern Europe.[7] Written in response to that failed Devolution Bill, *Joe's Drum* was ready to recommend that Scotland 'flourish, and add [its] own, independent weight to the world'. Yet in *Border Warfare* (1989), in following the 'theme, a thousand years long', of English oppression of Scotland, McGrath's principal concern remained with borders which run through countries, rather than only with those between them—ones highlighted in the conclusion in *Little Red Hen* that:

> . . . there's two Scotlands . . . there's the Scotland that's . . . been robbed and cheated and worked to the bone when it suits or thrown on the queue at the buroo when it doesnae suit—that's one Scotland; and

4. Robin Begg as William Wallace with Juliet Cadzow in *Border Warfare* at the
Tramway Theatre. 1989
(Photo: Alan Wylie)

there's a Scotland that owns factories . . . and sweat shops . . . and
grouse moors and mountains and islands and stocks and shares and says
what goes—and only one of them can be free at a time.[8]

As Margaret Thatcher's mercilessly sado-monetarist soliloquy at the end
of *Border Warfare* emphasized, though the play's principal lesson was that
Scotland was perennially 'bought and sold for English gold', the accent
always fell heavily on the terms 'bought', 'sold' and 'gold', and on the
thoroughgoing complicities of Scottish capital and ruling class with any
machinations originating with foreign oppressors.

So if McGrath seems such a thoroughly Scottish playwright, at least to
people in Scotland, it's partly because he intervened so crucially in the
1970s, and later, in debates which remained specific, and central, to
Scottish politics—and in many ways to its theatre revival—throughout the
last decades of the century. Playwrights, of course, are rarely celebrated
only for the acuteness or timeliness of their political interventions, but

rather for the ways these are staged. In this aspect, too, McGrath seems inextricably related to the Scottish context, though as a beneficiary of existing theatrical modes as well as a contributor to them. In 'From Cheviots to Silver Darlings', McGrath recalled finding on his first foray northward with 7:84, in 1971, that 'Scottish popular audiences have a totally different set of traditions of popular entertainment . . . a different language, not only theatrical and verbal, but political and social'.[9] When he returned to form 7:84 Scotland in 1973, it was certainly not to find a theatre scene dominated only by historical drama of nationalist nostalgia, or entirely lacking in the kind of political agenda 7:84 sought to publicize. On the contrary, throughout the previous summer, nightly in Glasgow and then at the Edinburgh Festival, huge audiences had enjoyed one of the great unsung—not literally unsung!—successes of modern political theatre, *The Great Northern Welly Boot Show*. The 'comedy, latent energy and class awareness in abundance' which Elizabeth MacLennan recognized in it were significant, at the time and later, in a number of ways.[10] For Glasgow audiences in particular, it celebrated an outstanding local political success: the 1971 occupation by the workforce, led by shop-steward Jimmy Reid, of the Upper Clyde Shipbuilders' Yard (UCS), thinly disguised as a welly boot factory in this production. For the early 1970s, the occupation was a famous and formative event: McGrath was later to record the immediate genesis of the *Cheviot* in Richard Eyre's suggestion of a production combining the history of the Highlands with recent events at UCS. The *Welly Boot Show* was also distinguished by the creative personnel it involved. The designer was John Byrne, creator of the pop-up book for the *Cheviot*, and later author of the *Slab Boys* trilogy. Some of the music was by Tom McGrath, author of a number of plays, most famously *The Hardman* with Jimmy Boyle. The songs, often drawing on a Scottish folk-music tradition, were performed by Billy Connolly—former shipyard-worker, late exemplar of a Scottish popular comedy tradition, and eventually, among much besides, also a playwright himself. Most importantly for 7:84, the *Welly Boot Show* provided several of the performers who went on to work with McGrath on the *Cheviot*—John Bett, Alex Norton and Bill Paterson. These were all already adept in a theatrical style using song, knockabout action, broad comedy and a rich humour latent in vernacular Scots to develop solidarity with audiences and to direct firm satiric vision on recent political events.

Description of the *Welly Boot Show* in exactly the terms earlier applied to *Ane Satyre of the Thrie Estaitis* is tendentious: there were obviously differences between 1554 and 1973. But it emphasizes how far the Scottish context may *always* have offered particular opportunities for direct, pungent commentary on contemporary politics; for particular solidarities of language or outlook between audience and stage; and for use of the distinctive 'traditions of popular entertainment', unusually prominent throughout Scotland's theatre history, which McGrath recognized. McGrath undoubtedly brought to Scotland a set of political interests and performance idioms developed for himself, based on work at the Liverpool Everyman, on earlier experience with 7:84, and on a whole range of mentors and models no doubt including Brecht, Piscator and Joan Littlewood. Yet to an extent he arrived in Scotland to discover that his idioms and interests had got there before him or had always been there. Differences between the *Cheviot*, or *The Game's a Bogey*, and that earlier work in Liverpool—or, still more obviously, the naturalistic manner of *Random Happenings in the Hebrides* (1969) indicate not only personal development and growing radicalization after 1968, but also rapid adaptation to a new tradition. McGrath's continuing indebtedness to this tradition and his conviction of his own settled role within it, were clearly confirmed by the Edinburgh Festival production of *A Satire of the Four Estaites* in 1996. With almost numeric exactness, its title highlighted McGrath's extension of a sequence of Scottish dramas, politically acute and broadly entertaining, stretching back to Sir David Lindsay's initiative in the sixteenth century.

If *A Satire of the Four Estaites* marked a kind of final term, or terminus, in McGrath's coalescence with Scottish traditions, there were also many important stages along the way, particularly in 7:84's 'Clydebuilt' season in 1982. This revived, or virtually rediscovered, drama illustrative of what McGrath called the 'strong cultural side' belonging to a 'long, rich and neglected tradition' of working-class struggle in Scotland.[11] The plays included were Joe Corrie's *In Time o' Strife* (1927), Harry Trott's *U.A.B Scotland* (1940), Ewan McColl's *Johnny Noble* (1946), Ena Lamont Stewart's *Men Should Weep* (1947) and George Munro's *Gold in His Boots* (1947). Each reminded Scottish audiences that their theatre did indeed have a rich, neglected and highly politicized tradition, running back a long way beyond the 1970s—to the Glasgow Workers' Theatre Group, in the case of Trott's play; to Theatre Workshop's Glasgow period in the late 1940s, for McColl's; and to workers' companies formed after the General Strike, eventually the Fife Miner Players, for Corrie's. Both *Men Should Weep* and *Gold in his Boots* were first performed by a company in some ways directly comparable with 7:84, Glasgow Unity. Initially amateur, Unity incorporated during the war a number of largely working-class companies, including the Jewish Institute Players and the Transport Players as well as the Workers' Theatre Group. Rather in the manner of *The Great Northern Welly Boot Show*, Unity's productions, including their greatest success, Robert McLeish's 1946 dramatization of the contemporary housing crisis, *The Gorbals Story*, addressed immediate political concerns in ways specifically directed at, and sometimes even involving as performers, the ordinary people who experienced them most sharply. Sustained in dramas generally much more naturalistic than 7:84's work, Unity's political commitments were nevertheless equally clear. The company's motto, 'the theatre is the school of the people—it makes them think and it makes them feel' came from Gorki:[12] in a series of plays portraying chronic poverty, Unity repeatedly confronted its audiences with Glaswegian versions of the Lower Depths, and with a politics of implication demanding just as loudly as 7:84, three decades later, the need for redistribution of wealth and for radical social change.

Glasgow Unity, in other words, provided a prototype—consistent with the imaginative and theatrical resources of its age—of the Scottish People's Theatre 7:84 sought to establish in the 1970s and 1980s. Like *A Satire of the Four Estaites*, the 'Clydebuilt' season was an act of auto-genealogy: a relaxed version of Harold Bloom's 'anxiety of influence', through which McGrath and his company rediscovered, or recreated, their theatrical forbears.[13] A 'long neglected' Scottish theatrical tradition would have slipped further from view without 7:84's work, which had itself always drawn on the potentials this tradition incorporated. Thoroughly plugged into Scottish social and political history, McGrath's drama was plugged into Scotland's theatrical past, in this way, in a circuit of reciprocal discovery thoroughly empowering for each. It was also widely enabling for later writers and directors, who found in 7:84's work all sorts of opportunities for combining elements domestic and international, established and innovative. Some of their indebtedness was indicated by Gerry Mulgrew, director of the popular experimental company Communicado, when he remarked in 1986 that McGrath's work had 'opened the door and provided the focus for a distinct and intelligent Scottish theatre. It engendered a whole popular movement whose reverberations are still being felt today'.[14] They are still being felt in Scotland now, early in another century.

All of which should explain why it is so easy to think of John McGrath as a Scottish writer, even exclusively so. Yet it's not really the purpose of this essay to claim McGrath solely for Scottish literature—though it would obviously be reasonable to claim sections of Scottish literature, at any rate substantial parts of recent Scottish theatre, for McGrath.[15] Any such claim might run counter to the kind of border warnings, discussed above, about narrowly national or nationalist interests, which were such an important part of McGrath's contribution to the Scottish political scene. Instead, exploration of McGrath's Scottishness may also have much to reveal, usually contrastively, about the English context, and about the nature of political drama more generally, within Britain and beyond. There seems, at any rate, surprising scope for enquiry of this kind. Some of the best of commentators on recent political theatre, and on McGrath's work—John

Bull, Maria DiCenzo, Baz Kershaw—do examine developments on both sides of the border, though not always in relation to each other. In other areas of theatre criticism, commentary of this kind is rarer, though Scottish critics should perhaps not complain too loudly about its sparseness. Dominic Shellard's recent *British Theatre since the War* (1999), for example, seems derisory in devoting to Scotland only four pages out of 260. Yet few Scottish theatre critics have paid much attention to England at all, or considered the implications for Scottish drama of developments made south of the border—apparently preferring to believe, like the early Soviets, that revolution, theatrically anyway, can happen in only one country at a time. In its political mode especially, theatre may be more intrinsically local in outlook than other literary forms, and was often made particularly so by McGrath—by his insistence that actors research and address local issues for every performance of touring shows, and by his development of quite different idioms for use in the Highlands and in the cities. This might offer some excuse for narrowly local vision among theatre critics, but it can impose unnecessary limitations and misconstructions on their work nonetheless. English critics, for example, might have been less excited by the apparent novelty of the Osborne/Wesker/Delaney school of 1950s kitchen-sink realism had they been aware that for a decade or more, already, Scottish drama had scarcely moved more than a few feet from a kitchen sink; or noticed that Scottish companies had brought all their wares—including the kitchen sink—all the way to London at least twice, in the transfers of *The Gorbals Story* to the Garrick in 1948, and of George Munro's even grimmer *Gay Landscape* to the Royal Court ten years later.

Any British-wide assessment of the 'Second Wave', as John Russell Taylor called it, which followed the Royal Court school—the politicized generation, McGrath included, who dominated theatre in the later 1960s, 1970s and early 1980s—might usefully begin with the first line of Howard Brenton's *The Romans in Britain*, produced at the National Theatre in 1980: 'where the fuck are we?'. As well as its immediate relevance within the drama, the question had an obviously metatheatrical aspect, significant for the entire production and certainly for the author himself. Of earlier work at the National, Brenton remarked that he found himself, along with his director David Hare and their cast, as if in 'an armoured charabanc . . . parked within the National walls'.[16] Critics have often pondered why Hare, Brenton, David Edgar and other members of a supposedly radical generation of English playwrights were so ready to move from early work with agit-prop, alternative or other small touring groups into parking spaces within the National Theatre, 'armoured' or otherwise. There remains more scope for enquiry into moves in a generally opposite direction. These define the careers not of a group of playwrights, but of the two most genuine radicals, politically and theatrically, in late twentieth-century British drama, John Arden and John McGrath. Each began with plays relatively conventional in style and in politics, performed in fairly established theatres: Arden with the pacifist problematics of *Serjeant Musgrave's Dance* (1959) at the Royal Court and *Armstrong's Last Goodnight* (1964) at the Glasgow Citizens; McGrath with the class-consciousness of drama such as *Events while Guarding the Bofors Gun*, performed at Hampstead in 1966. Each moved on, roughly simultaneously, to more radical socialist politics and to more innovative theatrical forms—Arden perhaps most clearly in *The Non-Stop Connolly Show*, produced for the Irish Trades Union Congress in 1975. Each was involved, or nearly became involved, in performances, bizarrely, though appropriately, just *outside* the country's grandest theatres. Arden picketed the Royal Shakespeare Company at the Aldwych during rehearsals for *The Island of the Mighty* in 1972; 7:84, apparently, were once invited to provide some form of street theatre *around* the National, as if its administration had realized at last that, like the Pompidou Centre in Paris, its interesting bits were to be found on the outside, rather than among the supposed cultural treasures ensconced within. Most importantly for the present argument, both Arden and McGrath eventually fled as far as possible from metropolitan theatre, towards the Celtic fringes of Ireland and Scotland.

It would be wrong, of course, to suppose that this was a move which simply provided McGrath with the theatrical equivalent of a tax haven. 7:84 were accepted within the established theatre in Scotland no more readily than they had been in England, nor did they seek such acceptance. On the contrary, the lasting legacies of McGrath's work included 7:84's initiation of a circuit of small, ad hoc performance spaces—often in parts of the country, the Highlands particularly, that had scarcely encountered live theatre previously—and the persuasion of the Scottish Arts Council, for a time, that touring to such venues was a responsibility for any funded company. The productions of *Border Warfare* and *John Brown's Body* (1990) also helped consolidate the use of an old engine-shed and former transport museum in Glasgow—first employed theatrically for Peter Brook's *The Mahabharata* in 1988—as 'The Tramway', a regular venue for experimental and progressive forms of drama ever since. All these developments extended McGrath's sensible conclusion that the most natural and necessary spectators of left-wing drama were ones who might never go near a conventional theatre, and that plays must therefore be taken to them. His metropolitan contemporaries in England, on the other hand, seemed readier to accept the supposedly bourgeois audiences who usually turned up to the established theatre, even if this meant sustaining thoroughly adversarial attitudes towards them—ones summed up in Brenton's metaphors of 'Petrol Bombs through the proscenium arch', as

5. Robin Begg and John Bett as Norman Knights 'the planted ruling class' in *Border Warefare* at the Tramway Theatre. 1989

6. Billy Riddoch as James Watt in *John Brown's Body* at the Tramway Theatre. 1990

well as of his company lurking in an 'armoured charabanc' at the
National.[17] Such attitudes could hardly have been further from the
collaborative, educative, cajoling forms of address in McGrath's plays, or
from his determination to allow audiences to identify their strengths,
problems and capacities for change for themselves. Radical contrasts were
equally evident in theme. The Hare/Edgar/Brenton faction seemed almost
to relish berating their audiences for Britain's late-twentieth-century
decline, and moved on with apparent alacrity to political self-criticism, in
Edgar's *Maydays* (1983), or to fantasy forms of utopianism, in Brenton's
Greenland (1988), when socialist politics faltered in the 1980s. For
McGrath, 'hopes can't just die/When a half of humanity's hungry and
poor': change and improvement were always shown as achievable, and the
bone didn't break.[18] *Border Warfare, John Brown's Body* and *A Satire of the
Four Estaites* all showed political conviction and theatrical inventiveness
sustained into the late 1980s and 1990s, often with renewed vigour,
despite the undoubted pressures of the time.

Much of the credit for this continued optimism and the open, enabling
forms of its communication obviously goes to McGrath himself. Yet some
also reflects on the Scottish audiences so much of his work addressed and
on the history which so disposed them towards it. 'A socialist country', in
the view of most of its citizens, as Elizabeth MacLennan recorded,
Scotland may simply offer a natural context for radical theatre.[19] A
country repeatedly on the wrong end of political and economic struggle
throughout the last millennium, as *Border Warfare* showed, and one of the
first to experience the Industrial Revolution, Scotland was inevitably a base
for much of the early development of the Labour movement, a staunch
supporter of it in later years, and ready towards the end of the twentieth
century to reject the Tory Party comprehensively, apparently unanimously, eventually to the last parliamentary constituency, some time
before the rest of the United Kingdom had quite recognized the urgency of
doing so.[20] Thinking over this generally radical history, and its origins, a
character in *Blood Red Roses* mentions:

> Culloden . . . the King's Birthday Riots in 1792, the Friends of the
> People agitation, the militia riots at Tranent, the Clearing of the High-
> land straths, the Weavers Uprising in 1820—right through to the
> marines landing on Skye and Tiree in the Crofters War in 1882, and
> the tanks in the streets of Glasgow in 1919 . . . the British Army
> never seemed to stop turning out for action against the population of
> Scotland.[21]

Could English history offer an equivalent list? Probably, though its
component episodes might be ones less sharply focused within popular

consciousness, less influential upon it and less usefully or clearly available to dramatists. What Sandy Craig describes as 'the lack of any deeply rooted sense of national cultural identity in England' may have been part of what persuaded both Arden and McGrath to leave.[22] Scotland's advantage in terms of radical political awareness, like Ireland's, derives not only immediately from the kind of historical experience listed above, but also from ways its influences tend to be directed: the opportunity to attribute acts of oppression to external forces—to a *British* Army, for example—obviously contributing strongly to local solidarity and readiness for collective resistance. Peripheral nations within the United Kingdom always have a political axe to grind: as discussed earlier, McGrath's work regularly helped ensure that this sharpened socialist commitments, rather than only nationalist ones. In appealing to a specifically Scottish identity, his drama was implicitly also appealing to a radical, or at any rate firmly anti-Tory one: its occasional apparent flirtations with nationalism were in this way more strategic, and probably less 'ambiguous', or 'ideologically ambivalent' than commentators such as Baz Kershaw have suggested.[23]

Yet *some* version of such feelings of local solidarity might be available, increasingly, almost anywhere in the United Kingdom, or in contemporary Europe, providing that this 'anywhere' perceives itself as controlled from somewhere else; as a province peripheral to a centre of power. As McGrath emphasized in 'From Cheviots to Silver Darlings', tensions between centre and periphery, local and multinational, were already crucial to life, identity and imagination in the late twentieth century, and likely to become more so in the twenty-first, within increasingly pan-European political and economic structures and globalized forms of media and capital. Scotland's positioning in relation to these factors is in many ways fascinatingly exemplary, rather than by any means altogether unique. Scotland's radical tradition helped McGrath create and sustain a theatre which might have thrived nowhere else, but which remains relevant to a much wider world. McGrath himself considered that the 'truly cosmopolitan . . . has to be local', and that the best way to make 'people all over the world . . . see what's going on' is to ensure that 'the way you tell it—the specifics of the characters and their lives—is very, very accurate, and local, and works locally'.[24] In the same year Hugh MacDiarmid suggested a theatre concentrating on Scottish *differentia*, he also demanded that 'Whatever Scotland is . . . /Be it aye pairt o' a' men see'. John McGrath's drama, pre-eminently, did allow the country to be seen, and to see itself, in this way, adding enormously, for thirty years, to the possibility he hoped for—that Scotland would continue to 'develop its own place in the world without losing its social morality and its cultural specifics'.[25]

CHAPTER SEVEN

Celtic Centres, the Fringes and John McGrath

Ian Brown

A contributor to the conference that gave rise to this book reflected on the 'irony' that two of the great English dramatists of the late twentieth century, John McGrath and John Arden, had 'fled to the Celtic Fringes'. I suggested that they had, rather, been drawn to the Celtic Centres. The thrust of this chapter is to explore what, besides John McGrath's personal interests and commitments, in the Scottish theatre tradition and social and political milieu may have positively drawn McGrath and made it particularly receptive and welcoming of so much of his drama. In doing so, it will explore something of the nature of that tradition and the ways in which McGrath's work both finds an appropriate home within it and develops it further.

Before doing so, it is well to remember that there were very clear personal reasons to draw McGrath to Scotland. He says: '[After National Service and Oxford University] I was taken by romance to a small village in the North Highlands, Rogart, in Sutherland. Here in the Highlands I discovered a living cultural identity that made instant contact with the traces of my Irishness and the feeling for nature—and much else—of my Welsh childhood.'[1] Such personal sympathy and the 'romance' that led to his marriage to Elizabeth MacLennan go some way to explaining an attachment to Scotland, but not quite to Scottish subject matter. McGrath begins to explain this when he observes: 'I'd spent quite a lot of time in the Highlands before anyone mentioned the Clearances. And then it was only indirectly. In 1961, someone I'd got to know came round for a drink, and said he'd discovered some old parish registers.'[2] Elizabeth MacLennan comments on the later result of this conversation over 'a drink': 'John had been researching and preparing the subject of *The Cheviot, the Stag and the Black, Black, Oil* for the fifteen years he had known me. He had the play all mapped out. We knew where we wanted to take it.'[3]

In other words, long before the establishment of 7:84 Scotland and the launch of *The Cheviot, the Stag and the Black, Black Oil*, the subject matter for the play was developing in his mind. MacLennan, however, gives evidence that the attraction of Scotland as a locus of McGrath's theatrical developments, beginning with *The Cheviot*, goes far beyond interest in specific subject matter:

> John, myself, David [MacLennan] and Feri [Lean] were impatient to start in Scotland with *The Cheviot* . . . Scotland is distinguished by its socialist, egalitarian tradition, its Labour history, its cultural cohesion and energetic participation in argument and contemporary issues. Within its separate educational, legal and religious systems is a strong but not chauvinist sense of cultural identity. Culture and politics are not dirty words. We felt our plays there should reflect and celebrate these differences in language, music, political identification and carry on the arguments.[4]

McGrath himself talks of this move in terms of a wider commitment to Scottish actors, problems, plays and audience when he outlines the reasons for going to Scotland in 1973 as: 'to find Scottish actors to create a Scottish company, to deal with Scottish problems, to make Scottish plays and so to get more directly involved with Scottish audiences.'[5] There is clear evidence, then, that there were powerful and complex attractions in the Celtic centre of Scotland that provided an attractive and positive locus for McGrath's work.

It is well, however, to address the very concept of Scotland as a 'Celtic' centre. The essence of the Scottish politico-national identity, as Michael Lynch, for one, has shown with great clarity in his *History of Scotland*,[6] is based on a (more or less and often fractious) consensual process of alliance and conjunction. The basic political formula in the Middle Ages was of semi-autonomous regions coming together through shared political and economic interests to form the national grouping defined by the boundaries of 'Scotland'. Thomas Owen Clancy and Barbara E. Crawford emphasize the point:

> In [language or landscape, politics, peoples or territory], Scotland during its earliest history is not a fixed and labelled destination, but a constantly shifting theatre of change. Even as late as the fourteenth century, Scotland as we know it was still evolving, first into a kingdom and then a nation, defining its borders and amalgamating its startling range of peoples and languages.[7]

Given that, ultimately, alliance rather than simple conquest, whether internal or external, formed this grouping, there had to be a form of mutual tolerance within the Scottish body politic, however intermittently hostile and on occasion, indeed, marked by the intolerance of battle and the violence of territorial and political warfare. This applied to the wide variety of Picts in Fife, the North, North-east and elsewhere, Cumbrian, Cymric, Dalriadan and Scoto-Irish Celts of the Borders, South-west, West, Islands and Highlands, the Angles of Lothian and the Nordic communities of the North and Islands. Indeed, it is worth remembering that Orkney and Shetland became part of the Scottish kingdom only as late as the fifteenth century. In other words, the nature of the Scottish identity was multicultural from the beginning, even if not by any means always harmoniously so. Thus it has remained, though often with bouts of internal dispute and conflict. Scotland is not in truth simply a *Celtic* centre. It has always been, and remains, a multinational nation, one where still in the far north of the mainland, for example, a simple assumption that Gaelic rather than Nordic culture forms its local roots will be met with (justified) demurral. Indeed, McGrath himself refers to Scotland as a 'nordic nation'.[8] In short, the Scotland that drew John McGrath is not simply Celtic but, in a complex and historically alive way, multicultural.

This Scotland has also been over the centuries a centre not only of its own culture, but also of a variety of international movements. Voltaire famously said of Enlightenment Scotland: 'It is from Scotland that we take our taste.' Such an international position was not then new. Bill Findlay has pointed to the key role of George Buchanan in the genesis of the French classical drama of Corneille, Racine and Molière.[9] Between its foundation and the Reformation in Scotland of 1560, the University of Paris had more than twelve Scottish rectors. The thirteenth-century St Andrews Music Book reveals a school of musical composition of continuing international importance. The artwork of the *Book of Kells* was almost certainly done on Iona and later removed to save it from Viking depredation. The parochial view that somehow North Britain and Ireland are not centres is a little out of focus. This observation is crucial to understanding why John McGrath might be drawn to work in Scotland. He was not moving to work in a Celtic Fringe, but moving to work in a vibrant culture with a strong sense of its multicultural past and present and of its central role in the development of international culture and politics.

However true all of this is, it might be argued that, nonetheless, for a theatre worker to move from England to Scotland when McGrath did was to move from a national context with a strong theatre tradition, however disenchanting to McGrath aspects of its operation were,[10] to one without such a tradition. This, however, is to misunderstand the difference between the strong theatre traditions of England and the strong, but different, ones found in Scotland. Much recent research has shown that, when McGrath came to work in Scotland, he was moving to work in a specific theatre tradition whose elements arguably had much to offer his theatrical practice. A superficial perception of the effect of the Reformation on Scottish theatre had masked understanding of this tradition. Certainly, James VI's departure to London in 1603 meant that his love of theatre benefited London's stage rather than Edinburgh's, while the public theatre in Scotland underwent a period of over a century of repression by the dominant ideology of a radical church. By the early eighteenth century, however, this repression was beginning to recede and from the middle of the eighteenth century it was over.[11] At that point, the forms of theatre were being redeveloped on the modes then current in London. Barbara Bell, however, points out the rediscovery early in the nineteenth century of a native tradition, what was to develop into the 'National Drama' with a repertoire based mainly on adaptations of Scott's novels:

> The Scottish theatre underwent changes during a twenty year period from 1812 to 1832 which were as revolutionary as any brought about by the alternative theatre movement in Scotland over the last two decades. Fundamental changes were made to the repertoire, to the organisation of theatres, to the fabric of the buildings and to the way in which people regarded the theatre—its relationship to their lives and shared experience. The changes were brought about through the use of the very popular theatre forms [John] McGrath identifies as forming the basis for his work.[12]

By definition the popular forms to which Bell refers had somehow been maintained throughout the period of repression. To understand this, it has to be recognized that a key point in the historic Scottish tradition, made by a number of critics and historians, in particular Donald Campbell[13] and Bill Findlay,[14] is that it has not been focused strongly on playwrights, but rather on performers. The power of the performer in the Scottish tradition is implied in the stock phrase 'the real Mackay', Charles Mackay being the actor who played Baillie Nicol Jarvie from 1819 onwards in the Edinburgh Theatre Royal adaptation of Sir Walter Scott's *Rob Roy*. Here, the performer occupies a crucial role and acts as a guarantor of quality, 'the real Mackay'. In other words, this particular tradition depends on the centrality of the actor who provides its performances, rather than the playwright who provides its scripts. This tradition continues to this day and was available to John McGrath.

The role of the actor in such a tradition is not simply to perform in plays. The real Mackay was also a highly popular comedian. This capacity of the performer to be both actor and popular entertainer continues throughout the nineteenth century. Bill Findlay offers a study of a mid-nineteenth century exemplar, James Houston, who had 'parallel careers on the concert and theatre platforms as, respectively Scotch comic and Scotch comic actor'.[15] Findlay observes that a factor that allowed the linkage of these two careers 'and which helped these careers overlap—was Houston's command of Scots. A number of reviews of his comic acting talent drew attention to this.'[16] The language issue is one to return to, but the tradition of the performer who is both skilled in popular and classic theatrical forms as in the case of Mackay is clearly maintained by Houston. In modern times, it has been represented by the work of Russell Hunter, Una McLean, Rikki Fulton, Elaine C. Smith, Andy Gray; the list continues and is very long. If practical evidence were required of its specific Scottishness, it exists in an experiment of Bill Bryden's at the National Theatre in the 1970s. Bryden believed the Scottish tradition of working across categories was transferable and directed a pantomime there with the leading National Theatre players. The sight of the misery of Robert Stephens, cast as an Ugly Sister, a fish so far out of water as to be beyond actorly resuscitation, was repeated throughout the company. The range of skills expected of a Scottish actor, however, provided a variety of competencies. Key members of McGrath's companies such as Bill Paterson, Alex Norton and John Bett represented that Scottish tradition.

McGrath himself talks of auditioning three 'actors I had seen in *The Welly Boot Show* the year before, Alex Norton, Bill Paterson and John Bett. They had worked together a great deal before, and combined an enormous number of skills, acting, singing, guitar, pipes, whisky, commitment, and others'.[17] From this, it is clear that McGrath was scarcely breaking barren ground in developing the aesthetic of *The Cheviot*. As Bill Findlay puts it:

> The UCS work-in inspired two important theatre events. *The Great Northern Welly Boot Show* (1972) was directly based on the events at UCS and provided a popular hit in Glasgow and Edinburgh. Combining drama and music with political satire, it foreshadowed *The Cheviot, The Stag and the Black, Black Oil* (and shared some of the same performers).[18]

When McGrath describes his working process in developing *The Cheviot*, the reader immediately recognizes that it needed actors trained in the Scottish theatre, in his words, 'good Scottish actors':

> I threw the material at the company, told them they were entertainers now, not Chekovian [sic] actors, and to work on their acts, and bring them in for us all to see. Being good Scottish actors—who had all

worked in many different situations, from Ibsen via panto to spieling on strip-shows, that is what they did.[19]

McGrath was clearly conscious of working with, and within, a well-established Scottish tradition.

The popular nature of that tradition itself is worth examination. Alasdair Cameron and Adrienne Scullion make a key point about this: 'We have continually argued that trying to create a great tradition for Scottish theatre is a lost cause but suggested that *popular theatre* is the key to seeing how Scottish theatre evolved and how notions of Scottishness were kept alive on the stage.'[20] They go on to observe:

> Barbara Bell's research has shown that adaptations of the novels of Sir Walter Scott (who it could be argued was the popularising force at the origin of a distinctively Scottish theatre) had declined drastically in popularity towards the end of the nineteenth century . . . supplanted by Boucicault . . . and Pinero.[21]

Cameron and Scullion, however, while noting Bell's observation of trends in legitimate theatre, make a case for the popular tradition's continuity in alternative theatrical venues, forming, as it were, a nineteenth-century Scottish Fringe. They argue that the audience for the National Drama did not disappear, but

> . . . had (re)turned to the 'popular stage' and that parallel tradition of Scottish theatre, the fairs and geggies . . . the actors associated with the National Drama still performed with notable success on Glasgow Green, and later at Vinegar Hill, on the geggie stages. These performers were still singing the same songs, appealing to the same audience, albeit in rather different surroundings . . . The geggies, in a relaxed and informal atmosphere, provide the populous [sic] with plays about their own country, spoken in a familiar accent for audiences who could not afford the London touring shows or lived in the country and could not travel to the large city theatres. In so doing they preserved a distinctively Scottish dramatic tradition.[22]

It is clear that such a tradition, given the values and sympathies, not to mention the themes, of John McGrath, would be one that would provide a secure base for his work as playwright and director.

That this tradition was not attenuated before McGrath's arrival is borne out, of course, by the work of such a popular theatre company as Glasgow Unity in the 1940s, to choose but one example. Cairns Craig and Randall Stevenson observe of the influence of that company:

Unity's example both encouraged a long line of Scottish companies, such as 7:84 and Wildcat, combining theatrical innovation with a strong political message, and helped establish a style of realistic drama . . . depicting the harsh realities of working life, in the west of Scotland particularly. Like many of its successors, Unity was also to run foul of the Arts Council, which had provided some its early funding, and the company had to cease work in the early 1950s. By then, however, it had helped initiate the Edinburgh Festival Fringe by putting on plays without official support at the first Edinburgh Festival in 1947.[23]

Part, then, of what offered a welcome to McGrath in Scottish theatre was certainly a long and strong tradition of prominence for the kind of popular 'Fringe' theatre he wished to develop. As Maria DiCenzo observes:

In theatrical terms, what Scotland could claim to be its own was a tradition of popular forms such as music hall and panto—live forms of entertainment in which music and comedy figure prominently. What 7:84 did was to take advantage of the familiarity with and entertainment values of these forms (and others such as the 'ceilidh') and to use them as vehicles for political analysis and commentary.[24]

Femi Folorunso suggests that the more modern vehicles of music hall and panto that McGrath could employ had deeper roots. In doing so, he emphasizes the importance of aspects of recent popular theatre in the Scottish tradition not only with reference to McGrath:

In nearly every modern Scottish play, recognisable bits and pieces of music-hall aesthetics can be found. Where they are not explicit—for example in techniques of performance—they are implicit in dramatic consciousness . . . From the irreverent jokes and scabrous humour in Liz Lochhead's *Mary Queen of Scots got her head chopped off*, to the witticisms and songs in almost every play John McGrath wrote for 7:84 Scotland . . . the impact of the music hall is everywhere discernible.[25]

Folorunso, however, specifically draws attention to that version of music hall entitled 'Scottish Variety' and places it firmly in a popular tradition going back four centuries: '. . . from its introduction until the late 1940s, it was the most popular and richest form of entertainment in Scotland . . . and . . . occupied the middle space in a direct line from the seventeenth-century popular entertainment to contemporary drama in Scotland.'[26] He goes even further to speculate on an origin for the specific popular theatrical form of the Scottish pantomime. This, he argues, can be seen to perpetuate elements of the weird, wonderful and supernatural that may initially have been inspired by Celtic folklore or descended partly from seventeenth-century circuses and mountebank shows.[27] However this may be, Folorunso dates the interaction of popular and text-based theatre to a very early period:

> We now know, for instance, that a pattern of utilitarian drama was established in Scotland before the Reformation. This pattern achieved its highest standards in Sir David Lindsay's *Ane Satire of the Thrie Estaitis*. A close scrutiny of the language and techniques of this play suggests very much the kind of imposition . . . of literary order on popular elements in order to make some urgent, serious political statements.[28]

DiCenzo's observation on the work of 7:84 can then be seen to apply to work of a much earlier period:

> One of the advantages of the Scottish [7:84] company was that it could merge class politics with specific regional/national problems for an audience more than ready to listen to and support them. Scottish issues provided a focus for the subject matter of the plays and popular Scottish entertainment (both rural and urban) provided the language through which to reach audiences.[29]

It is clear that the theatrical tradition that offered these 'advantages' to McGrath's work was deep-rooted. McGrath could respond to a long-standing history of Scottish theatre and his work in Scotland further developed and transmitted the potential of that history. Nadine Holdsworth observes that '*The Cheviot* is widely acknowledged as one of the most successful radical theatre pieces Britain has ever produced and is credited with redefining the nature of Scottish theatre's subject matter, aesthetic context of production and modes of reception.'[30] The point is also that McGrath's 'redefinition' grows organically out of the many earlier redefinitions that led to the existing 'subject matter, aesthetic context of production and modes of reception' that drew him to Scotland in turn to help develop its theatre.

In effect, then, a consensus view in the study of the performativity of Scottish theatre exists that it is possible to discern there a communality of audience and performers within which popular and so-called high-art forms are interlinked and even interdependent and that welcomes issue-based dramatic discourse. Such a performativity clearly has strong attraction for a playwright and director with the concerns and themes of John McGrath. (Indeed, in parenthesis, such a performativity can be seen to provide a possible explanation as to why Scots translation and performance of such writers as Molière and Tremblay have worked so very well, when in English their translation has not been seen to be so successful.) The richness of such a theatrical and historic resource was employed by McGrath time and again, integrating a range of techniques from a variety of Scottish cultural sources, from *The Cheviot* itself through to his own response to David Lindsay, *A Satire of the Four Estaites*. McGrath notes that these techniques have common features with 'traditional forms of working-class entertainment', such as 'music-hall, variety theatre, club entertainment, the *ceilidh* in Scotland, the *noson llawen* in Wales, panto, and through the Morecambe and Wise show on tele-vision'.[31] In his Scottish work, however, there is a culturally specific conjunction of dramatic conventions, forms and content which is particularly powerful. He himself draws attention to the claims of *The Game's a Bogey* in its 'critical recreation' of 'grossly reactionary club show elements' to produce 'a show of great sophistication in artistic and political terms, which was very far from being grossly reactionary'.[32]

The Edinburgh Festival and its Fringe, effectively founded by Unity amongst other companies, has been a more recent, but very important influence in the development of Scottish theatre. Craig and Stevenson offer one perspective on that influence in discussing the use of the Assembly Hall for Guthrie's production of Robert Kemp's version of David Lindsay's *Ane Satyre of the Thrie Estaitis* in 1948:

> Practically, because it had been designed for debate rather than as an acting chamber, the Assembly Hall posed immediate theatrical problems, solved by Guthrie's reinvention of the Elizabethan thrust stage, jutting out among the spectators so that the actors are surrounded by the audience. Involving the audience much more immediately than a proscenium stage, his tactics set a pattern regularly followed by later Scottish theatre, often drawing its spectators into close complicity with performers through shared outlooks or simple physical proximity. Such tactics were followed by 7:84 in their 'ceilidh house' style of theatre.[33]

The revival of Lindsay's masterpiece, since revived several times, had another effect besides that which Craig and Stevenson rightly refer to. This was to bring to the fore an example of earlier Scottish theatre in a satirical drama that, while played for the Court, was also played in public and drew on a wide variety of popular forms. This alerted Scottish theatre-workers to a resource of their own tradition of which many had been in ignorance. It is surely no coincidence that, as noted already, one of the last of John McGrath's stage plays was inspired by, and his modern version of, this play. The ways in which McGrath embraced and drew from the Scottish tradition could hardly be more clearly demonstrated than in the case of *The Fourth Estaite*, a play English newspaper critics had the greatest difficulty in understanding and uniformly condemned—to the glee of Scottish aficionados. McGrath observed that the play 'meant a great deal to people in Scotland. It was well received [by them]'.[34]

The use of the Assembly Hall to explore new configurations of the relationship of performer and audience was only the first of such spatial experiments presented at the Edinburgh Festival and Fringe. There, in the late 1960s and early 1970s alone, experimental work by Grotowski, Ronconi and Ellen Stewart's La Mama made use of non-theatre venues and unusual configurations and revisited the range of possibilities for audience-performer communication and interaction. Such experience was complemented year-round by the spatial experiments of the first Traverse Theatre (1963–69) in James Court and the flexible auditorium of the second (from 1969) in West Bow. Both these spaces changed and enhanced the vocabulary and grammar of performance dynamics. Scottish theatre by the time McGrath arrived, in common with the rest of Euro- pean theatre, was actively reviewing and reshaping audience-performer dynamics.

So far this chapter has focused very much on the theatrical tradition which attracted and welcomed John McGrath. The present configuration of Scottish politics might suggest that McGrath would also find a welcoming political climate in Scotland for his socialist dramatic themes. A number of commentators have made this suggestion. Maria DiCenzo for example observes, 'Scotland's long socialist tradition offered fertile ground for the [7:84's] work'.[35] It is true that the elections for the Scottish Parliament of 1997, under proportional representation, allowed a very clear picture to emerge of support there for the Conservative Party. It attracted only 16% for the vote, the remaining votes going to left-of-centre parties of one kind or another. A bald representation of the nature of Scottish political life as left of centre in a way attractive to McGrath is, however, probably too simplistic. In common with a number of other areas of Britain, Scotland certainly had a lively socialist movement in industrial areas at the end of the nineteenth and beginning of the twentieth century. Yet, the majority vote in Scotland could be Conservative (or as the party was then self-consciously called 'Conservative and Unionist') as recently as the 1955 General Election. When McGrath arrived, although Scotland did have a long tradition of communitarianism, arguably more important to McGrath's concerns than socialism itself, Scotland was not just a country of left of centre ideas. The change under way between 1955 and now, of which McGrath's work formed a part, was more complex than a simple shift from Right to Left.

This deeper complexity is grounded significantly in a long tradition of debate in Scotland about the nature of the state and the relation of its elements. Since 1707, much of this has focused, naturally, on the meaning of the Treaty of Union. Its nature, however, sharpened and refocused with changes in British society following the Suez Crisis of 1956 and the subsequent evidence of the demise of the post-1707 Anglo-Scottish Empire in which Scots had played such an important role. Changes in the constitution of the imperial order that had arisen out of the Treaty of Union in turn induced further debate on the constitutional nature of the internal political order. The Conservative and 'Unionist' vote in Scotland has declined more or less constantly not only since the general election of 1955, but since the Suez debacle of 1956. Further, the decline in the Conservative Party with its connections to the Orange Order and Unionism is matched by the decline in numbers since 1960 attending the Church of Scotland.[36] Elements of this were associated with both the Orange Order and Unionist Conservatism (the Roman Catholic Church still being, even now, a focus of Labour politics in the west of the Central Belt). In the late 1960s and 1970s, then, Scotland offered a sympathetic home for an artist interested in the political structures of, and power relations within, society at large. The Scots were, then as now, dynamically reconsidering the political settlement both within Scotland and within the United Kingdom. McGrath came to observe in 1989, 'Labour is wrong not to take a bold step against the Union'.[37]

This political debate has been intensified by the fact that, at times, there has been a misreading of the relationship of Scotland and England since the Union, one which sees Scotland as somehow subsumed within Britain and 'Britain' another term for 'England'. In such a reading, what Tom Nairn has called 'cultural sub-nationalism'[38] prevails. Cairns Craig, however, suggests:

> there is an alternative way of viewing these relationships: what nineteenth-century Scotland developed was a Scoto-British constitutional identity whose nationalism consisted in the long-drawn-out struggles to maintain the independence of precisely those institutions —church, law and education—which had originally been guaranteed by the Act of Union. The paradox, in other words, is that Scotland's *nationalism* was already enshrined *within* the Act of Union, and defence of the Union was the first and immediate resort for those defending the rights of Scottish culture. As Graeme Morton has argued, 'unionist nationalism' was the very basis of nineteenth-century Scottish culture, so that 'however strange it may seem to twentieth-century nationalists: Scotland wanted more union, not less. Scotland's mid-nineteenth-century nationalists believed their nation had entered the union of 1707 as an equal, and that was how they demanded to be treated'. Indeed, the movement for Scottish Home Rule developed not so much out of resistance to the Union but out of insistence upon it, and upon the fact that the treaty was being breached by the Westminster parliament.[39]

This perspective is transgressive, in terms of a centralized vision of the British State. It further offers a radical constitutional perspective for political debate of a kind clearly attractive to McGrath, himself a radical. Indeed, the importance in Scottish cultural and intellectual life of debate of all kinds offers a further attraction to a theatre worker like McGrath who, in the words of Nadine Holdsworth, 'calls for theatre to be a place where society debates itself and contributes to a climate of change in an acknowl-edged process of dialogue with the audience'.[40] His work after 1973, for instance, regularly deals with issues of the nature of nationhood, political authority, social identity and constitutional change. *Joe's Drum*, indeed, can be read as a cry of pain and anger at the legal, but anti democratic, manoeuvre that meant that the 1979 majority vote for a Scottish Assembly was refused effect. While never a Scottish Nationalist, McGrath clearly found in the themes current in Scottish life of the assertion of Scottish identity, independence of thought, subversion of a would-be hegemony and debate about the nature of the state and constitutional politics sympathetic to his work in theatre. He sets out his views on the value of non-hegemonized diversity when discussing Scottish culture in the context of the dangers of globalization: 'Diversity in nature, in human experience, in the language of living, in peoples, is one of the great sources of joy. A culture that is loved, guarded, and developed will tend to have more subtlety, more specific reference, more density than a demotic that has to serve the needs of half the world.'[41]

McGrath's interest in the use of the languages of Scotland is also expressed in his writing for the theatre. The attempt to suppress both the Scots and Gaelic languages enshrined in the 1872 Education Act, which privileged the use of English in schools and school playgrounds, placed both languages in a relatively oppressed position. Both are, however, languages of great age and with very substantial literatures. McGrath's opposition to cultural suppression found a new vitality in working in languages whose very use is not simply an artistic act, but, in Katja Lenz's words in relation to Scots, political: 'The decision to write a play in Scots is still a political step. With some authors, the choice of Scots is clearly a statement of national and cultural politics. In less radical cases, Scots serves to transmit a feeling of specifically Scottish identity.'[42] Fiona M. Douglas reinforces this point more generally when she says: 'Language can act as a strong cultural identifier and can function as a rallying point, an emblem of in-group solidarity, or a linguistic totem. By using Scottish words, a speaker signals that they are part of the wider discourse com-munity that is Scotland.'[43]

From *The Cheviot* on, McGrath would make use of Scots and some-times Gaelic to give theatrical expression through means of the languages themselves to his themes of resistance and the assertion of cultural identity against a would-be dominant hegemony. In this frame, his very use of Scottish languages whether Scots, English or Gaelic, becomes an assertion of the liberty of the individual and the rights of free expression. He observes: 'The Gaelic language now has fierce champions, and the regions of Scotland are developing a conscious sense of the value of their own tongue, songs, skills and history—and the Doric [the Scots dialect of Aberdeen and Buchan] is far from dead.'[44] McGrath's apparent enjoyment of the potential of the languages of Scotland extended to his use of Scottish popular music forms. This use extended from the traditional Gaelic music employed in *The Cheviot* to the popular modern forms providing compositional inspiration for such collaborators as David Anderson. In this, McGrath recreated the tradition of music in popular theatre referred to *passim* in this chapter. Thus, he shared experience with his audience through reference to commonly understood musical conventions. He would sustain his themes by freely using newly composed music in modern popular idioms, traditional music or folk song as the moment required without privileging one over the other. As with his use of languages, the ways in which he used music were in themselves political statements.

John McGrath worked often in the Fringe both in the sense of the Edinburgh Fringe Festival and of the Fringe Theatre of the 1970s and later. It must, however, be clear that he helped make those Fringes central to the theatre of the British Isles. In this, a very large part of his work was developed within Scotland and, as we have seen, the Scottish theatre tradition. Nadine Holdsworth makes this point very clearly when she says, 'McGrath's creative energies were primarily focused in Scotland'.[45] She observes: '*The Cheviot* was in tune with the Scottish psyche that was emerging in the wider context of national self-reflection, growing confidence and increasing political nationalism.'[46] This observation might be applied to any of his Scottish plays. As a result, despite his early background and origins, in any modern collection of essays on contemporary Scottish theatre, McGrath is identified as a Scottish playwright. Certainly, he was happy to be described in such a way: he provided his own entry, for example, for the Scottish Society of Playwrights' *Playwrights Register: Directory of Scottish Playwrights*.[47] He says in his *Introduction* to his plays in the collection, *Six-Pack*: '. . . although these plays are written for Scotland, I am not ethnically Scots, being an itinerant Liverpool-Irish person of Welsh upbringing, Oxford and London training and Scottish only by marriage, domicile and commitment.'[48] It is, however, surely sterile to debate whether McGrath 'belongs' to the Scottish or the English theatre. The point is that, just as Henry James, T.S. Eliot, Jonathan Swift or Bernard Shaw sit both in and between two literary traditions, John McGrath both inhabits and mediates between the different theatre traditions of Scotland and England. What is certainly also true is that, in Scottish theatre, he found practices, performativity and a set of values which encouraged him and allowed him to develop. Very much of his theatrical output is in the context of Scottish theatre, on Scottish themes of international significance and making use of the languages of Scotland and of the grammar and vocabulary of its theatre. When he was drawn to the Celtic-Anglian-Nordic centre, he found welcome, inspiration and achievement and a theatrical, intellectual, political, emotional and, even, spiritual home.

CHAPTER EIGHT

'Bursting through the hoop and dancing on the edge of the seediness'

Five Scottish Playwrights Talk about John McGrath

Ian Brown

The recording and transcription of these interviews was made possible by a research project grant from Queen Margaret University College. All interviews took place in Edinburgh and on the following dates: Stewart Conn, 10 July 2002; Tom McGrath, 9 July 2002; John Clifford, 18 July 2002; Liz Lochhead, 16 July 2002; Stephen Greenhorn, 16 July 2002.

Stewart Conn

Born in Glasgow in 1936 and brought up in Kilmarnock, Stewart Conn is a leading poet as well as a playwright. He was literary advisor to the Royal Lyceum in the early 1970s and for many years involved in radio drama production, becoming head of BBC Scotland's radio drama department before leaving in 1992. His many works include the seminal The Burning *(1971) and most recently* Clay Bull *at the Royal Lyceum (1998).*

John McGrath, to me, burst through the hoop by tapping something that I think was latent. His work was so exciting because there was a suppressed frustration in the 1960s at not having access to a brand of theatre that it was felt could exist, but didn't. There would be elements of farce in one play, or a stand-up comedian in another, or direct address to the audience in a third, but there wasn't an amalgam of ingredients and a mix of music that would actually provide a mosaic and a dynamic for an entire evening.

My earliest awareness of John was from *Random Happenings in the Hebrides*, which I found very filmic. I don't feel at this remove that it was earth shattering and changing theatrical form. Nor was his *Trees in the Wind*. The real burst was with *The Cheviot, the Stag and the Black, Black Oil*. That hit me smack. I was amazed not only at its daring, the evening's ingredients, what it did in terms of dramatic form and the putting together of disparate elements, but also at the Scottishness of the form. I had been excited before by theatre change and novelty, something full front at me, as at Joan Littlewood's Stratford East, *The Hostage* and *Oh What a Lovely War*, the use of songs, the use of music hall. I'll never forget the end of *The Hostage* when the soldier, shot dead—I still feel the emotion of it—stood up and went into the 'Bells of Hell'. I had never encountered anything like that before, with that tempo, but it didn't touch any Scottish empathy in me. What *The Cheviot*—and *The Game's a Bogey*—did was suddenly have actors talking directly to me. It was the mix, the inventiveness of characterization—the McChuck-em-up character, for example —the moment-by-moment wit, the impact and energy through the songs, the way in which the narrative was told. And it was the way in which the play was resolved in conjunction with two other things. One was where the play went, aiming for audiences in community centres, in miners' halls, that intensified the vibrancy of the performance in space, made a closer link and empathy between performers and audience than I had experienced before. It brought back something of a community involvement in theatre that Joe Corrie had had, but Corrie had done it within the formal drama. McGrath tapped something new and Scottish, new theatre form, new venues. The second thing was the interplay and relationship, the inventiveness and composite genius of the casting. Because in having Billy Paterson and Johnny Bett, and Alex Norton, what more can you ask! And not just in terms of acting—or composing as with Dave Anderson's music and Terry Neason's singing—but in writing and themselves creating it.

This is where, conceding the excitement and the energy, I have a dilemma with 7:84 from then on. It's the possibly inevitable dilemma of a company that starts with such éclat and such talent and how it continues in what it does next. I remember going to Lochgelly Community Hall to see the later *Joe's Drum*; I found the later ones frustrating and duplicatory. Their cast was adequate, but didn't have the spark of the original ones. Yet, I think it's more that the plays themselves, although they were different characters and settings, seemed a carbon copy in intent and statement. This is where I have to stick to my guns in what I believe as a writer that I have to do. I believe that for a kind of theatre that most satisfies me, an author has to divide himself among the characters. Chekhov is a supreme example. I don't think theatre is a soapbox and the two-dimensionality of the characters in the later 7:84 mode of performance, repetitiveness of message and emphasis on political placarding meant to me diminishing returns. Because of the specificity of the political message, even the choice of halls and who they are touring to, my suspicion is of preaching to the converted. I'm not persuaded that you can throw out the middle-class mode of theatre, and then assume that the working class has some psychological and emotional element the middle class doesn't have. Anymore than I think, for a play to be universal, does everybody have to respond identically, which I think John certainly implies, as I read his *A Good Night Out*. Of course, what he is wishing is an identical political response. There were wonderful tactics that he used, but I'm not persuaded of the theatrical justification of the end product in every case.

Paradoxes abound with me. When I produced *The Game's a Bogey* for the BBC's *A Decade's Drama* season in 1980, I had to reassemble the original 7:84 cast. We got them and, suddenly, there was this marvellous moment when one of the cast froze, and said 'Why is he (John) giving us rewrites when we wrote it?' This was an interesting comment on the durability of the joy of democratic creativity and its very creativity: it is very difficult to have everybody equal in the theatre. I didn't know John McGrath in a close personal sense: I would meet him occasionally going up the road; he'd be at the bus stop. I felt almost embarrassed at how charming he was and how deferential and nice and asking about my work. I was very aware of his work, knowing his energies and what he had done on television and what he was doing, and the brand of theatre he was doing, what he was achieving in meeting audiences and also his prolific-ness. I just felt ashamed and embarrassed at my own inadequacy, quite honestly, but he never made me feel that—that was within me. I can still not resolve this Liverpudlian going to Oxford at the same time as Giles Havergal and having an Oxford peer group and being involved in this brand of theatre and founding 7:84. And the aura that he had! He was one of the most handsome men that I have ever seen.

I have not heard anything bitchy of John, other than from people in the crucible of the company involved in the production, with all the tensions of a production going on. The word catalyst seems inappropriate for him, because he was so much more than a catalyst in his guiding energy, a creator and achiever. You think of the catalyst as not having such positive edges, but he was an extraordinary catalyst through what he did, not in the process of what he was doing so much as as a result of what he did. There was a paring down, becoming more realistic or, as in television, more documentary, as in *Z-Cars*, one of his great triumphs! It may be that this paring down reaches a point where there is such direct, almost documen-tary, interplay, that there comes a yearning for something of the magic of the theatre. The phrase slipped out. It's a phrase I suppose I would be guarded about if I were not talking to you, because I don't mean it sentimentally. I mean a power that can shake your spirit. Some of the most magical things that I have seen have been the most appalling and heart-rending. The Ninagawa *Macbeth*, do you still have the images of that in your head? I mean that by 'magic', *The Tempest* done as it can be. I don't mean a soft, cosy putting of a conjurer's red handkerchief over reality. The theatre can be powerful and still have that. Extraordinarily! I would not have the political, soapbox, element as be-all and end-all, and subjugate everything else to it. The better shows did follow the narrative; later, they became set pieces. And that is where the momentum slows and dies.

John lit. He was a fireworks display that shook me as a writer into a realization of my own non-dynamicness, and non-exploration of the boundaries of a medium that I was working, and happy to work, in. He did open up people's minds and gave great satisfaction, especially in the political climate of the time, by expressing in theatrical terms what people were shouting to see. *A Good Night Out* is the title of his book. He gave that. His was a drawing together of remarkable, simultaneous talents and a wonderful outlet for them but, especially given a changing political climate, the problem was that, once that had happened, how do you sustain the excitement when so much of it is gauged by the success of the political message?

Tom McGrath

Born in Rutherglen in 1940, Tom McGrath's past occupations have included poet, journalist and musician as well as playwright. In the 1960s, he was features editor of Peace News *and editor of* International Times. *In the early seventies, he launched and was first Director of the Third Eye Centre (now CCA). His many plays include* The Hardman *(1977) and* Animal *(1979) and his translations include Tankred Dorst's* Merlin *for the Royal Lyceum (1992) and Daniel Danis's* Stones and Ashes *for the Traverse (1995).*

I first met John after we had been doing *The Great Northern Welly Boot Show* in 1972. Billy Connolly and Tom Buchan had written the script and I had been the piano-player-cum-MD. We did it at the King's Theatre in Glasgow as part of Clyde Fair International and then as a co-op in the Edinburgh Festival. There was a certain style to the *The Welly Boot Show*. The format of music and very out-front type of acting was all new to me. I had a little action group then for setting up an arts centre, which eventually became the Third Eye Centre. I needed somebody from the theatre world and Kenny Ireland suggested we do an artists' register as a co-op because there were so many talented people at the time out of work. They are all names now, but they weren't in work. Then one day, John McGrath came. That is the first time I remember meeting him, this big man, very handsome big man. I'm sure everyone says that about John. He was a lovely looking man and very friendly, and with Liz, his wife, he said, 'I'm wanting to assemble some people for a show, and I understand you have some kind of contacts here.' And it was *The Cheviot, the Stag, and the Black, Black Oil* that he was preparing. So he asked if I had any idea where to get in touch with Alex Norton and I pulled out the register, gave him the whole lot, quite gladly, and the show was great. I did like it very much. The other thing was that John asked if I would play the piano in it and do the music. I was fully committed to opening the Third Eye Centre and with a family. So, I said I couldn't do it. I could see a continuation of a lot of the routines, the garrulous Texan and other things, that I'd seen the actors developing in performance in *The Welly Boot Show*. So, I knew that it was an interaction between the actors and the writer. And then there were people like Dolina singing and the whole Gaelic element coming into it. That I thought was very good.

John had an enormous impact in holding out for very popular forms of theatre, non-obscure forms of theatre, working-class involvement forms of theatre, socialist theatre. He had a great impact that way. I think also he had an impact in relationship to history, to awareness of the past. As to what brought him to Scotland, there is his wife's own involvement with Scotland and there is a very, very rich working-class history here and there was the whole history of the Highland people. Plus the fact that the oil was the key economic thing that was happening in the whole of Britain then. John came from afar. Essentially, he came from a different background and so things weren't so muddled for him and he didn't have the kind of complexity of a Scottish identity directly on his shoulders, you know. He was part of it, but also he could also observe. He had a very sensitive, but very sharp, eye.

I remember his earlier writing. It didn't have the very strong socialist parameters that all of his later writing had. And I often wondered what happened to that writer, because I'm more interested in vulnerability, confusion and things like that. For all the strength and social impact that he undoubtedly had, there was something else. The romantic in him was perhaps abandoned or put in a cupboard or something. But I remember being with Jenny Tiramani, who designed a lot with John at one point, working with her at the Theatre Royal, Stratford East. We were out in a car somewhere and she was driving and I went, 'Jenny, Jenny, stop the car'. She stopped the car, and I said, 'Look at that bird'. I jumped out the car and started looking at this hawk or something and I got back into the car and she said, 'That's exactly what John McGrath does! He's exactly the same.' She said 'The number of times I've been out in country roads and he's stopped the car, and he's out with his binoculars so he could see this hawk.'

In terms of Scottish theatre, he was the right person at the right time, without a doubt. You know, the rest of us could have all been sitting being poets and all the rest of it. Not to denigrate that, because I think a lot of the depth and the richness of the language is all to do with that poetic experience, but none of us was capable of that push and that drive at that time, getting things organized like that. I think we are a lot more capable now, but a lot of things have changed since then and he was part of that change. He opened up the Highland circuit. The work that he did with Giles Havergal when they did the *Clydebuilt* season was very important to him. To me, John was a man of great stature, which I think we needed. His great stature was really important to me, his theatricality, the fact that he could match up to a Dario Fo for a while, that he had that dimension to him. I saw that tremendous energy guided by a very strong intellect—and a good sense of fun!

He was very generous about other people's work. He certainly was in relationship to mine whenever he came to see it. I remember him coming in 1989 into *City*, a play I had on in Glasgow at the Tramway where he had also done *Border Warfare* in the same year. *City* was on for only about ten days after all that enormous preparation. We were going up the stairs into the event and he said to me, 'This is only on for ten days?' I said. 'Yeah.' He just shook his head: he couldn't understand why I had allowed such a situation to happen. Of course, an awful lot of it was away beyond my control, but John never lost control. He would keep very much in control of what he was doing. But, on the other hand, I had this belief, still have, that eventually, at the end of the day, something worthwhile will come through in some sort of obscure way. I don't believe too much in format.

John Clifford

John Clifford, born in Derby in 1950, is the author of over sixty plays, translations and adaptations for every dramatic medium and is Professor of Theatre at Queen Margaret University College, Edinburgh. His plays include Losing Venice *(1985) and* Inés de Castro *(1989), which he later made into an opera with James McMillan for Scottish Opera (1996). His translations include Calderon's* Schism of England *for the National Theatre (1988) and* Life is a Dream *for the Edinburgh International Festival (1998) and his adaptations include* Great Expectations *(1988) and* Wuthering Heights *(1995). Most recent plays have included, in 2002,* The Queen of Spades *and* Charles Dickens: The Haunted Man.

I first came across John McGrath's work as a research student in St Andrews. I was absolutely immersed in seventeenth-century Spanish playwrights and beginning to get a bit discouraged and depressed about my thesis. I was looking for a direction and developing strong left-wing beliefs of one sort or another. 7:84 came to St Andrews and put on *The Game's a Bogey* in the student union. It was just one of those moments in theatre. They happen about once or twice a lifetime; something just completely bowls you over, you just go 'Oh, my God'. I was so moved by that show, Bill Paterson playing John MacLean. I just think it's their best show actually. I thought it was stunning, funny, very informative and very moving, and it completely, completely, altered my view about what theatre could do. I didn't consider myself a playwright at the time. When I wasn't doing my research, I was trying to write stories and novels, and not getting very far. But this was like a complete thunder stroke really. Soon after that, in fact, I gave up my thesis. I decided I was just doing the things that were expected of me according to my class. So I stopped being a PhD student and firstly became a bus conductor on the buses between Leven and Dundee. So I was really taking this whole business seriously. Very naïve, but I was becoming part of the working class and all that stuff about solidarity. After that, I became a student nurse in Kirkcaldy and I stuck that out for a couple of years. Now actually, of course, it was a completely wrong direction for me to take in lots of ways, because I couldn't stand nursing: I was profoundly frustrated. During that period, I saw one of the later shows, I don't know which one, in Methil community hall and I think it had an audience of six. It was empty. They were just obviously not making any connection with this particular audience they were aiming for. And there was I. I had abandoned everything and joined the working classes and I found that actually it wasn't the direction I could take. But having said all that, it was an immensely valuable time for me. And I did go back and complete my thesis. And I read *A Good Night Out* and I care for its ideals.

Some theatre is very depressing: it presents a really bleak, violent, nihilistic, upsetting view of the world and you swallow it, I suppose because it's good for you and the more depressing the better. You read critics and they use words like 'bleak' or 'searing' as terms of praise and for me those aren't terms of praise at all. They show that in some real respect, the play has failed because I'm convinced—and I owe quite a lot of this to John's influence—that going to the theatre should give pleasure. I mean this in a very full way, the way that he meant, intellectually stimulating, about things that really matter, so that there's a lot to discuss afterwards in the bar. It should be emotionally pleasurable: you go through a very intense and very full emotional experience that is very multi-layered, so it's not just devastating, and bitter and appalling. It's sometimes very funny, as well as sometimes very sad. It sometimes makes you very angry; sometimes it surprises and shocks you. It's emotionally rich, and spiritually rich, and that's another form of pleasure.

I think it was extraordinary what he did. It wasn't that he invented small-scale touring, but the fact that he embarked on those extraordinary tours opened up a whole new touring circuit to theatre. It opened up the possibility of reaching out to new audiences in a way that I find very inspiring. His was a take on history that was completely different from the conventional view. I suppose, being as I've always been somebody who has never been able to think the same as anybody else, I've always had a very strongly individualist slant on the world, which is both a strength and a great weakness. It was very difficult for me to find my voice as a playwright because the kind of plays I wanted to write was not the kind of plays I ever saw. Even though I never wanted to write like John, at least his was another dissenting voice that was making itself heard. And that's enormously strengthening, somewhat encouraging. We were parallel lines. We never really met each other; we never really worked together; we never collaborated. I don't even remember meeting him socially. He was this man that was so important to me in terms of what he had achieved; I was very shy in those days, very shy. So even if I had met him, I don't know what on earth I would have said to him. It would have been very difficult for me to talk to him.

I remember watching *Z-Cars* as a boy. I thought *Z-Cars* was the most exciting, just amazing. Real issues were being debated dramatically on television. I had a very difficult time when I was growing up, but certain artistic things kept me alive and *Z-Cars* was one of them. And it was years later that I understood that he had been responsible for it. So again, he had been really important for me although I hadn't a clue that it was him. In some ways, I didn't warm to the later work, but the man as an artist and a creator was really important for me. It's a measure of what a complex and fascinating character he was. He was hugely inspiring when the focus was on the individual, the human predicament. It's to do with warmth and compassion and humour and all the qualities that are life-enhancing. Which is very important in my work. That's how theatre should be and that's how his best work was for me. I suppose there was a kind of didactic doctrinal side to it which I did find very exciting at first, because I was trying to make sense of all my ideas about how society would be and we were living in a commune, and it was all part of that. Well, that helped shape my thinking enormously. But then, I suppose as I got older, I've become less and less impressed by ideology in whatever shape it comes because life is just so rich and complex. I think if you try and shoehorn it into ideology you miss out, while art, theatre, is such a fantastically rich form of expression. I just value that richness really.

Liz Lochhead

Born in Motherwell in 1947, Liz Lochhead began her writing career as a poet and performer. Her first play was Blood and Ice *(1982) and since then her plays have included the seminal* Mary Queen of Scots Got Her Head Chopped Off *(1987) and* Perfect Days *(1998). Her adaptations include* Dracula *for the Royal Lyceum (1985) and her two Molière versions for the same theatre,* Tartuffe *(1986) and* Miseryguts [The Misanthrope] *(2002). Her award-winning version of* Medea *for Theatre Babel (2000) has led to other forthcoming translations of Greek tragedies into Scots.*

John McGrath was for me, firstly, the author of *The Cheviot, the Stag and the Black, Black Oil* and the big change that meant. Of course he's got all kinds of other significances. I think probably his big long-lasting legacy will be the whole idea of touring drama in Scotland, which didn't really quite happen before he proved that you could take things out there on the road. I think, too, he probably was very much an influence on people who were my big influences, like Gerry Mulgrew of Communicado, rather than a direct influence on me. I think everybody in Scotland really was grabbed by the idea that you could use our old traditions, that the music hall and the ceilidh could somehow be married together. I think that was genuinely new and I went to see lots and lots of his plays and enjoyed them thoroughly. I think I enjoyed them much more than they personally influenced me. I don't think I've got the same taste in drama at all. I think I now believe that drama is not really the medium for putting across political points, but what I do take from him is that you've got to be a 100% passionate about what you are doing. And you have got to write about what you are genuinely interested in. In this, he was just fantastic. And then of course as a producer, his *Clydebuilt* series was a big influence on everybody of my generation. In the same way that *The Cheviot* restored a voice to us all, the *Clydebuilt* series restored this history. I think his achievements will be felt for ages and ages, and at different times, different things that he did will come into prominence. I loved the film of *The Bofors Gun*. I mean, he wasn't that much older than me, but I was a very late starter, so I feel like I'm a kind of full generation or more after him, because he really knew what he wanted to do early on. And the things that he did in *The Bofors Gun* and *Z-Cars* were just tremendous. When he died, I thought, 'I wish I could go out to the video shop and watch that and drink a glass of wine and toast him.'

He was always very good at the formal experiment, like opening up what you could do in the theatre, getting away from the three-act or two-act form, and there were the big promenades. I wasn't so keen on them personally. They're just not my taste in theatre. I think it's the smaller things that I personally loved. The up-closeness of *The Bofors Gun* or some of the plays that Elizabeth MacLennan did that were very personal. I think of the television drama, *The Long Roads*, with Edith MacArthur, where she was the old lady who was dying. There you got the 'State of Britain' film. I thought that was really marvellous and subtle. He really cared about the individual. Some of his work was very thoughtful, very intimate and that's when he really spoke to me. It was those things that I found very, very moving, because they were complex and uncomfortable at times, but they dealt with some of the big issues through individuals. What is there bigger than dying as a small person in the big world? That night that we all celebrated him it was a great night, but it made me want to actually see some of these intimate things.

I liked him very much. I think he probably had more of an effect on me as a person even than as a dramatist, because I was very aware of the fact that he was *so* 100% passionate and committed about what he was doing, like producing *Carrington*. I remember meeting him on a plane then and the absolute all that he gave it. That was the surprising thing: you wouldn't have thought you would have John McGrath producing something about posh Bloomsburyites. But, you see he wasn't the simple man that I think we try to make him: we could put him into a box far too easily because of certain of the big things that he said. But I think he was a very complex figure. I think he will probably be remembered for his big statements and for 7:84, but I think we shouldn't forget some of these other things. People try and put him in easy categories, you know, 'political theatre and that's all you need to think about'. Because he did wear his political heart on his sleeve the way he did, it is easy for people who think they disagree with him to therefore discredit that. I don't think they can if they actually look at the drama.

Stephen Greenhorn

Stephen Greenhorn was born in Fauldhouse, West Lothian in 1964. His first play Heart and Bone *(1989) won a Fringe First Award. Since then, he has written extensively for the stage, his plays including* The Salt Wound *(1993) and* Passing Places *(1997). His writing for television, includes episodes for* The Bill, *the series* Glasgow Kiss, *and the devising of the Glasgow soap,* River City.

To me as a playwright, John McGrath was 7:84 and the main effect that he had on me was *A Good Night Out*. It became a kind of manifesto against lots of things that I thought were wrong with theatre and that seemed to exclude me from ever practising anything in theatre. It was only when I read it that I saw there was an alternative vision that made sense to me of what theatre could be and the kind of sources it could draw on. Simple things made sense, like the fact that I had been living in a mining village in West Lothian: growing up there I would habitually get a train in to see stuff at the Lyceum in Edinburgh and we would always have to leave halfway through the last act because the last train was going home. It was only McGrath who pointed out that you have to consider the whole experience of the audience in terms of putting these shows on, about how they get there, how far they have to travel, how they are going to get home. The social fact that this might be the one night in the week where they get out the house, therefore you have got to provide. It was understanding the fact, when I was finally working with 7:84 with *The Salt Wound* on tour in 1993, that, when people drive for forty miles, you need to provide an interval so they can have a tea-break and a chat. They don't want to arrive, see a show, and go home. It's a whole night out. That book was the first time that I had read something that echoed my feeling of being marginalized by traditional forms of theatre, but that there was an alternative if people chose to explore that.

As a playwright, he wasn't a huge influence on me because I was too young to be caught up in the whole *Cheviot, Stag, Black, Black Oil* stuff. I knew about it, but it was something that was happening beyond me at a point where I was so young that it didn't have any impact on me. What did have impact was during the Miners' Strike. I went to see *In Time o'Strife*, the Joe Corrie play that they had revived around the time. That had a big impact on me by the fact that what Corrie was writing about, and what 7:84 had chosen to revive and point out, was exactly what was going on in my village at the time: who was and who wasn't going to break the strike? So it seemed to me that that was the first Scottish play that I'd seen that really spoke to me about issues that were real and resonant and relevant for the life that I was living. After that, when I went to study in Glasgow, I started reading through McGrath plays and it was only then that I came across *Joe's Drum* and *Blood Red Roses* and all the other stuff. It became an exercise about discovering the text rather than having seen the shows, because I missed them when they were out and about. It was about finding a form that was flexible and laid-back, and playful and incorporated all sorts of aspects of music, and comedy and cabaret as well. It was that breaking down of form and the recognition that, if you want to broaden your audience base, then you have to start thinking about structures and not being rigid about the structures that you are applying and, also, about the places that you play.

I suppose the other big thing about 7:84 for me was the fact that they were the only company that ever toured anywhere near where I lived. They came to Shotts, which was a neighbouring village. At one point, I think they actually played at Fauldhouse Miners' Welfare, though I can't remember which show they took there. Whereas every other theatre company assumed that you would have the means to travel to see them, 7:84 had the initiative to actually go and try to find the audience that wouldn't be able to come and find them. It was about that notion of seeking out a new audience and knowing that you can't just put on a classic five-act drama that's necessarily going to be immediately resonant with people whose experience of narrative structure is different.

I don't know if the experience of 7:84 gave me a push to come into theatre, or whether I would have come in anyway. Several things happened at once and, ironically, the point that I became involved in 7:84 was just after John McGrath had left. I ended up working with the script reading group that they had. That was quite a strange few years where I was still a student and then a recent graduate, and was writing myself. Then Iain Reekie took over and he and I spent five years arguing the toss about how 7:84 as a company should be carrying on the ideology that John had set up, but without being constantly hampered by the reference of his own work. When I was doing *The Salt Wound* for them, Iain was forever beleaguered with the suggestion that it is not really 7:84 because it was not John McGrath. My simple response was always that, of course, it was going to be different because I am not John McGrath: 7:84 was commissioning a different writer. When John was there he was doing his own plays. This created a house style because he was doing so many of them and, when Iain was commissioning different writers, then the style was going to change. I'm not sure that any other company would have taken Iain on as Artistic Director and, if that hadn't happened, I am not sure that I would have carried on writing plays, because at that point, I had given up. I had stopped. I had worked a bit for TAG, and a bit for Maggie Kinloch when she was up at the Byre. But it was within structures and audiences in which I felt I was alien. It was only 7:84, the company, that I felt offered me the chance to find a voice of my own and address an audience that I wanted to speak to.

I think John McGrath's still influencing Scottish theatre. He did things with people like Nicola McCartney where he was directly encouraging, commissioning and developing work with her. I never had that situation with him, but the other influence he had on me as a dramatist was the fact that he was quite happy across several different mediums, as I am. He wasn't snobbish about doing TV and one of the most exciting things about him was discovering about why he had set up *Z-Cars* and the fact that you could set up popular drama with ambitions about what it was going to tackle. And equally about the fact that you can write and do popular large-budget films, but with an ideology about what you want to say. I think that ability to move between media and, if you like, dance on the edge of the seediness and money-oriented market that TV and film is, yet try and operate there without being completely overwhelmed, is a challenge that still exists today. I think that that's worth trying to pick up and take on. What he challenged was the assumption that, if you went and worked for TV or film, you had just to assume that you were going to get fucked over and it was going to be just awful anyway. But I wouldn't compare my past work on *The Bill* to *Z-Cars*! The TV stuff that I aspire to do is about creating popular drama that draws in an audience because it is quality popular drama, actually has something to say. John helped me want that.

PART FOUR

Case Studies

CHAPTER NINE

The Television Adaptation of *The Cheviot, the Stag and the Black, Black Oil*

Robin Nelson

The television version of *The Cheviot, the Stag and the Black, Black Oil* has long been acclaimed as an extraordinary TV piece. It is frequently cited in Television Studies as a rare example of non-naturalistic drama on television, a medium in which the codes and conventions of various naturalisms and realisms have dominated. In addition, the television adaptation, like the theatre play, is polemical and unusual in being overtly political in content. It powerfully mobilizes a strong argument from a specific point of view, that of Scottish rural and industrial working people. It challenges establishment institutions and effectively points out why the Scottish people should not have faith in them with regard to claims about the benefits of North Sea Oil production off the coast of Aberdeen in the early 1970s. In the summary of one contemporary newspaper reporter, '[t]he message comes over with unforgettable power—anti-capital, anti-Church, anti-judiciary, anti-London, anti-hunting, anti-shooting, anti-landlord.'[1] For the BBC in 1974–5, indeed perhaps at any time, the *TV Cheviot* is strong stuff, appearing to breach both normative principles of composition and the Corporation's much-cherished reputation for 'balance' in its role as a Public Service Broadcaster.

For many years, I have been aware that, at the time of adaptation, there were tensions between the key makers, John McGrath and John Mackenzie (respectively writer/adapter and director/producer) and the institutional forces of the BBC. Revisiting the *TV Cheviot* following the untimely death of McGrath with the aim of teasing out the political issues, it was initially difficult to discover what had happened. The BBC Written Archives has a script and some related information but not a full production file and it has

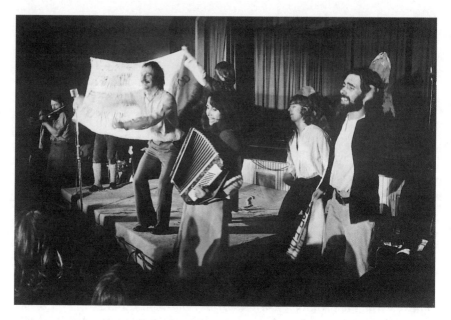

7. The Company in the Opening Song of *The Cheviot, The Stag and The Black, Black Oil* at Dornie Village Hall. 1973

been necessary to track down a range of sources, some residing in memory traces.[2] More than a quarter of a century has passed since the making of the *TV Cheviot* so it would not be surprising if memories had faded. In a conversation with Cooke,[3] however, McGrath's recollections are precise and the documentation now discovered appears to bear out his account. Before telling the story of how significant parts of the *TV Cheviot* narrowly avoided consignment to the cutting-room floor, however, it is helpful to establish how the adaptation for television came about in perhaps surprising circumstances and to delineate its key features.

The TV Cheviot, BBC1, 1974

It might seem puzzling that, having turned his back on national television[4] because of its limitations in terms of socio-political intervention, McGrath would entertain the idea of a *TV Cheviot*. After a decade of struggle to find the right conditions to build a political theatre, he had finally fulfilled his political aims with 7:84 Scotland and *The Cheviot* in a localized and specifically-targeted touring theatre praxis. It thus seems odd on first reflection for McGrath to have returned to TV drama.

The answer to this puzzle lies perhaps in two parts. McGrath ultimately spied an opportunity in a *TV Cheviot* for the kind of non-naturalist television drama to which he had long aspired, but in the first instance the idea of an adaptation for *Play for Today* was 'entirely accidental'.[5] Given the critical acclaim of the whole *Cheviot* project, it is easy to naturalize the shift from theatre to television in terms of an inevitable transfer of 'quality product' to a broader audience. In fact, the decision was taken rather quickly and, as frequently proves to be the case when 'seminal' television productions are researched, the process of production involved serendipity. Moreover, there was no unanimity on the idea of 'quality product' as we shall see.

Television director John Mackenzie saw *The Cheviot* on stage and, like many others, was enthralled by the piece. He was impressed by the talent of the theatre company and struck particularly by the impact the piece had on a local audience just north of Glasgow. Experiencing live 'how moved they were',[6] he wanted to try to convey through television to a broader public the extraordinary impact of the theatre event. Meeting McGrath subsequently, Mackenzie recalls a brief discussion of this idea but it was only when another *Play for Today* project fell through shortly afterwards that an opportunity arose.[7] Executive Producer Graeme Macdonald agreed to re-allocate the resources from the postponed project and Mackenzie, suddenly finding himself effectively producer and director of what became the *TV Cheviot*, revisited 7:84. Time was extremely tight and, fitting his vision to the circumstance, McGrath proposed:

> . . . to use the stage play as an alienating device. I didn't want to make television naturalistic soup out of what was a very determinedly anti-naturalistic piece. And I said it would have to be done in front of an audience because it was about the interaction between the stage and the audience. And that would give us the liberty then to cut away and shoot scenes on film which would help it along.[8]

McGrath, working summarily with *Play for Today* story editor Ann Scott, quickly developed a screenplay which, after some deliberation within the BBC, went into production. Though there were occasional tensions between the two Johns over direction, McGrath acknowledges that Mackenzie was 'one of the few directors who've ever asked me into the cutting room because he knew what I was trying to do was not normal'.[9]

As the project developed, then, it is clear why, notwithstanding the normative constraints of the television medium, McGrath took the opportunity for a *TV Cheviot*. Devices of documentary realism, dramatized film inserts and, in particular, shots of audience members were used in an attempt to catch and convey the spirit of *The Cheviot* project but to do something more televisually. The juxtaposition between different forms was: '. . . consciously Brechtian . . . Brechtianised television. It wasn't a

Brechtian stage play, but it was a Brechtian way of approaching television.'[10] The 1974 television adaptation follows the published *Cheviot*
playscript quite closely, some small changes in the narrative order
clarifying the line of the story. Although avoiding any meta-commentary,
the presentation approximates to documentary coverage of a specific
performance of *The Cheviot* at Dornie village hall. Whilst the overall
impact rests on the juxtaposition of a range of modes quite rare in a
television drama, sufficient familiar features of treatment remain to guide
viewers in to the piece. The titles, initially under a pilot's voice-over,
establish location with a distant image of Scotland as if on the display
screen of a spacecraft, and then cut to a helicopter circling a castle later to
be identified as the Dunrobin home of the Sutherlands. The arresting,
though conventional, establishing grammar of Long-Shot to Mid-Shot to
Close-Up takes viewers through a visual cross-fade under sea sounds to a
coastal landscape which picks up in the distance 7:84's white transit van
approaching the venue. A sound cross-fade leads to a Close-Up of Allan
Ross, the company's fiddler, playing the 'live' audience into Dornie,
identified by the sign on the exterior wall of the village hall.

Before the television audience 'enters' the hall it is confronted by a
shock of images. A montage challengingly links a JCB digger shot in
Extreme Close-Up, a Scottish soldier and colourful explosion at sea.
More specifically identifiable, an oil-rig, Cheviot sheep and a hunted stag
visually prefigure the battles of *The Cheviot*: land clearance, cultural
tourism and oil prospecting. The shooting of the stag is linked in sound
montage to the shot of the gun, which ignites the oil flare of the rig's
exhaust pipe. This feature parallels an action in the playscript by Billy as
'Texas Jim' who fires a pistol as an oil rig appears on the mountains of *The
Cheviot*'s touring theatre pop-up book set. This set is visible in the
television version but is reduced by the dominant televisual conventions of
Two-Shots, Mid-Shots and Close-Ups of performers to a vague backdrop.

Once the television audience is invited inside Dornie village hall, the
performance is presented as if taking place as a theatre piece in front of
the live audience. The show itself was shot by Brian Tufano under
Mackenzie's direction on film, in sequence, over three weeks. To capture
audience response, people from audiences who had already seen the show
were invited to come again to Dornie village hall and were skilfully filmed
watching a performance without faking and without unwarranted intrusion
of the camera. In an effort to recreate something of the sense of shared
space and identity created by the form, content and performance style of
The Cheviot in its ceilidh setting, individual audience members are picked
out by the camera in a variety of responses. Elderly women sing along to
the Gaelic songs. Rural workingmen, cigarette in mouth, are shown in rapt
concentration. The audience claps along with the livelier songs and

laughter is both audible and visible. Technically the strategic inter-cutting between Close-Ups of the performers and members of the audience is a simple and apparently seamless editing device. In sum the audience is shown being entertained, moved and alerted whilst the television viewer is invited by the inter-cutting device to locate her or himself in a position of identity with the collective.

Three additional televisual strategies subsequently combined with the already mixed-mode of the theatre piece: the live audience reaction shots cut into those documenting the performance, noted above; inserts of dramatized exterior action; and documentary-style Vox Pops.

Turning to the second key feature of the *TV Cheviot*, a range of television inserts shot on film on location punctuates the recording of the Dornie hall event. The first category of these consists of exterior reconstructions of historical events which are merely narrated in the theatre version. For example, there is a dramatized reconstruction of redcoat soldiers depicted chasing a Scottish youth in order to remove his plaid. Similarly, the well-dressed gentleman figures of Sellars and Loch are shown in conversation riding fine horses across the land. In another example, a physical attack by the police on women resisting eviction in the Clearances is dramatized along with their victory of ducking the local constabulary in the river. For the most part the dialogue in these film inserts follows that in the playscript though, on occasion, a voice-over (typically Bill Paterson or Alex Norton) narrates.

In some instances, the visual inserts do more than merely make visual for television the events handled verbally in *The Cheviot*. Replacing Patrick Sellars' monologue and mock poems to heroic victory, an actor playing Sellars addresses the camera claiming that 'nobody suffered in the Clearances' whilst the camera pans across derelict crofts to pick up the splendour of Dunrobin castle. This montage invites the television audience to draw conclusions perhaps in a manner parallel to, but different from, the engagement constructed between performers and audience members in Dornie village hall.

The third feature of the television version, in one sense related to the play script but in another sense quite distinct, is the use of Vox Pops televisual documentary techniques. These do not appear until the third section of the *TV Cheviot*, dealing with oil in the 1974 present. Whilst the theatre version of *The Cheviot* draws on documentary material, it is reported by the actors. In the *TV Cheviot*, extensive use is made of collages of Vox Pops allowing local people from Aberdeen to relate their ex-periences directly to the television audience with the ring of authenticity.

The first sequence of some five minutes duration relates the process of people being displaced from their hometown by the steep rise in house prices. Newly-weds such as Agnes and Laurie McGeogh, in seeking to establish a family home, find it 'virtually impossible to buy a house at all'. Sounding a distinct echo of the Clearances, others are forced 'to emigrate' (Iain and Pat Read) by the invasion of highly paid oilmen mostly from America. These latter are represented in the Vox Pops collage by the nattily-dressed Casing Crew Supervisor, Al Butler, who initially praises the locals as 'the only honest people left in the world'. Subsequently, when the disillusioned Scots begin to ask questions about the benefits to them of off-shore oil-production, Butler's tone changes and, in veiled threat, he sneers, 'Do the UK people want to learn the job? Or do they want us to fly people in to do the job for them?'

Following a collage of shots featuring the logos on the rigs and equipment of Shell, BP, Esso and more multinationals, the second Vox Pops sequences, again almost five minutes in duration, presents local riggers who have first-hand experience of the working conditions. This material replaces '*Alex as Aberdonian Rigger*' in the play script reporting similar content. Although the riggers are relatively well paid when on the rig, they are not paid for their shore leave, so that the remuneration overall is relatively poor. Working conditions are such, as one rigger tells from his personal experience, that a broken arm is bound up with a couple of American magazines and the man issued with a couple of painkillers for the three-day wait until the next airlift to shore. In sum, 'we get all the scab jobs' and 'they treat us like animals'.

The strategies of the televisual adaptation of *The Cheviot* may be unremarkable in themselves. Visual story-telling in place of verbal is a mainstay of the medium, historical reconstruction is the pride of period drama and Vox Pops are a standard of news-gathering and documentaries. The use of an established televisual documentary technique of actual people relating directly to camera their personal experience in a drama, however, proved to be contentious since it served to authenticate the narratives and political implications of *The Cheviot*. The use of documentary strategies with implicit truth claims in combination with the fictional associations of even historical drama caused major problems at the BBC as we shall see, and for a while threatened the whole *TV Cheviot* project.

Milne, the Memo and the Grey, Grey Areas

Prior to its transmission, the *TV Cheviot* was viewed by Alasdair Milne, then Controller BBC1. Such scrutiny was not in itself unusual, since under the BBC's in-house system of referral upwards, producers typically ran issues by executive producers who in turn referred material up to directorate level, as appropriate. Thus it would only be surprising if material like that of the *TV Cheviot* had not been referred by the Executive Producer of the *Play for Today* series, Graeme Macdonald. Alasdair Milne viewed the film on the night of 25 February 1974 and the next day pronounced himself 'not happy about it on a number of counts'. Milne's memorandum to 'H.P.D. Tel' (Head of Plays, Drama—at that time, Christopher Morahan) and 'H.D.G. Tel' (Head of Drama Group—at that time, Shaun Sutton) makes objections about both the content and form of the piece. Though he claims he 'accepted from the start that this play was a polemic', he feels 'we can't use television for the straight forward projection of this kind of political tract'.[11]

Milne is precise about the passages which he wishes to be cut and, on the shooting script now held in the National Library of Scotland, these exact passages are square bracketed by hand in green pen. They are linked by a concern on McGrath's part to broaden the context of the debate about the Highlands and locate what had happened to the people there in a pattern of international events, the causes of which McGrath attributes in Marxist terms to the 'savage progress of capitalism'.[12]

The passages marked for excision in the television script are as follows:

1) OLD MAN: The technological innovation was there: the Cheviot, a breed of sheep that survive the Highland winter and produce fine wool. The money was there. Unfortunately the people were there too. But the law of capitalism had to be obeyed. (p. 14)

2) STURDY HIGHLANDER: In Australia the aborigines were hunted like animals; in Tasmania not one aborigine was left alive; all over Africa, black men were massacred and brought to heel. In America the plains were emptied of men and buffalo, and the seeds of the next century's imperialist power were firmly planted. (p. 29)

3) MC1 (Master of Ceremonies) In the eighteenth century speaking the Gaelic language was forbidden by law.[13]
(*Chords*)

MC2 In the nineteenth century children caught speaking Gaelic in the playground were flogged.
(*Chords*)

MC1 In the twentieth century the children were taught to deride their own language
(*Chords*)
Because English is the language of the ruling class
Because English is the language of the people who own the highlands and control the highlands and invest in the highlands

MC2 Because English is the language of the Development Board, the Hydro Board, the Tourist Board, the Forestry Commission, the County Council and, I suppose, the Chicago Bridge Construction Company.
(*Chords*)

MC3   The people who spoke Gaelic no longer owned their land.
MC1   The people had to learn the language of their new masters.
        (p. 52)

4) MC1   By economic power. Until economic power is in the hands of the
        people, then their culture, Gaelic or English, will be destroyed.
        The educational system, the newspapers, the radio and television
        and the decision-makers, local and national, whether they know
        it or not, are the servants of the men who own and control the
        land. (p. 55)

McGrath's internationalist political position is evident in these passages
and confirmed by his concern to avoid any strong association of *The
Cheviot* with nationalism and the Scottish National Party. This concern
is made clear in his introduction to the published playscript when he
speaks of the performance given, on invitation, at the SNP's annual
conference. When invited by the SNP Chairman to perform *The Cheviot*,
the 7:84 company pointed out that they 'were not nationalists and would
attack bourgeois nationalism'[14] but the invitation stood and was accepted.
McGrath then relished:

> Liz squaring up to all 500 of them [the delegates] and delivering
> 'Nationalism is not enough. The enemy of the Scottish people is Scottish
> capital as much as the foreign exploiter' with shattering power.[15]

Beyond his international socialist commitment, McGrath is open also
about the politically charged analysis incorporated in *The Cheviot*. Indeed,
he points out that, '[d]irect Marxist analysis of the Clearances (cf *Das
Kapital*) . . . were not only grasped but waited for, expected'[16] by
Highland audiences.

In asking for the passages above to be cut, Milne appears to have been
unnerved by the overt Marxist and Internationalist dimensions retained in
TV Cheviot. But he apparently found it difficult to refute the applicability
of McGrath's economic and political analysis, effectively a reworking of
the famous 'All that's solid melts into air' passage of the Communist
Manifesto which brings out the destructive, inhuman ravages of the
capitalist system.

The account of Scotland's history offered in *The Cheviot* resonates with
the *Manifesto of the Communist Party*'s analysis of the 'constant revolu-
tionising of production, uninterrupted disturbance of all social conditions'
under which 'all fixed fast-frozen relations, with their train of ancient and
venerable prejudices and opinions . . . are all swept away'.[17] Particularly in
the television adaptation, McGrath looked to invite audience members to
make connections beyond the specifics of the Highlands' experience to the

displacement of a range of indigenous peoples worldwide and the underlying causes of that displacement. Hence the passages above which stress the undermining of indigenous culture (the Gaelic), economic displacement (from Cheviot sheep and oil in Scotland to European settlement of rich agricultural land in Australia and America) needed to be connected, for McGrath, with a social and economic structure that energized change to the benefit of the 'ruling class' and at the expense of the indigenous people.

It was ultimately the discursive position of *TV Cheviot*, the apparently true account of Scottish history told from an oppositional political standpoint, that disturbed Milne. He appears to have been relatively untroubled by the breach of normative TV drama conventions for which the *TV Cheviot* is celebrated in the history of television drama. His concern with form does not challenge the non-naturalistic presentation of the theatre play itself or McGrath's consciously Brechtian televisual treatment, but he objects to the adaptation diving 'feet foremost into the confused area between fact and fiction'. Beyond the passages marked for excision above, Milne is 'even more concerned' about the documentary additions to the original playscript. His feeling on this point is strong:

> Every one of the interviews connected with North Sea Oil is overtly chosen to show how grubby, mean, unfair and generally depressing to the standards of life of good and decent people the whole North Sea Oil project is. We have manipulated in the name of drama a series of factual statements to suit a chosen theme.[18]

Milne proposed that the second half of the piece needed 'radical reappraisal'. On learning that one of his key contributions to the *TV Cheviot*, namely the substantial documentary inserts, was in question, John Mackenzie was not best pleased. In McGrath's account, Mackenzie stormed into Milne's office in a fury, but his invective left the Controller unmoved.

At the time of this confrontation, John McGrath was away and, on his return, he took a more measured approach. As an Oxford graduate and former BBC employee, McGrath was schooled in establishment institutions and was well able to take on the BBC on its own ground and according to its rules. Having read Milne's memorandum, McGrath felt he could answer all the specific points of objection raised since he had research evidence to support all his claims. For example, the allusion to aboriginals being forcibly driven from Tasmania could be supported by historical documentation and its relevance to *The Cheviot* theme could be defended in terms of its direct parallel of displacement of indigenous peoples. A meeting was set up between McGrath and Milne who invited the Controller of BBC2, Aubrey Singer, to sit in. McGrath went quietly and rather academically through each of Milne's specific objections presenting his research evidence point by point. On reflection, McGrath felt he slowly wore Milne down until he finally said something like 'Look this piece sounds as if you don't want the oil to be dug out of the sea'. Showing himself to be reasonable—and one might say balanced—by agreeing to change one questionable line, McGrath had effectively won the debate. For the record, the passages proposed by Milne for excision, and cited above, remain in the transmitted *TV Cheviot*.

Turning to Singer, his BBC2 colleague, however, Milne sought a second opinion. Giving insight into the mindset of the BBC at that time, Singer said something like: 'Well, you know Alasdair, the more extreme the point of view expressed in this play, the less likely the audience will think it's the BBC's point of view. So I think we're quite safe to put it out.'[19] That the five specific passages cited by Milne for excision remain intact in the transmitted *TV Cheviot* might be taken as a testament to McGrath's urbane rationality and persuasive charm. Alternatively, it might mark the self-assurance of the BBC as an institution of the establishment in relation to the perceived position of *TV Cheviot* as extremist polemic. The story does not end there.

Having effectively lost the battle over the form and content of the *TV Cheviot* since there appeared ultimately to be no real substance in the original objections, there was little, short of crude censorship, that the BBC could do about the drama itself. So, in accordance with Singer's position, it appears to have set about distancing itself and constructing the *TV Cheviot* as an institutional 'other'. The showing of the *TV Cheviot* on 6 June 1974 was preceded by a fifteen-minute documentary about the 7:84 company, a film insert into an episode of *Midweek* entitled 'oil profits' (22.45 5 June 1974, BBC1). Following the showing of *TV Cheviot*, furthermore, a post-transmission discussion with Paul Barnes and Chris Dunkley was held as part of *In Vision* (23.30, 6 June 1974, BBC2).

The transcript of *Midweek*, which unfortunately does not document the film insert on 7:84, is interesting in setting the context in which the political stance of *TV Cheviot* was evidently unacceptable to the establishment. Ludovic Kennedy's introduction speaks of: 'Britain becoming an oil-producing nation. . . . What's been discovered is being regarded as our crock of gold, the means to make Britain self-sufficient and [sic] energy and transform the balance of payments.'[20] With the impact of the oil crisis of 1973 being felt, the political significance to Britain of a substantial off-shore oil supply was immense. There were differing estimates about the scale of the oilfield but Professor Peter Odell, a member of one of the first study groups, forecast that there was sufficient oil to keep Britain bright and warm for sixty years. It is little surprise, therefore, that Milne's reading of the *TV Cheviot* as, 'this piece sounds as if you don't want the oil to be dug out of the sea' caused him and the BBC great concern.

The edition of *Midweek* details the political manoeuvring and bungling involved in the issue of licences between 1964 and 1973 by both Conservative and Labour governments. The terms were broadly so generous to the oil companies that, in the summary of Vincent Hanna, 'Lord Balogh estimates that the oil companies will make between sixty and eighty thousand million pounds in pre-tax profits in the North Sea over the next twenty years. And the cost to them will have been about a tenth of that.'[21] The ensuing *Midweek* debate identifies the need to maximize income for Britain. In Hanna's up-beat concluding summary:

> Well, whatever methods we use—stiffer taxes, a state interest in oil or a National Hydrocarbons Corporation, the effect has to be the same: to get a fair share of North Sea profits for the British taxpayer . . . So that's the dream and a dream likely to come true . . . Billions of barrels of oil pouring into Britain by 1980 bringing unlimited energy and a surplus on our balance of payments. And 80% of the profits ending up in your pocket. Which leaves plenty over for the oil companies.[22]

The link into the documentary on 7:84 acknowledges, however, that, 'There's just one more snag . . . A lot of people don't think it's Britain's oil at all'.[23] The Scottish National Party had given notice that it would repudiate any agreement made by the United Kingdom government about oil found off the coast of Scotland. The tenor of the segue is that it is difficult enough to negotiate a good deal for Britain with the oil companies and, now we're in sight of achieving untold wealth and prosperity for British taxpayers, an oppositional group is threatening to destabilise the situation. Enter 7:84.

As noted, the content of the documentary is not included in the transcript of *Midweek* and there is no video record in the National Film and Television Archive. Some sense of its discursive position lies in McGrath's memory. McGrath's perception is that the BBC's need to clarify for viewers the political stance of the company underlay the despatch of a crew to film 7:84 in the Outer Hebrides. McGrath reports that:

> . . . they tried all kinds of dodges to get us to look like Maoist 'Shining Lights' as in Peru, or something like that, and they thought we were waving claymores (laughs), and we didn't have any of it. Then they tried a really dirty trick which is that we had a song which contained a verse which came close to libelling a landowner and, without telling me, they invited the landowner and his lawyer to the show that night.[24]

Having been tipped off by the sound recordist leaning over the rail on the boat from Mallaig to Skye, McGrath persuaded the company to drop the song that night to avoid the hassle of any possible lawsuit. 'And of course they [the BBC] were furious and they interviewed me and said on camera "Are you afraid of the landowners?" and I said "No" and they said "Well, why did you cut that song?" I said, "We'll give you a BBC reply: because it wasn't working artistically."'[25]

McGrath is clear that the BBC was aiming in the making of the *Midweek* documentary insert to discredit the 7:84 company. In the absence of a transcript or video, it is difficult to judge the BBC's precise discursive position in the final piece but the fact that the BBC called upon the Head of the Scottish Landowners' Federation, amongst other Scottish establishment worthies, to confront McGrath in the *In Vision* post-transmission discussion lends some credibility to McGrath's view that the aim was at least to construct 7:84 as extremists who sailed close to the wind as far as the law was concerned. If this is the case, it would square with the importance to Britain, stressed in *Midweek*, of getting 'a fair share of North Sea profits for the British taxpayer'. Overall on 5–6 June 1974, the BBC appears to be constructing a dominant liberal view that the bungling of politicians thus far—which *Midweek* fully acknowledges—should be forgotten in order that a new regulatory framework might strike a better deal for the British taxpayer. There was room for the oil companies themselves to make a handsome profit in the region of 20 per cent of production takings, so everybody should be happy. In constructing such a consensual position, the last thing the BBC wanted was a wild, left-wing drama challenging many of the assumptions on which that liberal consensus rested.

That the BBC wished to distance itself from 7:84 and *TV Cheviot*, pointing up and marginalizing its 'extreme' position along the lines sketched by Aubrey Singer, is evident also in the *Radio Times* feature for the week commencing 30 May 1974. In an otherwise bland and descriptive piece which at least recognizes the popularity of the touring *Cheviot* with Highland people, Peter Gillman's article is nevertheless headed in bold, 'Enter stage Left: the North wind of change'. It announces that: '[t]his Thursday's *Play for Today* is a personal view of Scotland from a group of Scottish strolling players . . . A RED FLAG mysteriously inscribed '7:84,' flaps wildly in the north wind that scours the landscape.'[26]

National press coverage of the *TV Cheviot* sustains the refrain of 'loony lefties'. Sean Day-Lewis observes that, 'John McGrath's bitter *The Cheviot, the Stag and the Black, Black Oil* quickly sighted its enemy, the ruling class, and maintained a relentless barrage in that direction for ninety minutes'.[27] Even Nancy Banks-Smith saw the play as 'partisan propaganda' though she does recognize its message for the Scots to be 'as crucial as Christianity to a morality play'.[28]

With the broader audience, the *TV Cheviot* was a great success. The BBC's own research shows the broadcast gained 8.3 per cent of the UK audience when average audiences at the time were 6.8 per cent (BBC1) and 12.1 per cent (ITV). Besides above average viewing figures, *TV Cheviot* received an overall Reaction Index of 70 when the *Play for Today* average index was 54:

> The story of Scotland's exploitation past and present came over with considerable force, according to the large majority of the sample, in this unusual blend of drama, music and film. Whether or not they wholly agree with the 7:84 company's version of Scottish history (and to some, certainly, it seemed 'pure propaganda' and 'very very biased') they found it entertaining, admired it as satire and thought it brilliantly put over.[29]

Seventy-three per cent of the sample watched the whole play and in-dividual commentators found it, 'one of the most interesting and enthralling programmes of the year'; 'I thought I would not like it, but would love to see it again'; 'I am surprised that the Government allowed the BBC to televise this truly superb creation'.[30]

Amongst the many letters sent to McGrath, including a good number from expatriate Scots, the response is also positive. Three are worth citing not as representative but for their particular relevance to this article.[31] Mary Spowart of Grangemouth, Stirlingshire wrote on 7 June 1974: 'Our family sat enthralled from start to finish. It was TV at its best. For once we felt we were taking part in the production.' Mrs Catherine Power of London SE 27 remarked in a letter to John McGrath, dated 6 June 1974, that 'No one could fail to observe the natural and enthusiastic audience participation, in such contrast to the self-conscious audience participation which has been tried in a few of the London theatres.' Rose Jones writing from London SW 10, on 8 June proposed that *TV Cheviot* was

> incredibly well done—quick, funny, yet with a poignant sting. A very good village entertainment because of the direct involvement—not with fancy words—but live and with meaning fully displayed—and therefore valuable for everyone. . . . [T]he best was that feeling of continuation . . . the references to all the other countries were (*sic*) exactly the same thing has happened under various guises, under capitalism.

To McGrath, who had left television partly because of the constraints of its naturalist habits, these letters must have come as music to the ear, vindicating his conscious attempt in *TV Cheviot* to make Brechtian tele-vision drama. The last letter not only picks up on the international dimension of a play which many regard as deeply Scottish, but unknowingly vindicates the inclusion of precisely those passages Milne wanted cut.

Finally on post-transmission correspondence, a note from Alasdair Milne dated 8 June responds to McGrath who no doubt could not resist pointing out the success of *TV Cheviot* 'Many thanks for your note. I must say I was surprised, and not a little pleased, at the reaction to *THE CHEVIOT*. I remain of the opinion that the final shape was not entirely satisfactory but I am very glad we did it.'[32]

In TV Drama Studies, *TV Cheviot* is most frequently cited as a rare example of non-naturalist television practice, illustrating the kind of exciting, challenging television drama the audience might have had, if only the cosy naturalist habit might be broken. Such a view resonates with the 1970s debate about the 'classic realist text' and the proposition, particularly in the domain of film theory at the time, that experiment with form was the only way to a politically challenging or 'progressive' drama.[33] Interestingly, Milne seems to have been undisturbed by those compositional features of *TV Cheviot* for which it is renowned and more concerned with an aspect which troubles television little today, the blurring of a distinction between fact and fiction. Following the success of the *TV Cheviot*, further formal experiments might have been expected. A letter to McGrath dated 29 July 1975, from BBC producer Brian Rose, expresses, on behalf of the controller of BBC2, an intention to make a series of recordings of small theatre companies on location 'to overcome television's coldness as a medium'. But, as Alan Bennett might put it, 'they didn't, did they!'.

For students of television, the most interesting aspect of the story of the adaptation of *The Cheviot* into the *TV Cheviot* is, perhaps, that Milne's objection to the piece was its blurring of fact and fiction, his sense that, '[w]e have manipulated in the name of drama a series of factual statements to suit a chosen theme.'[34] What this stance effaces is that all television programmes hold a discursive position, though, in the case of establishment institutions, that perspective is unacknowledged and often unrecognized. As indicated above in the discussion of 'oil profits' in *Midweek*, a balanced coverage seeking different views and exposing some of the ineptitude by which several governments appeared to have given away the bulk of North Sea oil profits to the American oil companies, ultimately arrives at a consensual position which appears fair and balanced but, from a Scottish point of view at least, is strongly partial (in both senses of the word: 'in part' and 'adopting a specific position').

The BBC, though not part of the official establishment—indeed proud historically to have operated at arm's length from governments —traditionally takes the position of informed, liberal consensus. The corporation is noted worldwide for the integrity of its news reporting and its efforts to establish the truth of the matter by means of seeking the balance between opposing points of view. Whilst this is without doubt a laudable aim, it has from time to time led BBC executives to slip into the assumption that the BBC position is central and neutral whilst that of others who disagree is biased and marginal. Such appears to be the case with the *TV Cheviot*.

The stance of McGrath and the 7:84 company on the rights to North Sea Oil and historical matters of ownership and displacement of land in Scotland and elsewhere in the world was ultimately unacceptable to Milne not because it was factually wrong, as McGrath's victory in the script discussion demonstrates, but because it inconveniently undermined the position which the government of the day was trying to construct. Influence may be felt even at arm's length. What Milne saw as the blurring of a line between fact and fiction was rather the muddying of North Sea waters, already murky through deals with the, mainly American, oil interests. McGrath's and 7:84's clarity of vision was simply at odds with the cleansing process otherwise proposed by governments and financiers. In terms of the distribution of oil profits, history shows that, with regard to the benefit to ordinary indigenous Scots, McGrath and 7:84 had it just about right.

CHAPTER TEN

A Practical Realism
McGrath, Brecht, Lukács and
Blood Red Roses

Stephen Lacey

In the course of a long and varied working life, John McGrath became
identified with a resolutely anti-naturalist theatre tradition that has its
roots in the popular (conceived in political as well as aesthetic terms).
'Anti-naturalism', though it is an inelegant phrase, has also characterized
much of his work for television (and this includes his writing about
television drama), again for ideological/political as well as formal reasons.
However, this does not mean that his work on screen resembles his work
on stage at the level of dramatic method; indeed, much of it (from the
early *Z-Cars* to the principal text under discussion here, *Blood Red Roses*)
is much more recognizably illusionist (though not naturalistic, in the sense
McGrath would use the term) than his work for the theatre. I want to
argue in this chapter that there is no contradiction here, since one of the
unifying factors behind his work has been the need to discover and explore
what one might call (though not without some anxiety, given the problems
attached to the term) a practical realism, appropriate to the medium and
to the times. I want to explore what this means in relation, primarily, to
McGrath's television adaptation of his stage play, *Blood Red Roses*,
which was shown in three parts in November 1985 on Channel 4 with
simultaneous release in re-edited form in the cinema. It is the longer
television version, with its distinctive narrative structure that follows the
conventions of the drama mini-series, that I am mostly concerned with
here. However, to pursue questions about realism requires a certain
definition of the terms I have been using so freely and a consideration of
the traditions in which McGrath's work can be located.

McGrath was frequently seen as a 'Brechtian' practitioner in the rather
loose sense that the term is often used of post-war political theatre in the

UK. However, if the cap fitted, it did so rather uneasily. McGrath himself was always slightly dismissive about his debt to Brecht, preferring to locate his main influences elsewhere, especially with Joan Littlewood. The parallels between McGrath and Brecht are nonetheless obvious: both explored the potential of theatre as an urgent ideological intervention into wider political and historical debates; both were committed to an idea of popular theatre, relocating the theatrical event as a popular celebration (Brecht's championing of the boxing match, McGrath's love of the ceilidh); and both explored a pluralistic approach to theatrical form, borrowing from, and including in the single event, a variety of techniques and strategies. However, despite the similarity in their cultural politics, McGrath's work (in whatever medium) does not always look or feel like Brecht's, and this is partly because McGrath was much more alive to the possibilities of emotional engagement, openly acknowledged and exploited for political purposes. In particular, McGrath was open to the use of *identification*, especially in his plays of the 1980s (*Swings and Roundabouts* and *Blood Red Roses* are clear examples) and in some of his work for television, within an approach that was still resolutely anti-naturalistic and committed to an understanding of the individual in relation to his/her political and cultural context.

It is in Brecht's attitude to realism that we find the closest connection between them. Brecht wrote about realism in a number of contexts, but his clearest statement comes in the form of an essay submitted to, though not published in, a German-language review, *Das Wort*, written during his period of European exile in the late 1930s. The essay is a direct challenge to the theoretical positions of Georg Lukács, the Hungarian Marxist critic and activist. For Lukács, the great realist novels provided the only true model for a historically aware realism that could fully engage with and represent the complexities of a given society. Brecht took issue with the prescriptive nature of Lukács's arguments, pointing out that not all cultural forms (and especially not the theatre) could be malformed to fit the requirements of the realist novel, and it is difficult to refute his analysis at this level. His conclusion was that realism could only be adequately understood if it was defined in political, and not 'formalist', terms. Realism was primarily an ideological strategy, concerned with 'laying bare society's causal networks/showing up the dominant viewpoint as the viewpoint of the dominators:'[1] 'For Time flows on, and if it did not it would be a poor look-out for those who have no golden tables to sit at. Methods wear out, stimuli fail. New problems loom up and demand new techniques. Reality alters; to represent it the means of representation must alter too.'[2] For Brecht, Realism was inextricably connected to the popular, which he also defines in political, rather than formal, terms. 'The words *Popularity* and *Realism* therefore are natural companions . . . "Popular" means intelligible to the broad masses, taking over their own forms of expression and enriching them/adopting and consolidating their standpoint . . .'.[3]

It seems to me that this attitude towards the ideological significance of cultural practice informed all of McGrath's work, even though he was more interested than Brecht in the actual forms of popular culture. But it produces certain ironies, for in order to construct a realism for television—and exploit the narrative possibilities of the drama series for a mass audience—McGrath adopted, in the case of *Blood Red Roses*, an approach to narrative that can be best analysed using some of the terminology of Brecht's opponent, Georg Lukács.

There is not the scope here to do justice to the range of Lukács' theory (any more than Brecht's) but it is important to note that his analysis of the nineteenth-century novel, though it faltered in the presence of the experimental political drama of the early twentieth century, was subtle and complex. Lukács theorized the relationship between the personal and the social and between the 'intensive totality' of fictional narrative and the 'extensive totality' of the social world in the novel, in ways that have relevance to the contemporary drama series. It is certainly possible to argue that, whilst the single television drama may be rooted in the aesthetics of the stage play, the drama series, as it has developed since the 1970s, can be aligned with the novel for certain purposes. This is especially true of the potential of the series format to create narratives that connect personal stories to their historical contexts, much as the realist novel does. To explore these, and other, issues, we must turn to the text(s).

Blood Red Roses was first staged in 1980 by 7:84 Scotland, and toured nationally throughout Scotland. It is the story of Bessie McGuigan (née Gordon) and her family and takes the form of a 'saga'; that is, it is a contemporary tale told within the structure of a traditional story, beginning with the return of a soldier (Bessie's father, Sandy) from the Korean War. The narrative follows Sandy and Bessie from the Highlands to East Kilbride and parallels Bessie's growth from adolescence to adulthood (which is also her development from instinctive rebel to ideologically aware political activist) with the history of post-war Scotland. This history includes women's growing resistance to male hegemony and the struggles of the Scottish working class to resist the increasing rapaciousness of global capitalism. Bessie marries Alex McGuigan, a communist shop steward, has two children and becomes a shop steward herself, successfully organizing international resistance to the activities of her employer (a local firm that becomes a small part of a multinational company). Bessie's triumph is short-lived and the factory is closed down as the chill winds of recession begin to bite. Bessie is unable to get a job and Alex leaves her for another, more conventional, woman. The play ends with a historical pessimism but personal optimism; the working class has just voted in a Tory Government committed to the reversing of the hard-won victories of the post-war years, yet Bessie is pregnant with her third child (by a man, no longer on the scene, who is much younger than she). In his introduction to the published text, McGrath noted ruefully that the militancy celebrated in the play was 'distinctly out of fashion' in an era dominated by the growing Thatcherite hegemony, but that 'it seemed important . . . to take a longer look at one of these militants, and at the whole question of what "fighting" means in the age of the multiple warhead'.[4]

In adapting the play for television in the mid-1980s, McGrath was able to take advantage of the political and institutional space opened up by the arrival of Channel 4 in 1982. Having no production arm of its own, the Channel actively promoted independent producers and McGrath formed Freeway Films in 1982 partly at the suggestion of the first Head of Channel 4, Jeremy Isaacs. McGrath was able to be both writer and director of the adaptation and the outcome was a three-part mini-series, each episode of one hour's duration, re-edited into a 150-minute version for the cinema. Channel 4 provided most of the financial backing for the project, with top-up funds coming from Lorimar, the same company that produced *Dallas*. The irony of Lorimar's involvement in both screen versions was not lost on McGrath (although he insisted that, having

8a. Bessie McGuigan (Elizabeth MacLennan) and fellow workers on the picket line. *Blood Red Roses*: Freeway Films for Channel Four. 1983

8b. Celebrating the defeat of a multinational in East Kilbride. Gregor Fischer, Elizabeth MacLennan, Myra MacFadyean. *Blood Red Roses*: Freeway Films for Channel Four. 1983

approved the script, Lorimar did not interfere), since he intended *Blood Red Roses* to be an ideological antidote to the politics and narrative structure of the mini-series: 'I wanted to challenge the content and values of the mini-series format which is usually a portrayal of somebody's rise to power and fame; a confirmation of the ideology of the right'.[5]

In narrative terms, the series follows the main events of the stage play, but continues beyond them. In revisiting the story five years further on, McGrath was able to acknowledge the politics of a changing historical situation, in which Thatcherism was even more entrenched. We witness the birth of Bessie's third daughter, the heavy defeat of the Labour Party in the 1983 General Election and Sandy's illness and eventual death from a stroke. One significant innovation is that the central narrative is placed within a flashback structure, with the main events introduced by Bessie in voice-over from Sandy's funeral. Overall, the television series does what most televised versions of plays do, which is to 'open up' the narrative, showing what is talked about or represented metonymically on stage. However, many of the central events—for example, the departure of Bessie's mother, the move to East Kilbride, the first meeting of Bessie and Alex, the birth of the first two children—are common to both versions; indeed, much of the dialogue from the stage version is repeated in the screen one. But beyond this, the dramatic method is significantly different.

Theatrically, the play consists of short scenes, punctuated by traditional folk songs, and introduced by an 'announcer', who places each episode in its immediate political and historical moment. It also makes considerable use of monologues, particularly by Bessie and her father. It is in the monologues that the metaphorical resonance of the story is most explicit, especially in those delivered by Sandy, whose growing awareness of the contradictions of his life as a soldier allows him to draw parallels between different kinds of 'fighter' and to internationalize the struggles in which they are all engaged. These monologues are absent from the television version, although they have a residual presence in Bessie's voice-over, and there is no real screen equivalent to such an obviously theatrical strategy.

In contrast, the screen *Blood Red Roses*, like nearly all television drama, does not stray far from the constraints of illusionism. That is, it obeys the laws of spatial and temporal consistency and plausibility (these things can happen in the real world), characterization (people are 'believable' and identifiable human beings) and environment (it uses actual locations). It maintains, in short, a coherent fictional world that, with the exception of Bessie's voice-over, is never ruptured or rendered problematic in the way that the stage play is. But this does not mean that the series is 'naturalist'. McGrath wrote on several occasions about his hostility to naturalism, on television and on the stage, but his critique was on ideological as much as methodological grounds. Naturalism on television is 'a way of writing about the world which circumscribes the area you're allowed to write about . . . Such an approach excludes the intrusion of history: it erects a closed, charmed circle of emotional relationships without reference to anything happening outside'.[6] Clearly, however illusionist *Blood Red Roses* may be, it is not naturalism in this sense, since the purpose of its depiction of character and environment is to open out the personal narratives of Bessie, her family and all those with whom she comes into contact, into the history of a nation at moments of crisis and change. The episodic structure of the play gives each event a gestic significance, lifting it from its immediate context and offering it up for social analysis. These key scenes maintain their gestic importance in the series, but are inserted into a narrative, which emphasizes a continuous struggle that is more visibly present on the screen. In all its versions, *Blood Red Roses* is an 'epic', not in the strictly Brechtian sense, but because it is not 'rounded off' into a single, uni-focused drama, but rather cuts a swathe through post-war history, telling its story through short, detailed scenes, chronologically ordered (with the exception of the flash-forwards to Sandy's funeral) and often years apart. The cumulative weight of the events, as well as their specific political significance, gives the story its historical resonance; we are watching the story of a nation, not only an individual, the story of post-war capital told from the point of view of those who suffered under it.

How can we talk about this relationship between personal and historical narratives in *Blood Red Roses*? Often in television drama, history is simply a backdrop to the more important stories of the central character(s), but this is not the case here. McGrath places the narrative amongst the working class, following them not, by and large, in the domestic setting (like a great deal of post-war social realism that is indebted to the naturalist stage tradition) but in the workplace. Bessie and her co-workers are forced to respond to the increasingly remote activities of international capitalism (and this is a major factor in Bessie's radicalization). The factory she starts work in on leaving school is eventually bought by a larger company, which is swallowed up by a multinational. These developments become a source of dramatic tension; at the end of episode one, when it becomes clear that the firm has been taken over and jobs are under threat, Bessie leaves the viewer with the question, 'Who are these people and what are they planning to do to us?'. Much of episodes two and three is taken up with answering this question, which includes the story of Bessie's attempts to play capitalism at its own game and mobilize international trade union support to prevent closures and redundancies. This is paralleled by the development of technology and the media, which are here viewed as adjuncts to the increasingly repressive activities of capital. In one telling shot, Bessie looks out across the heads of a strike meeting she is addressing to a bank of telephoto lenses, trained on her by a national media mobilized against the working class. And developments in information systems are used by employers to blacklist Bessie throughout Glasgow.

The story of Bessie is a clear example of one that is narrated in the sense that Lukács used the term. In the course of a comparison between the ways in which the novelists Zola and Tolstoy depict a horse race, Lukács draws a distinction between 'description' and 'narration'. Description, which is the method of Zola and of the naturalist school of writers, is the representation of social reality by the accumulation of data, collected and transcribed by the writer, and then juxtaposed with the personal story of the central character. Narration, by contrast, is the method of Tolstoy and other realist writers of the nineteenth century, and represents social reality by seeing it from the point of view of a character, the protagonist, who acts as the structuring presence at the heart of the narrative. As Lukács observed, 'In Zola the race is *described* from the point of view of an observer; in Tolstoy it is *narrated* from the standpoint of a participant'.[7] In other words, narration requires that the novelist embeds his/her character in the events represented, creating a point of view on them. The choice of description or narration is not a neutral one for the writer, since the ideological consequences of each are different. Lukács argued that the descriptive method could only describe social problems as 'facts', their origins remaining unexamined; narration, in contrast, allows the reader access to problems through the experience of the participants, especially that of the central character(s). The question of point of view, as constructed through the actions of the protagonist, is key to this view of narrative—and to *Blood Red Roses*.

Although *Blood Red Roses* is about more than one individual, it has an undisputed protagonist in Bessie Gordon/McGuigan. But what kind of protagonist is she, and how is she connected to history? The central events of the play parallel the actions of a multinational company, ITT, in Scotland in the late 1970s. Bessie is based on a woman who led the successful opposition to ITT's closure plans, but was later victimized when the company eventually got its way. 'When the fuss had died down . . . the multinational closed down the factory, sacked everybody and simply went away. They made it clear that the reason for the close-down was the woman who had fought them. She not only lost her job—she became a local villain instead of a heroine.'[8] However, the series is not a thinly disguised biography and does not aim for the direct fidelity to historical fact that a documentary-drama might require. Its relationship to history is more complex and Bessie is an amalgam of different militants McGrath encountered, as well as having conscious echoes of archetypal Celtic fighting women. In fact, Bessie is a *typical* character and her typicality is rooted in McGrath's view of contemporary working-class political culture: it is also demanded by the series' realist fictional form. The idea of typicality is central to Lukács's conception of character in the realist novel.

'Typicality', however, is a term that requires careful and precise definition. The 'typical' is not, in McGrath's or Lukács's terms, synonymous with the 'average' (an ideologically loaded term and one that is much used in the discussion of naturalism). 'Average' implies a statistical norm and an average character is one who complies with a generally understood and agreed sense of 'plausible' and sociologically defensible behaviour, with all the attendant difficulties that these terms suggest. Bessie, though clearly a 'credible' character, is not average and typicality requires a character to be *inside* history in a more complex sense. As Lukács argued:

> The 'center' figure need not represent an 'average man' but is rather the
> product of a particular social and personal environment. The problem is
> to find a central figure in whose life all the important extremes in the
> world of the novel converge and around whom a complete world with all
> its vital contradictions can be organized.[9]

Lukács is linking typicality here to both the internal coherence of the text,
and, more importantly, to its ability to represent the dynamics of social
and political change. A typical character is one who *grants the reader/
audience access to the forces of history* at a given moment, whose situation
enables the writer (and, by extension, the film-maker) to connect the
personal to the social, and relate changes in one area of society to those
happening in another within a single narrative. Bessie McGuigan is
typical, then, not because she is an 'average' working-class woman (if such
a fearsome militant had been an average figure, female or male, then
post-war history would have been very different) but because her history
and actions allow us a particular, and privileged, view of post-war history.

At nearly every point, the development of Bessie's personal narrative
parallels that of Scotland to reveal a society in transition. The population
drift from the Highlands to the expanding New Towns of the Lowlands,
which, driven by brute economic realities, accelerated in the post-war
years, is represented in the plight of Bessie and Sandy. Having returned
from the war with a miserly disability pension and no economic prospects,
father and daughter are forced to leave their Highland home (having been
deserted by Bessie's mother). The cultural trauma of this move is surprising (to a non-Scots audience) and permeates much of the early part of the
narrative. The Gordons are transported to what they experience as an
alien country. On arrival at Glasgow, they set out to walk to East Kilbride,
not realizing that being 'near Glasgow' does not mean that it is a few
streets from the station. The derogatory 'chuechter' (Highlander) rings in
their ears and is echoed in Bessie's treatment at school in her new home
town (in a scene that is not in the stage play, Bessie confronts a PE
teacher, who attempts to victimize her because of her origins).

The changing character of Scottish society in the post-war period
permeates the texture of the series, often unremarked by the characters,
but clearly present for the viewer. East Kilbride functions as a metonym,
standing in for the transformation of the post-war urban landscape in the
name of redevelopment. As Bessie grows up, the town grows with her, its
changing landscape intruding, both aurally and visually, into her personal
story.

At other points in the narrative, the events that shape Bessie's life are
juxtaposed with wider historical ones. This is particularly true of the births
of Bessie and Alex's children; the first occurs on the night of Harold

McMillan's re-election in 1959, the second coincides with the 1964 Labour victory and the third child arrives on the eve of the 1983 General Election, which saw Margaret Thatcher returned to power with a massive majority. The juxtaposition is often humorous: at the birth of their first child (Janey), Alex rushes into the maternity ward to greet wife and baby with the words 'It's Harold Macmillan for another five years!', to which Bessie replies 'It's Janey McGuigan for life'. Bringing personal and political events into alignment in this way, produces two complementary effects. On the one hand, a key event in Bessie's life is placed not in the expected emotional/psychological context (although emotion is certainly present in the scene) but rather in its historical/political one, and this is a pattern that runs across the series, embracing not only births but also other key events, including Sandy's death (he dies as he is watching scenes of the miners' confrontation with the police during the doomed 1984 strike). On the other, the way that these events are represented raises questions about the limitations of particular political and social positions. At Janey's birth, it is her own mother that Bessie longs for. Alex's response is inadequate: holding his new baby in his arms, he can only say 'We're gonna need you to get rid o' these Tories.' He cannot kiss his wife and Bessie, as so often in the series, sees the connection between the political and the personal, confiding to the midwife that 'What's politics for if he couldna do that?'

For Bessie, the appropriate political response is one that recognizes that politics must be lived, not simply debated and that it must encompass all aspects of her life, including her identity as a woman. There is a strong, practical feminist consciousness in both Bessie and *Blood Red Roses*, which the series format allows McGrath to develop across the narrative, embracing several strands of the plot. It is clearest when Bessie is combining her role as activist and mother. In one key scene, Bessie is attempting to organize international resistance to attempts to lay off workers in her factory by telephone from her living room. A difficult conversation with a Portuguese trade unionist is juxtaposed with domestic chaos. The scene is humorous yet we are aware of the seriousness of the call both to Bessie and the activist who is risking a great deal in contacting her (this sequence is set before the restoration of democracy in Portugal). Alex, who we are reminded is a militant unionist, can offer no support because he is inept at handling his children and dealing with basic household chores (it is Sandy who takes control). The dilemma for Bessie is laid bare and the scene ends with a confrontation. Bessie has been told that Alex is having an affair, which he denies (though we later find it to be true). Bessie acknowledges that she has been unable to fulfil her 'feminine' duties, but the onus for resolving this is placed with Alex, who is confronted with his inability to share responsibility for home and family.

This is not only a personal failing, but also the limitation of a certain kind of traditional (male) political activism, which is radical in the workplace but conservative in the home.

However, *Blood Red Roses* is careful not to be anti-men and avoids a crude male/female opposition. Sandy learns how to help bring up his grandchildren and Alex is portrayed sympathetically as a man who is a victim of his own inability to change (a state of affairs of which he is agonisingly aware). In a later sequence, when Bessie is fighting to retain her job secured under her maiden name, it is Alex who argues on her behalf and offers emotional and practical support. In short, Alex's politics are not invalidated by his inability to overcome his cultural and ideological formation, but, in stopping at the front door, they are seen to be crucially limited.

Blood Red Roses is women-centred in other ways as well. The series places Bessie alongside other women, in particular her mother, her Aunt Ella and best friend and cousin, Catriona. It is Catriona, who dies of cancer in episode two, with whom Bessie is systematically juxtaposed. Catriona is vulnerable and timid, unable to voice her needs or fight for them. Much of Bessie's anger against injustice is fuelled by her determination that others should not suffer as she did. 'Everything I've done in the rest of my life has been in memory of Catriona', she says in voice over at her funeral. 'So that no other girl would get as little from life as her'.

The Luckácsian path to realism is not an easy one to follow, nor, in taking it, is McGrath exhausting all the possibilities of realism, viewed from other perspectives. The sheer difficulty of creating a personal narrative that resonates at the historical level in the way that *Blood Red Roses* does is indicated in a later McGrath play for television, *The Long Roads* (BBC1, 1993, director Tristram Powell) and I would like to consider it briefly here. *The Long Roads* is the story of an elderly couple, Peter and Kitty McVurrich, who leave their home on the Isle of Skye one last time to visit their five children, who are scattered across the UK. Kitty is dying of cancer, so the journey is a form of 'taking stock' as well as a farewell to children who have chosen very different paths to their parents and to each other. It is also a journey through Britain in the early 1990s and so is a 'taking stock' of British society at the end of the Thatcher era as well. Like Bessie McGuigan, the McVurrichs, coming from the margins of contemporary social life, are in no sense 'average' British citizens. Their journey takes them from the periphery (from Glasgow, the home of a policeman son, to a daughter who lives on the edge of economic disaster in Liverpool, and on to Peterborough, the home of a second son who is in the process of becoming wealthy in a high-tech industry) to the centre (two daughters live in London, though in vastly different circumstances, one in affluence, the other on a run-down estate). It is through this journey that McGrath constructs his elderly couple as 'typical' protagonists, whose situation allows access to the main currents of social, economic and cultural change in the period. Their point of view on events becomes the viewer's and what is strange and incomprehensible to them—the vagaries of a decaying rail network, the violence and poverty of urban life in Glasgow and Liverpool, the callousness of wealth—appears defamiliarized and unnatural to us when viewed through their eyes.

Yet the difficulty of using a personal story to access an historical one is apparent, as well. The length of *The Long Roads*, at ninety minutes as against the three hours of *Blood Red Roses*, works against it here, and the first three stages of the journey are dealt with briskly and unsentimentally. This led to one of the main press criticisms of the play, that it was too crude in its political analysis. As Jennifer Selway noted in the *Observer*, 'Some may find the distinct class delineation of the McVurrich children over-schematic.'[10] This is the kind of criticism that McGrath often faced and it may have its origins in ideological resistances to the play. Yet McGrath's own comments indicate that something else is at work, too: 'I wanted to talk about the landscape of a very divided Britain, and when I started I was involved in that', he said in interview. 'But I slowly became more involved in the relationship between Peter and Kitty. It's a political play, but only in the broadest sense'.[11] When the McVurrichs arrive in London, the pace and focus of the narrative alters, becoming much more concerned with how Peter and Kitty reform their bruised relationship as Kitty prepares for her death. This is handled with extraordinary delicacy and feeling (and not a little humour). If *The Long Roads* is realist at this point, it is not so much because its protagonists are typical in the Lukácsian sense, but because McGrath is giving voice to the often muted social experience of older people. During an influential essay, Raymond Williams argues that one of the main criteria by which Realism has been defined is that of 'social extension'; that is, the representation of hitherto ignored social experience, initially class experience.[12] From this perspective, Kitty and Peter are doubly marginalized—by their class and culture and by their age. In giving the McVurrichs and those like them a voice, McGrath, with great intelligence and sensitivity, represents the emotions, sensibilities and challenges of old age in a way that is still rare.

At the beginning of this chapter I argued that McGrath was not afraid to use identification. Given the centrality of Bessie to the narrative and the series' illusionist form, identification is clearly an issue in both *Blood Red Roses* and *The Long Roads*. However, identification here is not simply a result of either naturalist habit or a by-product of the form, but rather a central political strategy, especially in the case of *Blood Red Roses*. It is hard, I would argue, for any member of the television audience to stay with *Blood Red Roses* and *not* identify with Bessie McGuigan. Of course, identification is a complex and problematic process and nearly always involves more than emotional empathy (although that is certainly present in all versions of the text). It is more a question of how the series uses Bessie to construct a point of view on the events it represents and offers a perspective from which to interpret them. In one sense, *Blood Red Roses* uses viewer identification with Bessie to dislocate expected responses. By placing even the most personal events, such as births and deaths, in their historical context, the series directs us to political, rather than psychological, interpretations. At another level, the series was conceived with an acute awareness of the immediate context of reception. Made in 1985, at the height of Thatcherite triumphalism and in the aftermath of the defeat of the miners, *Blood Red Roses* was offered against the grain of the prevailing political climate. In particular, it articulates a counter to the dominant view of industrial militants (and the role of the mass media in perpetrating this view is acknowledged by the series in the way Bessie is demonized by the press). In asking us to view events from the standpoint of a protagonist who would, in other circumstances, be a popular hate-figure for many viewers, McGrath was using a familiar dramatic tool for his explicit political purposes.

In conclusion, *Blood Red Roses* is committed to what Raymond Williams, with reference to Lukács, calls the 'classical realist project':

> Showing a man or woman making an effort to live a much fuller life and encountering the objective limits of a particular social order, and depicting the creative contradiction between the impulse towards another life, seen not as an individual but as a general aspiration, and the structural constraints of a society.[13]

Here, it seems as though the social order is victorious. Bessie acts against the forces that have tried to dismantle the institutional and ideological resistance of the working class, aware that it is the latter that is the most damaging; 'Working people don't see themselves as part of a class any more', she laments towards the end of the last episode and what concerns her the most about an unsuccessful vote to take strike action in defence of her job is that more than half the workforce abstained. It is to McGrath's credit, however, that the 'creative contradiction' is not allowed have a pessimistic outcome. The final sequence of the series sees Bessie, her eldest daughter and new baby, joining a Nicaraguan solidarity march. The protest is a collective celebration and the camera sweeps across a mass of union banners, taking in marchers of all ages and colours. It is also accompanied by the haunting pipe music of Chilean exiles, Inti Illimani, a reminder of resistance in the face of oppression. As Judith Williamson noted, 'It is the memory of the cost of that battle which gives the banners their meaning: a memory which the film has supplied'.[14] *Blood Red Roses*, in all its versions, stands as a testament, 'a profoundly moving record of a real history which must be remembered and made visible, not to convince others but because memory is necessary to keep going for those whose history it is'.[15] Williamson's comment stands as a judgment on all McGrath's work.

CHAPTER ELEVEN

A Good Night In

The Long Roads

Robert Dawson Scott

Since long ago, a child at home,
I read and longed to rise and roam,
Where'er I went, whate'er I willed,
One promised land my fancy filled.
Hence the long roads my home I made;
Tossed much in ships; have often laid
Below the uncurtained sky my head,
Rain-deluged and wind-buffeted:
And many a thousand hills I crossed
And corners turned—Love's labour lost;

Robert Louis Stevenson[1]

In the extensive literature that John McGrath's work has provoked, he is unhesitatingly positioned as a radical, forever challenging orthodoxies, generally from a progressive standpoint. The titles of the books and articles in which his work is discussed tell their own story: *Disrupting the Spectacle; The Politics of Alternative Theatre; Radical People's Theatre; Stages in the Revolution; The Politics of Performance; The People's Story; Unruly Elements; Return of the Radical* and so on.[2] Nor do his own theoretical and critical writings indicate anything other than a warm embrace of this positioning.[3] 'Revolution cannot be reduced to theatre', he wrote in the aftermath of the euphoria of Paris in 1968 which he witnessed at first hand, 'but at times like this, theatre can aspire to express revolution.'[4] He pursued his iconoclasms on a dazzling array of fronts, both political and aesthetic.[5]

However, while his political engagement and commitment is beyond doubt, it seems to me there are two weaknesses in reading McGrath's life and work entirely in these terms. The first is that it tends to underplay, or at best to take for granted, his prodigious gifts as a writer. As it is, one of the more familiar criticisms from his detractors, both political and aesthetic, was that he was no more than a purveyor of crude agit-prop. He may well have been a polemicist and an ideologue but he was also a technician, a practical man of the theatre and the moving image. In the theatre, *A Good Night Out*, for example, remains even today not only a manifesto but also a user's manual. In film, his success in establishing the Moonstone film-making workshops was just one indication of how well he understood the inner workings of that medium too.

The second difficulty is that it tends to depersonalize him. Political histories, by their very nature, concentrate on ideas rather than the people who have them. But in McGrath's case, this is not simply a sentimental point. At times, he held together the two 7:84 companies in England and Scotland through difficult, not to say penurious, times by the sheer force of his personality. Both before and after those times, he worked extensively in television and film production, a field in which what are loosely called 'people skills' are critical. These skills also enabled him to access the largely hidden stories of Scotland which became such a rich source of inspiration for him.[6] In other words, this facet of his make-up both made the work possible and informed what went into it.

There are, of course, traces of his writerly skills and his humanity in almost all his best work if one cares to look. But in my view *The Long Roads* throws both into especially sharp relief. This ninety-minute television drama was first broadcast on BBC2 at 10pm on Sunday 31 January 1993. It tells the story of Peter and Kitty McVurrich (played by Robert Urquhart and Edith McArthur), an elderly couple from the Isle of Skye in Scotland. Early scenes allow us to understand that Kitty is seriously ill. The couple leave their island croft to make a farewell visit to their five grown-up children and their families who are scattered across the United Kingdom. Through their eyes, we encounter the five very different locations, lifestyles and attitudes in which and with which their children have ended up and which serve as a snapshot of contemporary Britain. During the trip and as a consequence of it, the central relationship deepens and ripens. Finally, the old couple return to Skye and Kitty dies, at peace.

The film was that rare thing in McGrath's output, an original drama written directly for the screen.[7] It is undoubtedly different from the main body of his work; he himself promised it would be in the original treatment for the film, a document which shows how clear his intentions were from the very beginning.[8] The most obvious difference from most of his other work is that it is entirely naturalistic.[9] Characters speak to one another in realistic dialogue, the narrative is linear, locations are real (it was filmed entirely on location). The televisual grammar—the sequence of establishing shot, close-up, reaction shot etc.—is also essentially conventional, not significantly different from any mainstream television drama. Furthermore, the film is, in McGrath's own words, 'not political in a direct way'.[10] It is framed in personal terms. The characters are individuated rather than symbolic. Only the youngest daughter, Marie, shows any signs of politicization but even that is only in terms of her own character. No doubt it is partly because of these differences that the film seems to have become detached from the *urtext* McGrath catalogue. There is, at least, a dearth of comment on it despite the fact that it was the one work for the screen which won him an award for his writing.[11] I hope that highlighting some of its qualities may, in addition to illuminating aspects of McGrath the writer and McGrath the man, help to stitch the film back into the main catalogue of his output.

We first need to review the circumstances of its creation. The beginning of the 1990s saw McGrath emerging from a bruising time. He had lost both the English and Scottish 7:84 theatre companies as a result of what he believed, with some justification, was naked political aggression. The English company had closed altogether after the loss of its Arts Council of Great Britain funding in 1984. The Scottish one continued but it was, in his words, 'a different company' since he had been forced to resign from it at the point of a Scottish Arts Council funding gun in 1988.[12] This was not just an artistic setback. It had been the central focus of his life for the best part of two decades. There were financial implications too. 7:84 had been a source of income as well as inspiration and purpose. But, as if his misfortune might be catching, he found access to the rest of the nation's stages almost entirely closed to him.[13] Only the Scottish history epics, *Border Warfare* (1989) and *John Brown's Body* (1990), both originally intended for 7:84 Scotland, were picked up by Wildcat Stage Productions (the music theatre production which had split off from 7:84 Scotland a decade previously and was run by McGrath's brother-in-law, David MacLennan).

It was a time, too, of more general despondency for anyone on the left of British politics. Margaret Thatcher was herself forced out of office in 1990. But the political philosophy which bore her name was still surfing the economic boom in the south-east of England that was to crash so spectacularly on 'Black Wednesday', 16 September 1992. It is not surprising that *The Bone Won't Break* is a very much more downbeat series of lectures than *A Good Night Out* had been at the beginning of the decade. There was bad news on the personal front too. Both his parents had died, his mother in 1985 and his father three years later, something that was to bear heavily on the genesis of the new film, as we shall see.

McGrath did still have Freeway Films, the production company he had set up in the early 1980s to exploit opportunities offered by the launch of Channel 4. This had been a successful enterprise, with a number of completed broadcast projects ranging from poetry readings to the filming of *Blood Red Roses* (1985). But if Channel 4 had been good for McGrath, it had had an even more profound impact on the British *paysage audiovisuel* as a whole. Specifically, the almost complete demise of the single drama on the BBC meant that the new channel had a clear run at such authored work. However, in the new dispensation of Film on Four, such projects were more likely to be called film than drama.[14]

In that context, it is worth re-examining McGrath's attitude to television drama and film in general. In the much quoted 'Rather a Bad Night in Bootle' interview with Cathy Itzin in 1975, McGrath famously dismissed the mass media as 'so penetrated by the ruling class ideology that to try to dedicate your whole life . . . to fighting within them is going to drive you mad.'[15] But he added two important riders. The first was to preface the remark with the words 'at the moment', holding out at least the possibility that things might change. The second was in the missing phrase represented by the ellipsis. It reads, 'as distinct from occasional forays and skirmishes'. Room for tactical intervention, then, if it could be organized. Earlier in the same interview, in a less quoted passage, he adds 'These mass entertainment media are not to be ignored, or you ignore them at your peril, because they contain within them the accumulation of fifty years' experience of mass entertainment . . . There is a lot to be learned from the technique of entertaining people from big movies.' He was referring specifically to his experiences in the 1960s writing for Hollywood studios but the same could be said of television. In other words, while the institutions of television or film production were problematic, the medium itself was there to have advantage taken of it.

Television or film may not have suited his main project in the 1970s and early 1980s, politically, temperamentally or aesthetically. But now, as the theatre turned its back, there were opportunities offered by a new channel which had what amounted to a statutory obligation to resist the 'ruling-class ideology' that McGrath had found so disagreeable.[16] All in all, it was a touch ironic that *The Long Roads* was eventually made by the BBC. McGrath did originally develop it with Channel 4 where David Rose, his long-time producer, was Head of Drama. Following a change in personnel, however, and after some prevarication, Channel 4 turned down the finished script.[17]

The BBC had by this stage responded to Film on Four's occupation of the high ground of serious television drama by establishing the Screen One and Screen Two strands. McGrath had nothing against reaching a mass audience. (And he did; nearly as many people watched *The Long Roads* on one night as the aggregate live audience over 7:84's entire lifetime.)[18] Nor was it as if the film was inconsistent with the principles set out in *A Good Night Out*: make sure your audience is somewhere they feel comfortable;

find a language with which they are familiar; entertain them. In this case, the audience was at home, in front of the television set, watching a drama with a simple structure using a grammar and vocabulary familiar from most other television drama which slipped easily into the Sunday night flow. It was, in effect, a good night in.

There was one further calculation as to form. The very nature of what he wanted to write about—families, love, death, the very bedrock of humanity—was, he considered, likely to be better served by a naturalistic film populated by individuals, rather than types. This may have been no more than a writer's instinct at work. But part of the unwritten history of McGrath as a writer which *The Long Roads* reveals is that he was able to emerge from twenty years in the theatre and deliver an award-winning original script, in a different idiom, for a different medium, hardly pausing to change the ribbon in his typewriter. It is true that he had never entirely left television behind; there had been a trickle of commissions from the BBC in the 1970s (not least the televising of *The Cheviot* itself) before the Channel 4 work began. But this original screenplay was something quite different. And if further evidence of his technical skills are required, he also produced a film adaptation of Beryl Bainbridge's novel *The Dressmaker* (1989) and a version of *Robin Hood* (1991) for a major Hollywood studio, all within the same relatively short time-span.[19]

McGrath sent the finished script of *The Long Roads*, to Mark Shivas, the editor of Screen Two, who accepted it almost by return of post and happily bought out Channel 4's residual rights. 'It seemed terribly true and real—and it was about people not particularly written about at that time,' Shivas recalls.[20] Pre-production began almost immediately. McGrath is credited not just as writer but also as co-executive producer, with Shivas, of the finished film. This may seem like a detail in the Byzantine complexity of film credits but it is significant here. Normally the title is reserved for the person ultimately responsible for the project, typically someone from the studio or broadcaster which is funding it; in this case, Shivas. For a writer to be executive producer as well indicates that he or she has retained a high degree of control over key artistic decisions such as casting, design and the choice of director. In this case, it underlines that, although he did not direct it, *The Long Roads* is very much McGrath's overall vision, conventional look and narrativity included, not just his script.[21]

McGrath had good reason to be so clear about what he wanted for this film. He had been thinking about it for the best part of thirty years. The idea was born when he saw a Japanese film called *Tokyo Story* (1953), directed by Yasujiro Ozu. The film is essentially about the collapse of a family in post-World War II Japan. An elderly couple come to visit their children in Tokyo where they are received coolly. The children learn later that the mother has fallen ill upon her return home and go to visit their parents but arrive too late to say their good-byes. Ozu is careful not to make judgements of anyone, suggesting that perhaps such scenes are inevitable and that, if anything, it is for the parents to make peace with the future. McGrath was so taken with the film and its take on family relations that he invited a group of friends to watch a 16mm print at his home in London in the early 1960s.[22] 'I've spent more than twenty years thinking about this play [sic]' he told a journalist at the time of *The Long Roads* broadcast. 'But I didn't actually write it until my own mother and father died in the mid-Eighties. After your parents die, your feelings about them change. You suddenly realise they are persons with their own agenda, not just the emotional appendages of their children.'[23]

Such sentiments indicate just how close to his heart this project was. The deaths of his parents in the 1980s, both from cancer, clearly released his pent-up feelings and allowed him to make what turns out to be a very personal film. Kitty McVurrich is not a portrait of his own mother but there are considerable overlaps. Kitty, who also has cancer, is shown to have brought up her family mostly on her own because her husband was away at sea. They live in a remote community, Skye, in straitened circumstances. She tries to reassure Fiona, her daughter in Liverpool, who is living well below the poverty line and resorting to minor shoplifting and massage parlour work to make ends meet, by telling her of the endless nights she spent knitting while her husband was away at sea to put food on the table. Her speech about being left alone concludes, only half jokingly, 'I should have done the massage but I don't think we had any.' McGrath's mother was forced to move with her two sons, one still a baby, from Birkenhead to an isolated mining village in North Wales at the beginning of the war while her husband went off to fight. One can imagine that the circumstances were tough for her too, even if the hardships were those imposed by wartime austerity rather than Conservative economic policy. McGrath himself remembered he and his fellow evacuees being spat on by local children when they arrived.[24]

Kitty is also a Gael. She sings a lullaby in the language to soothe Fiona, and McGrath carefully replicates the occasional archaisms which are characteristic of Gaelic speakers using English as a second language. McGrath's mother was of Irish descent, not Scots, and certainly not Gaelic. But the family's Irish connections were strong and the sense of there being a homeland in a different culture was a real one within the family. There is a family link with Peter, too, the merchant seaman. Some of McGrath's male relations were also involved with 'the boats'—seamen of one sort or another, in Dublin, Belfast and Liverpool.

The creation of these two characters is the film's biggest single triumph. Old people are rarely found at the centre of film and television drama.

Generally they are minor characters, often comic relief or sources of folk wisdom. McGrath makes us see the world through their eyes and makes them real by showing their strengths and weaknesses. They are clearly heroes, as, one suspects, McGrath's parents were to him. But he shows this, paradoxically, by making them anything but heroic. Kitty is stoic in the face of constant pain from her illness, but she is not spared the indignities, vomiting in public, collapsing at inopportune moments. In a key moment, she shows the greatest weakness of all, contemplating throwing herself out of a top-floor hotel window before Peter pulls her back, gently and tenderly rather than melodramatically. For his part, he is clearly ill-at-ease in the face of her condition, drowning his sorrows in the local pub in an early scene. But he has buckled down to taking care of her and in particular to making this trip which she is so set on. Typical of the deft writing working within the conventions of the form is the way in which McGrath releases information. It is only at the end of the film that we learn that Peter has defied doctor's orders to let Kitty make the trip. A less subtle writer would have told us that at the beginning, leaving the characters open to easy judgements (whether of the 'silly old fool' or the 'aren't they brave' variety), which would have obscured the emotional journey on which the pair embark amidst their physical journey.

If there are few films which feature elderly people, there are even fewer which feature a love affair between elderly people. The first point at which you realize that the mood of *The Long Roads* is not going to be irretrievably grim, as it threatens to be once the first establishing shots of Skye are over, comes after the Liverpool sequence, the second of the visits. Peter and Kitty are discovered sitting on a railway platform waiting for a train. Without warning, he simply puts his hand in hers. From that moment, as they start to enjoy the enforced time they have together on the journey, the flower of their mutual affection, which has until then been hidden in the bud, gradually blooms in an autumnal sunshine. There are even, daringly, indications of physical desire. This fulfilment of what has probably been half a century of partnership provides the balm to the less than comfortable portrait of Britain provided by the rest of the film and to the varying degrees of disappointment they find in their children. Even in describing it, the potential for cloying sentimentality is obvious. Yet time and again, throughout the film, McGrath keeps such dangers at bay with his control of the material.

There is no doubt that he was also well served in all this by his actors. Critical analysis has found it difficult to engage with performance in the past, though Simon Frith[25] and John Caughie[26] have both, from their different standpoints, gone some way to opening the door. For most ordinary viewers, however, who, as we have seen, are accustomed to naturalistic drama and therefore enjoy relating to characters, it is a major point of entry into enjoyment of any film or play. In this case, the television reviewers, the nearest thing we have to representatives of the audience, were unanimous: 'tremendously moving' (*Daily Mail*); 'sensitive love story . . . beautifully handled' (*The Sunday Times*); 'It is very true and touching with performances that make it almost unbearably so' (*The Mail on Sunday*); 'played to perfection' (*The Times*); 'Urquhart and MacArthur were very moving as they crept back towards a love for each other which years of hardship had dimmed' (*Daily Telegraph*).[27] MacArthur was also nominated as best actress in that year's Scottish BAFTA awards for her performance. There is perhaps scope for another study to pin down just what it is in these performances which makes them so affecting. Whatever it is, rather like the rest of the film, it is nothing showy; both actors appear to do very little. But their very stillness, suggesting dignity and acceptance, itself provides a fixed point in the turbulent and confusing world they and the film inhabit.

McGrath captures that world in the vignettes of the visits to the children and also in scenes where the couple are seen en route (mostly in trains, rather than by road, another tiny reversal of expectation[28]). There are four visits, rather than five; we never get to Marie's flat in east London. Let the first one, to Iain, the McVurrichs' eldest son, a policeman in Glasgow, serve as example. Our introduction to him, even before we know who he is, is in the middle of a violent arrest, intercut with the old couple's arrival by bus in Glasgow on a motorway flanked by grim tower blocks. Clearly this is a brutal world. Sure enough, once the action moves to Iain's home, his young children are to be found watching a boxing match on television. Their grandmother's attempts to remind them of gentler games on the beach on Skye when they were younger fall on deaf ears. Iain's wife Mandy (described in the script as an ex-policewoman) is also part of this harsh world, barking instructions at her husband and children, living in a flat which, while not especially impoverished, lacks anything which Doris Day might recognize as 'a woman's touch'. Earlier, on the phone to her husband, complaining about her in-laws' clearly unexpected arrival, she memorably enjoins him (one police officer to another) 'Iain you're not in the witness box—you can tell the truth'.

The next day, on a trip to the Burrell Collection, the jewel in Glasgow's cultural crown, the children's reactions reduce life to its bare essentials and Iain's own car is broken into in the idyllic parkland setting which is home to the gallery.[29] What hope is there? The old couple feel uncomfortable and unwelcome and leave ahead of schedule early the following morning (a tiny plot detail which has the effect of delivering them to their other offspring a day earlier than expected, ensuring that each encounter cannot be, as it were, rehearsed). Iain has understood why they came to visit and realizes he will never see his mother again. But the moment passes and he is unable to say goodbye.

All this and more is accomplished in no more than ten minutes of screen time. Each subsequent visit is similarly crammed with rich fragments of observation and telling moments, creating a series of believable worlds in a very brief time frame. Together they build up a picture not so much of contemporary Britain as of several different Britains which know very little of each other. Iain would probably recognize the desperate housing scheme where his sister lives in Liverpool. But Deirdre's plush Eaton Square flat (and her house in the country which we only ever see on a home video), paid for by her husband's commodity trading, might as well be on Mars (and vice versa). The divide between north and south is, of course, no accident either.

This may begin to sounds as if it is verging on the political, and of course it is, in the sense that McGrath's portrait of the state of the nation is as beady-eyed as ever. But whereas in his other work this might preface a call to arms or an explanation of the causes of this state of affairs (or even a song) here the consequences are played out in human terms. Fiona is humiliated, first by the loan shark who catches her unloading her pathetic shoplifting haul—food for her children's tea—then in front of her mother and her husband when the massage parlour pimp turns up asking her why she hasn't been back to work. Deirdre, in opting into the gold rush of her husband's futures trading, feels guilty for betraying her roots when she is prevented by her new life from taking her parents in for the night. On the other hand, at least she has a family of a sort even if her kids have been packed off to boarding school. In the case of Roddie, the technocrat, it is clear that in opting for his corporate lifestyle and his frigid wife, he has sacrificed even that. In the anguished aftermath of learning of his mother's impending death, he attempts, in a cruelly embarrassing scene, to make love to his wife and conceive a child; in the midst of death, we make new life. But his wife pushes him off her, using the language of the nursery; he is crushed.

For anyone who has not actually seen the film, it must be tempting to assume that these vignettes are caricatures, the better to get across the different locales, both mental and physical, that the characters inhabit. I cannot speak for other viewers but for me one of the pleasures of the film is the way in which it overcomes that problem by the technique of gently wrong-footing you just as you think you have identified the particular television shorthand in use. It is this that also keeps at bay the sentimentality that would threaten any story involving an elderly couple saying goodbye to their children for the last time and ending with a death, even without a love story woven into it. But there is also a sly humour, much of it dependent on the very difference of Peter and Kitty's world from the world they come to visit. Their world is Scotland, and in particular Highland Scotland.

I want to take a little detour, before approaching some tentative conclusions, to discuss the representations of Scotland in the film because, apart from the jokes they generate, I believe they are both quietly subversive and highly personal for McGrath. But to do that we need briefly to remind ourselves of the context in which *The Long Roads* appeared. Despite the renewed interest in Scottish film and television production in the 1990s that Duncan Petrie has catalogued[30], at the time the film was broadcast, representations of Scotland, and especially of the Highlands, were relatively rare and still not entirely free of the critique levelled at them by Colin McArthur in his seminal *Scotch Reels* collection.[31] Hugh Hebert has argued that *Tutti Frutti* (1987), John Byrne's marvellous serial about a Scottish rock and roll band, 'brought Scottish screen drama in to the mainstream' whereas before, works by Bill Douglas and McGrath himself had seemed like 'strangers dropping in'.[32] That may have been true of urban Scotland but, judging by what else was on the year *The Long Roads* was broadcast, there were still some old prejudices clinging on among commissioning editors in London about the rest of the country. On the BBC, *Strathblair* was a series not so different from today's *Monarch of the Glen* except that it was set in 1950s Perthshire. On ITV, a new version of *Dr Finlay's Casebook* was just getting under way, 'updated' from its original 1920s setting to post-war Scotland—much the same as *Strathblair*, in fact, and also set in Perthshire. As with many prejudices, there was a germ of truth behind it. The industry joke at the time was that the only alterations they had to make to the mainstreet of the Perthshire village of Blair Atholl, where *Strathblair* was filmed, to give it the right 1950s feel was to modernize the lighting and the shop fronts.

Strathblair and *Dr Finlay* were self-contained, their own little worlds. Usually, if ever the wider world and rural Scotland, especially the Highlands, collided, it was someone from the metropolis going to find out about themselves, a trope unaltered from *I Know Where I'm Going* (1945) to *Local Hero* (1983). Highlanders going forth, excluding historical epics, were confined to films like *Geordie* (1955) which, try as one might, are hard to extract from McArthur's kailyard. The idea of looking at contemporary London and the rest of Britain, in whatever decade, down a telescope whose viewfinder was sited in Skye, was a complete reversal. In context, it is a genuinely radical step.

To be sure, McGrath has some fun with the idea, when, for example, Kitty, on a train full of urban commuters, authoritatively discusses the details of sheep castration by biting or praises the *haute cuisine* at the London hotel as 'quite good'. Most importantly, however, these are not two Ealing comedy Islanders just off the boat from Great Todday.[33] There is a neat reminder of this, when Peter and Kitty are dropped off by mini-cab at Roddie's house on an executive housing estate in Peterborough. A lively conversation has clearly sprung up between Peter and the Asian driver during the journey. Peter, once again the man of the world, is able to say goodbye in the man's native tongue—which naturally surprises and delights the driver.[34] Then a neighbour appears. Kitty, working on a Skye assumption that neighbours know one another's business, asks if Roddy had left a message. The neighbour hurries her child inside muttering about the odd people you see these days. You could see this as indicative of Peter and Kitty's otherness. But the woman's reaction is so hysterical—what kind of threat does an elderly couple pose, exactly? —that, if anything, it reinforces the sense of alienation associated with such housing estates and suggests that the community on the Isle of Skye has rather more to offer; it is, one might say, rather less insular. In that vein also is Roddy's prediction of computer programmers working from crofts on Skye, which, coming from him, reinforces the idea that Skye is not a remote inaccessible landscape but part of the modern world.

Altogether this is a far more positive, modern (despite the fact that the protagonists are elderly) non-patronizing and (to most Scots) recognizable vision of Highland Scotland than had been found on almost any screen hitherto. When they finally get to the London hotel, the young German receptionist, as well as being completely unable to pronounce their names, both knows Skye and thinks it is in England. Anyone in Scotland will tell you that you don't have to meet a German in London to find that level of confusion about what goes on north of Watford. This is, if you like, one for the Scots. I have touched on McGrath's lifelong love affair with Scotland already. I think this film may in part be his homage to that landscape and language and culture whose long roads he criss-crossed so often in all those years of small-scale touring with 7:84, so often in fact that he probably knew them better than most Scots. He also knew that it would be wrong to ignore those aspects of Highland life which still lean to the mystic or the unknowable, however much it may undermine his otherwise humane and sympathetic construction of it. When the McVurrichs return home, the postman tells them there has been a hare on the doorstep. In the Gaeltacht, as in several other European folk cultures, the hare is a harbinger of bad luck and sometimes death. It certainly is to Kitty. You may see that as superstition, but you could also see it as evidence of the kind of knowledge, rather like her very language, which does not fit easily into the rational world and which is all the more valuable for that. After all, it is the rational world which, as we have seen is so painful for Peter and Kitty's children.

In the end death comes to us all, highland or lowland. McGrath sets himself the challenge of showing how old people, especially those who know they are close to death, often observably arrive at a kind of serenity, an acceptance of life in all its forms, including of course the paradox that death is the most life-affirming moment of all. Acceptance is more than simply toleration. The latter implies putting up with something until the opportunity comes to change it at some point in the future. Acceptance implies that you accept that things are not going to change. You could add, as part of McGrath's construction of the Highland Scotland discussed above, that the nature of life on Skye, close to an indifferent nature where the hens have to be fed (and the sheep castrated), lends itself to a kind of acceptance. And yet, even there, McGrath has one last twist, as Peter finds the sadness of having finally found his wife, only to lose her for ever, too much to bear. It is worth quoting the final scene in full, stage directions included:

> (*Shot 112. Exterior Machair, Skye, daytime*)
>
> (Peter walks alone through the glories of the Machair in late spring—the flowers glisten, the sand shines white, the sea, the birds play in the tide, the waves sparkle in the sun, the small birds are singing, the bushes are bright with blossom; he is overwhelmed by the beauties of the world. He cries, as he picks her some wild flowers.)
>
> PETER: Oh God, why did you make the world so wonderful—and then make us leave it?[35]

The Long Roads amply demonstrates McGrath's skills as writer in its economy of language, its richly drawn characters, its deft handling of difficult issues, its wit and also, in a wider sense, in the way he puts on the mantle of the chosen style so effortlessly. And it is a film on a human scale; of family values, of being and becoming, connecting directly with his own life and family. But just as it is possible to discern these qualities in his other more celebrated works, as I mentioned earlier, so here it is possible to discern the radical McGrath, in the representation of Scotland, in the elevation of old age, in the analysis of contemporary Britain. It turned out not only to be a rare work written directly for the screen but also his last major original work.[36] It would be odd for such a superficially un-characteristic film to be his epitaph. But, with its inevitably elegiac tone, it does feel rather like it.

CHAPTER TWELVE

Three One-Woman Epics
The Political Performer

Olga Taxidou

In the one act play, *Plugged in to History*, written in 1972, the main character Kay, says:

> When I read the papers, I feel plugged in to history. I feel the course of events coursing through my veins. I feel taken over, crushed, by many men. I feel occupied, a house, squatted in, defiled. I feel like a deserted ball-room being defecated in by a halted army. I feel like South America after the Yankees have finished with it, like Dresden after the bombing. I feel like a shed of cats. I feel like a mid-night zoo. I feel like a clump of trees outside a barracks, full of soldiers in rough khaki having under-age village tarts. I feel like Pompeii the next morning. I become a human news-tape, mile after mile of me, torn out, ripped off, abandoned. Do you know why? Do you begin to? It's because I feel everything, all the way through me.[1]

Kay transpires as a precursor to the characters in a series of one-woman plays written by McGrath and performed by Elizabeth MacLennan in the 1990s and in 2001–2. These plays, the last that John McGrath was to write, bear the mark of his relationship to history as the above title suggests. They are also a homage to the significance of the performer in his work. *Watching for Dolphins* (1992), *The Last of the MacEachans* (1996) and *HyperLynx* (2001) were all co-created with MacLennan and all exhibit some of the concerns that have marked McGrath's work. In many ways they can be seen to bring together his main preoccupations: *Watching for Dolphins* deals with the activism of the 1960s and 1970s from the perspective of the 1990s; *The Last of the MacEachans* revisits the notion of the 'organic community' and the relationships between local and international cultures; and *HyperLynx* deals with the impact of globalization on our lives and structurally links that to the events of 11 September. All these plays cover huge historical movements. They are epic in their scale and all are performed by a single actor. I am interested in examining how the scale of the themes covered is translated into theatrical conventions for performance. In other words, I want to look at how these characters are connected to the historical process and what kind of languages of performance this approach has helped to create.

McGrath has repeatedly stated that his theatre is markedly different from Brecht's. His references to Brecht appear more out of a sense of duty and almost always reluctantly. On the one hand, he might be responding to the ways Brecht and 'Brechtian' aesthetics have been appropriated throughout the cold war to signify anything and everything about political theatre. There are surely many traditions in political performance beyond the Brecht/non-Brecht divide. On the other, in terms of performance conventions McGrath's work is in dialogue with traditions that Brecht was not particularly interested in, like his whole engagement with popular culture, his borrowing from television and cinema etc. One of the ways in which his work is significantly different from Brecht's is in his use of dramatic 'character'. I would like to delineate this particular aesthetic through a reading of these one-woman plays. Thematically and formally epic, these recent plays are a continuation of the experiment in dramatic character initiated by early plays like *Plugged in to History*. It is a language of performance that has been created through a lifetime cooperation with Elizabeth MacLennan. Her contribution to McGrath's particular aesthetics of political theatre cannot be overestimated. At the same time, since the themes of all these plays are grand and historical, the notion of character proposed is one that constantly negotiates between the personal and the political, between the local and the international.

Like Kay, the protagonists of these plays combine an instinctual, almost physical, relationship to history with an emotional and intellectual approach. Interestingly enough, they are not simply 'epic' characters in the received sense of the term. They are psychological in at least one sense; they rely on a coherent reading of character in order then to transgress it. They all flirt with what would traditionally be interpreted as 'madness'. They have sides to them which are quirky, unstable and unreliable. At times they consider drastic measures, like violence, to confront the historical issues raised. They are complex and contradictory, eliding between psychological moods and political analysis. Kay, like Reynalda, Meg and Heather in *HyperLynx*, is certainly more than a naturalist character or even a strictly 'epic' type. These women seem to borrow from both traditions in a combination of narrator, role, character and performer. The bringing together of all these conventions creates a type of performance through which the personal life of the role and historical life she represents fuse into one. The resulting performance, however, cannot be reduced to its components. It equally requires a complex reaction on behalf of the audience.

Watching for Dolphins was first performed at the Museum of Scotland in 1992 as part of a broader series of events organized by MacLennan that dealt with the cultural and political identity of Scotland. Reynalda is a woman in her early fifties who

> was brought up in one of the best English, radical, non-conformist intellectual families, but has gone through a lot since then. She has played her part in most of the liberation struggles and revolutionary movements of the 60s, 70s and 80s, and through committing herself to them more completely than most, has learnt from her experiences a great deal more than her limited background might imply.

When the play opens Reynalda is about to open her grandmother's bungalow in Wales as a bed and breakfast. It is her way of coping with the New Economy of the 1990s. Her only commodity is herself and her heritage so she decides to put it up for sale. Or does she? This is not a straightforward tale of compromise and survival. While Reynalda is preparing the three-course meal for the opening night of her B & B we get a survey of the politics of the left from the 1960s to today. It is not always a pleasant journey that we are asked to follow. From the grand gestures and aspirations of the 1960s Reynalda is reduced to running a small private business: 'Demonstrations, rallies, meetings, car-stealing, border-hops, failed kidnappings, graffiti campaigns: I've gone through most of them in my time—but this little gesture is the most obscene. I'm afraid of it. I don't want to do it. But . . .'[2]

But there is more to Reynalda than we are led to believe. As this is not simply a confessional monologue, Reynalda becomes a kind of kaleido-scope through which we view different aspects of the whole left cultural project of the 1960s and 1970s. And for this she relies on the conventions of the epic tradition. However, there are other sides to Reynalda, sides that complement but also sometimes undermine the epic bravura in its forms and in its grand historical thematic sweeps. The first word that Reynalda utters is 'mouth-watering' and from then on we enter a physical, bodily world of culinary and other pleasures. She says:

> Mouth-watering! They've got to be drooling for it like Pavlov's dogs . . . when I think of all the bodily functions the average B&B has to absorb—Appalling to think what might go on in my little bungalow . . . Mouth-watering will probably be the one to encourage . . . B&B may only be ten pounds, but 'Evening meal' at eight pounds 50—there's where I make serious money!

The question is: will it be tonight? I mean, will anyone stop? Come in?
Stay?³

It is this multifaceted aspect of Reynalda that makes her go beyond the
epic tradition in performance. Her physical, bodily side together with
her utopian tendency make her more than a clear-cut and direct
spokesperson for the cultural left of the 1960s and 1970s. The play
concludes with two imaginary conversations she has with two different sets
of guests. These are Judge and Frau Schenker and Vice President and Mrs
Offaly. The judge was involved in the Baader Meinhof trials and Joe
Offaly 'works for a firm that once owned all the bananas in Nicaragua,
what a lot of bananas, a lot of copper in Chile and millions of acres of
sugar-cane in Cuba!'. For obvious reasons these two couples become
emblematic of everything that Reynalda has been opposing all her life. The
startling twist at the end which gives this play a slightly fantastic edge is
that she is contemplating assassination. She ends with: 'Judge and Frau
Schenker, Vice President and Mrs Offaly I am your servant. I am your
assassin . . . ?'⁴

   How are we to read this final evocation of violence? Has she been taken
over by her fantasy? Is this a final gesture of desperation or is it a
legitimate reaction to her predicament and to the historical dimension it
carries? Since it comes at the end it carries a certain gravitas that then is
read back into the rest of the play. All the one-woman plays referred to
here carry moments such as these where the protagonist transgresses, has
flights of fancy or madness. Like Kay who feels the historical process with
its ruins and catastrophes running through her veins, all these characters
are 'plugged in to history'. This, however, does not only give them insight,
knowledge and hope, it also unsettles them, it shakes up their being,
physically and emotionally. It also comments on the aspirations that these
characters have about progress, hope and change. McGrath's unflinching
faith in human agency and its ability to change the world for the better is
clearly punctuated by these moments of negativity. These in turn are
always read against an equally stubborn faith in the 'principle of hope'.
Reynalda says:

   I went on a boat to Cyprus once, from Marseilles. As we rounded Sicily,
   there appeared a school of dolphins, playing with us, roving freely
   through the warm seas, frisking like kittens, having fun, moving as one
   . . . Then, just as suddenly, they went away. I spent the rest of the
   voyage standing at the rail, hoping to catch another glimpse.

   I feel like that now. Every night I read the newspapers, watch my telly,
   phone my friends—'just to keep in touch'. But I stand here now, at the

rail, at 52, watching for dolphins. I scan the sea, but it's polluted, empty.
But they are there. They will come.[5]

This almost Romantic hopeful aspiration is inflected by the last word of
the play which is 'assassin'. Throughout his working life McGrath has
been associated with Marxist or at least socialist aesthetics. He sees
cultural practices as sites of struggle and critique. However, it needs to be
stressed that he has always been attracted to the 'unorthodox' Marxists
like Benjamin, Bloch and most recently Cornelius Castoriades. All these
thinkers embrace the Enlightenment but also see its other side. This
Dialectic of the Enlightenment recognizes the great discourses of
emancipation and critique but also sees violence, oppression and empire as
part-and-parcel of the same project. They are not simply an aberration, a
lapse in judgment or an abuse of power, they are constituitive elements of
Enlightenment thinking. And it is this double process of evoking history as
a nightmare and as a site of hope and change that I would claim these
characters embody. McGrath writes in a recent lecture, one of the last he
was to give, on the limitations of our received tradition of democracy:

> First of all, a democracy needs *Borders*: a *demos* or community seeking to
> run itself on democratic lines draws a boundary, and almost all those
> within are citizens with rights and responsibilities. Those excluded are
> non-citizens. Exclusion however is both geographical, i.e. those outside
> the borders, and internal, i.e. certain people within.
>   . . . Who is included, who is excluded, is a site of contestation, now as
> it was in Ancient Greece.[6]

It is this landscape of democracy as a site of contestation that these
characters inhabit. This allows them at once to enact the principle of hope
while also evoking the horrors that form part of the same democratic
inheritance. Equally important for the purposes of a Marxist aesthetic is
McGrath's evocation of a 'social imaginary', as the phrase has been
interpreted by Castoriades. This grants culture and particularly theatre, in
all its collective and civic dimension, a privileged position in the construction of a historical consciousness. Castoriades writes, in a section also
quoted by McGrath:

> I hold that human history—therefore also the various forms of society
> we have known in history—is in its essence defined by imaginary
> creation . . .
>   Each society creates its own forms. These forms in turn bring into
> being a world in which this society sees itself and gives itself a place. It is
> by means of them that society constitutes a system of norms, institutions
> in the broadest sense of the term, values, orientations, and goals of

collective life as well as of individual life. At their core are to be found in each instance social imaginary significations, which also are created by each society and which are embodied in its institutions.[7]

It is this heightened position to the whole category of the 'imaginary' which can be interpreted as the 'creative', without necessarily resorting to the sublime, that McGrath finds attractive in the thought of Castoriades. Also the structural connection that his work makes between the individual and the collective is crucial for McGrath's notion of character. More-over, Castoriades' late work, which is an attempt to reconcile history, particularly in its Marxist renditions, and psychoanalysis, proves very useful for McGrath.[8] To quote from the same lecture, McGrath reinforces his faith in the main tenets of the project of the Enlightenment. He writes:

> I can't end there. Apart from being a ridiculous optimist, I embrace Ernest Bloch's Principle of Hope, and believe the dialectic of society can never be stopped or suppressed for too long . . .
> From all of this you may detect that I am brooding on a new play. I have always argued that a writer needs to reinvent the theatre every time he or she writes a play.[9]

The last play that McGrath wrote, and probably the one he was brooding over while reading Castoriades, was *HyperLynx*. Again it features a female protagonist through whom we get a sustained critique of globalization. Heather is a high-ranking civil servant who works for MI5. She has been asked to investigate the anti-globalization movements but somehow gets too involved and starts to see the point of the protesters. She has plans, or fantasies, to act as a type of double agent who will somehow blow the whistle on the multinationals. The events take place on 11 September 2001 and while she is taking us through her dilemma she learns of the attack on the World Trade Centre. Indeed the play was originally written as a reaction to the events of Genoa 2001 and a second act was added after the 11 September attacks. The play is ingenious and almost unique in linking the two, globalization and terrorism, in ways that most political analysts shy away from. Heather, like Kay, has unique insights into history. Again her experience of the violence of history is a physical and sensory one. She says:

> I see the office window through the eyes of a 30 year old Yemeni suicide pilot, seeing the black girl, flying closer, closer to concrete and steel. I see the ground rushing toward me as I leap from my window on the 98 floor. I see a thousand people hurrying down a stairwell, they stop, they look, they see a whole building collapsing on them, huge lumps of concrete and steel, dropping onto them. I see ten, twenty thousand

sights only the condemned will see, their final visions of the world, in
their last moments. What cameras can never see. I see what they see.
That is what death looks like . . .[10]

Her connection to the historical process is what makes Heather see
beyond her own restricted world; it allows her to see what 'the condemned
will see'. Like the experiences that run through the body of Kay, in *Plugged
in to History*, what we are shown is not a pretty sight. However, this is
balanced against intellectual rigour and the clarity of the analysis that
follows. The play ends on an unflinching note of optimism. After a survey
of US foreign policy and the links between globalization and terrorism,
Heather decides to return to her office. It is there that she thinks she can
offer most:

> The worst crime of all is not seeing, not trying to understand, of blinding
> yourself with your own lies.
>   America has done that since they shot the first Indian, took his land
> and called it civilisation. It is a land founded on genocide, and hypocrisy,
> still driven by it: perhaps this is where they really need help, with some
> clarity, honesty of thought, to put intellectual rigour above cosy self
> deception, by spelling out what is really happening to humanity.
>   I think I can go back to the office now.
>   To work.[11]

This stance underscores McGrath's fundamental belief in the power of
knowledge and education, both basic principles of enlightenment thinking.
The call 'To work', which ends the play, is McGrath's answer to the old
question, 'What is to be done?' However, we are not simply led to believe
that it is a clear-cut matter of education. The death and destruction that
we have witnessed earlier, through the same character, undermine the
straightforward call to more knowledge and enlightenment at the end.
Indeed, I would claim that the dual quality that these characters enact
might also pose a classic liberal dilemma; one that McGrath was fighting
against but also working within all his life.
    Kay, Reynalda, Heather and Meg (from *The Last of the MacEachans)* all
have flights of fancy. They all flirt with transgression and they all have this
physical/bodily relationship to history. This allows them to experience the
horrors of the historical process in an almost empathetic manner. At the
same time, they can step back, distance themselves from it and present us
with a critical analysis. Both strands of presentation, I would claim, exert
the same power on the character and the audience alike. And it is in this
respect that they could be read as enacting a liberal dilemma. There is, so
to speak, in McGrath's work an unflinching faith in the powers of
progress, education, compassion, equality and the desire to work with

what is available, within the great liberal institutions. Parallel to this is the insight that these very institutions may have created many of the horrors that the characters are asked to address. The creation of this type of character is a way that this issue is tackled in terms of narrative. It might also be a gesture towards all the complications involved in working within welfare capitalism and the contradictions and possibilities that such a project may entail. Indeed, McGrath's work, can be and is emblematic of the relationships between the so-called 'counter-culture' of the 1960s and 1970s and the overwhelming demise of welfare capitalism. And it is an arena of politics and culture about which he had a lot to say.

All these characters inhabit such dilemmas and contradictions and it is their multifaceted nature that makes them appealing and very 'actorly'. Indeed they allow the actor to take risks, to challenge the audience and to display the art of acting in all its dimensions. In writing these pieces with a specific performer in mind, McGrath allowed for the art of the performer to also interact with all the themes and forms displayed on stage. The role of the performer herself and the possibility of the 'political performer' is examined and experimented with. These one-woman plays in their combination of epic, psychological and stylized acting create a kind of language of performance that is at once distancing and emotive. The relationship to history that this mode of acting represents tends to be more complex than the direct 'resurrection' of historical figures for the purposes of the stage. Drew Milne[12] [has argued] that the evocation of 'real' historical figures in McGrath's later work (*Border Warfare* and *John Brown's Body*) flirts too closely with traditional, and somewhat conservative, farce. This, he argues, sets up a difficult relationship with the past and tends to turn characters into caricatures. What was once a historical tragedy turns into theatrical farce, to paraphrase Marx's words. The characters of these one-woman shows propose a notion of character that is markedly more complex and contradictory. Through the specific working relationship with the performer, the kinds of characters presented in these plays propose a critical relationship towards history, towards the art of acting itself and towards the audience.

The Last of the MacEachans was presented at the Theatre Workshop in Edinburgh during the Fringe in 1996, at the Citizens Theatre in April 1997 and then toured Ireland, France and Italy. It was performed almost simultaneously with McGrath's adaptation of David Lindsay's *Ane Satyre of the Thrie Estaitis, A Satire of the Four Estaites*. This play deserves a study in itself for its uses of satire and farce for the purposes of political critique. *A Satire* was performed at a huge, newly opened conference centre as part of the so-called 'official Festival', while *MacEachans* played in a small venue on the Fringe, underlining a dynamic that is always present in McGrath's work about high and low cultures and about the relationships between central, hegemonic cultures and peripheries. Indeed these are the themes that *The Last of the MacEachans* revisits. Through Meg, who is quite literally the last of the MacEachans, McGrath and MacLennan interrogate another long-standing concern of theirs, the notion of the 'organic community' as this has been termed by Antonio Gramsci, amongst others. In his quest for a language for popular theatre, outlined in his two major books *A Good Night Out* (1981) and *The Bone Won't Break* (1990), the relationships to popular culture, to concepts of nationhood and organic communities forms a central thematic and methodological category. However, this has always been an area of Marxist aesthetics that has aroused much controversy and debate. The notion that popular culture is almost always and almost inherently critical is a dubious one at best and has been contested by McGrath himself. The relationship to 'traditional', 'organic' and primarily 'local' cultures is another matter altogether as it is one that has fuelled many a 7:84 play. And Scotland, particularly during the years of Thatcherism, proved a very attractive site of the unfolding of all these issues. Again the relationship that McGrath's project proposes between local and international cultures,

9. Elizabeth McLennan as Meg MacEachen in *The Last of the MacEachans*.
Edinburgh Festival: Freeway Stage. 1966

between nationhood and straightforward nationalism deserves a study in its own right.

Meg MacEachan is a character who enacts some of the tensions that such a vexed relationship to tradition may entail. Through her relationship with her son, a fencer and occasional poacher, we see her sometimes hilarious, sometimes painful relationship to the North Highlands. The play opens with Meg watching *Braveheart* on video. As she talks us through the Hollywood version of Scottish history with the predictable stereotypes and clichés she is also introducing some of the main concerns of the play: cultural identity; multiculturalism; the sense of locality; globalization; the need for change and adaptability. The fact that she does so through the use of television is significant. Television for McGrath's generation is another cultural site of contestation. And it figures dominantly throughout all three plays. The ways television is alluded to no longer point to the high hopes and aspirations of the 1960s and 1970s. McGrath is part of a generation of writers for whom television presented a great challenge. It offered a way of using popular culture critically and it reached a mass audience. Indeed, it was hailed as the alternative national theatre, to use Raymond Williams's phrase. The writings of Raymond Williams and McGrath himself explore the formal possibilities and critical potential of this popular medium. McGrath writes in *A Good Night Out*:

> Television drama is a greatly under-explored area. Most of the attempts to grapple with it seem to me to have either misunderstood or ignored completely the nature of the communication taking place: but television drama, in this country at least, exists as a relatively powerful social force and as a challenge to every dramatic writer who is at all concerned with writing for a mass audience.[13]

Writing the above in the 1980s, McGrath already had accumulated nearly twenty years of television work. The hugely successful *Z-Cars*, which he wrote in collaboration with Troy Kennedy Martin, was an early indication of the impact that television could have on the alternative culture movement. The televising of *The Cheviot, the Stag and the Black, Black Oil* proved a high moment in the history of British television drama. John Caughie suggests that the televising of *The Cheviot* presented a model for resolving television's fraught relationship with theatre and for creating a form of television drama that underlined the progressive potential of the medium. It brought together a variety of forms like drama, historical reconstruction, documentary, reportage and theatrical performance. It is worth quoting extensively from Caughie's analysis:

For the development of the formal effectiveness of documentary drama, *The Cheviot* . . . represents a radical separation of the discourses of the documentary: the television production is at the same time a drama, a documentary on the way in which the theatrical performance circulated in the Highlands, a historical reconstruction, and a documentary on working conditions in the North Sea oil industry. The elements are not integrated to confirm and support each other, but are clearly separated out and allowed to play against each other . . . It is the possibility of this collision of documentary drama, of the refusal of integration, which makes the documentary drama a potentially political form.[14]

McGrath continued his relationship with television. He was on the Channel 4 board in the early 1990s. In 1992 he wrote and directed *The Long Roads* which was specially written for BBC 2. This was a 'state of the nation' film, tracing the effects of Thatcherism on people's daily lives. It is the story of a dying Scotswoman and her husband who set out on a journey from the North of Scotland to London to visit their children in various parts of the country. It has been compared to Ozu's *Tokyo Story*, and indeed it examines relationships between generations, between local and central cultures, using the format of the road movie (in this case with the help of British Rail).

It is a similar terrain that Meg MacEachan covers, only the references to television in this and the other one-woman plays are less celebratory and positive. The reference to *Braveheart* is not coincidental as it underlines how the whole idea of an 'organic culture' can be appropriated by Hollywood and the culture industry. The references to television in *Watching for Dolphins* are even more scathing and critical. The optimism about the emancipatory and critical potential of television folds over in this play into the narcissism of postmodernism. Reynalda is attacked by a Channel 4 crew who want to make a documentary about her life. Although formally the presence of C4 allows Reynalda to create new characters from her previous life, the framing that this provides in the end acts as a raid on her sense of self, as she is constantly made to repeat her 'failures' for the sake of the filming:

Oh dear me
  NO—
  CUT—Thank you very much . . .
  (*Own voice*) No, I can't get teaching work anywhere . . . Am I sorry? Only for our society, and for the children—
  What? Repeat? Oh for sound—OK No, I can't get teaching work anywhere . . . Again? Must I? No I can't get teaching work anywhere . . .[15]

Gone are the great aspirations that television presented in the 1960s and 1970s. Heather in *HyperLynx* says:

> When I watch television I feel I am vomited over: bellyful after bellyful of yesterday's images in half-second pieces; an endless rush of stale, foul-tasting verbiage from prurient, cynical, nasty celebrities. I feel drenched with gobbits of inane chatter from screaming, cackling, hopped-up youths. I feel I've been coated with a dog's dinner of old lies and new superficialities. I don't want to, I can't go home to my TV. I'd rather go home to stare into an alchies' lavatory pan.[16]

This is quite a damning portrayal of a medium that was once considered as potentially radical. I would claim that the same critical relationship is established towards 'organic and traditional' culture as this is filtered through the character of Meg MacEachan. The relationship she has with her son is a complex and sometimes contradictory one. It is very visceral; both warming and hurtful. Her son leaves the Highlands after a drunken night and ends up in Pictou, Canada. However, he is not presented in heroic terms. In going away he is also leaving a son behind. Meg hopes his mother will let her see him although she claims she wouldn't be surprised if she didn't. Like her relationship with the North Highlands and, I would claim, like McGrath's relationship with 'traditional and organic cultures' (particularly various traditions of Scottish culture), Jimmy, Meg's son, is both a source of wonder and redemption but also sadness and disappointment. She says towards the end of the play:

> Whenever one of the old folk pass on, we always say 'there aren't many left like her, or him'. And now it's a bitty more true than ever it was . . . and as the place changes, so the natives are hunted out, like the last of the Mohicans, driven out by the White Settlers . . . I don't say it with hate, nor a desire for the ethnic cleansing—though there's a few Gaelic Serbs over in the west: no I say it with sadness . . . that's all . . . Nor can I say my Jimmy was driven out by them. It might as easily be my doing . . . No, he's away to Nova Scotia the same way he went to the pub, or up the hill, or away to Inverness, the way his will pushed him, and—aye—nothing could hinder him.[17]

This is a very different analysis of immigration from that presented in *The Cheviot*, and the overall tone of the play, like that in *Watching for Dolphins*, reflects the sadness that Meg experiences. In general both these pieces have been read as elegiac; the first as a melancholy reflection of the failures of the 1960s and 1970s and the second as a contemplative reading of McGrath's commitment to 'organic communities'. These readings seem to dwell on only one aspect of these plays. Yes, they are more melancholy

10. Elizabeth MacLennan as Reynalda in *Watching For Dolphins*. Edinburgh
Festival and Tricycle Theatre: Freeway Stage. 1992

and self-critical but this need not be a negative trait. These pieces all
rely on the impact of the performer. Their self-reflective and somewhat
brooding side is counterbalanced or complemented by the presence and
impact of the performer herself. Also the pieces themselves could be read
in dialogue with each other as there is a marked intertextual relationship
both in terms of the character and the overall narrative.

Despite her sadness at witnessing a way of life die, Meg MacEachan is no lamenting character. She has no hesitation in leaving the North Highlands and starting a new life in Cape Breton. She fantasizes about her new life and still dreams of dying in Jimmy's arms. Her account of this sequence is very lyrical and has a slightly Strindbergian flavour to it.

> I'll make patchwork quilts through the long winter nights for Margaret to sell to the posh ethnic boutiques in Toronto, and I'll keep a weather eye open for a wealthy widower with a wee bum and a sense of humour to keep me entertained though I'll not marry him unless he plays the fiddle, and then I'll practice on my old accordion and we'll play Highland music for the tourists and the weddings and the Burns nights, and at one of the Hogmanays in the far distant future, Jimmy will roll in with a bottle of Famous Grouse and we'll dance till I drop, and I'll be ninety-two and I'll have gone far too far and I'll have a great big heart attack and I'll die in his arms.
>
> . . .
> And that'll be me.[18]

Again Meg's character surfaces as a highly poetic but stubborn and determined creation. Her commitment to a sense of locality and identity can be easily moved geographically. Indeed it moves from a sense of tradition that is rooted in time and place to a reading of culture as something that results from immigration and diaspora. She doesn't bat an eyelid at the appropriation of her local culture by the tourist trade. Indeed there are ways in which her 'escape' to Canada can be read as parallel to some of the 'white-settlers' retreats to the North Highlands. Just as Heather's final call 'to work' acts as a comment on the play that preceded it, Meg's final statement to the audience is all about change, adapting and hope. In a self-mocking and ironic gesture that quotes the criticism of McGrath's work that sees it as 'moralising' she ends with:

> They say there was a bird that lived on an island in the Indian Ocean, and it never learnt to do what every other bird has to do: it never learnt to fly . . . So it grew bigger and fleshier and its wings grew shorter and stumpier, and it laid its eggs on the ground, until one day some Dutch sailor found the island and hundreds of these dodos, that couldn't fly away, and one of them fed thirty men, and the Dutch sailors kept coming for more and more and more roast dodo, fried dodo, boiled dodo, kippered dodo, pickled dodo, dead dodo—until, in one hundred years there was not one dodo left on the island, and that had been the only place they were to be found, so there were no more dodoes left in the whole wide world: they were extinct.
> So the moral is: Learn to Fly.[19]

And, of course, birds migrate. The notion of identity and culture that is being examined here is one that relies on change, on shifts in populations, on conflict and adaptability. It is more a hybrid view than one that is grounded in geography or ethnicity.

Reynalda, Meg and Heather are all creations that have a strong inter-textual connection. Thematically they voice McGrath's lifelong concerns about issues of cultural politics, local and international identities, the workings of globalization and terrorism. Together with *Reading Rigoberta*, an adaptation of Rigoberta Menchu's biography that was performed in 1994, they form a group of plays that also explores McGrath's notion of dramatic character. This lifelong experiment was conducted with Elizabeth MacLennan, a performer who has helped to forge this particular aesthetic. In his quest for a theatrical language for political theatre these plays point towards ways in which dramatic character can evolve. Using modes which are neither directly Brechtian nor straight naturalism, these characters explore the relationships between the individual and history. They also, of course, explore the complex relationships between actor and playwright. McGrath was a prolific playwright, director, theatre theorist and political activist. These are aspects of his work that almost always figure in any analysis. Less attention has been paid to the ways all these ideas help to forge a specific aesthetic. These one-woman plays created with the collaboration of Elizabeth MacLennan are also experiments in the notion of the political performer. This dynamic relationship between performer and playwright has helped to create a very complex and sophisticated notion of 'dramatic character'; one that nods towards the epic tradition but also carries with it the legacy of McGrath's and MacLennan's own work.

PART FIVE

Working with John

CHAPTER THIRTEEN

Working with John

Susanna Capon

Material for this chapter was taken from the proceedings of 'Plugged in to History', a conference to celebrate John McGrath's work, held at Royal Holloway, London University on 19 and 20 April 2002. In one of the conference sessions, actors, designers and writers who had collaborated with John McGrath spoke about this experience. These contributions were followed up with further interviews after the conference. The interviews, which took place in London unless otherwise stated, were carried out as follows:

Pamela Howard (her contribution, made on tape since she was working overseas at the time, was later expanded into an article in New Theatre Quarterly*); Bill Paterson, 9 December 2002; Troy Kennedy Martin, 11 November 2002; Jack Gold, 19 November 2002; John Bett, 8 November 2002, Brighton; Jenny Tiramani, 17 December 2002; Elizabeth MacLennan, 20 January 2003.*

Pamela Howard

Pamela Howard is a scenographer, director, writer, educator, exhibition curator and international producer who has created theatre in many countries and many languages. She designed Border Warfare *and* John Brown's Body *at the Tramway, Glasgow, for John McGrath. We include part of her* New Theatre Quarterly *article.*

John McGrath described himself as a visual writer. He stated emphatically that he never wrote a scene until he could see it in his head. That might seem like a constriction for any designer working or even collaborating with him, but in fact it was a liberation. It was as if one did not have to work out the size of the canvas, but rather construct the compositions that had to fit within the frame. His vision for the shape of the scene was the concretization of the dialectic of the words. He saw his epic history play

11. Filming of *John Brown's Body*. Tramway Theatre: Freeway Films/Wildcat
Production for Channel Four.

Border Warfare, written in 1989, and charting 600 years of relations
between Scotland and England, as beginning in 'a primeval Scottish forest
with wild animals'. He imagined a procession of the ghosts of Scotland
winding their way through the forest—hooded monks pushing an old pram
in which the baby was a huge thistle. This kind of stage imagery is familiar
perhaps in the Polish or French theatre, but definitely not in the British
literary tradition. John's visual language was a combination of truthful
images and fantastic inventions, often combining painting and sculpture
with theatre crafts. His first scripts were written very much like film
scenarios, with breathtaking leaps of location, and crowded with real and
imagined characters who would have to be doubled and trebled by the
small group of actors that the company could afford.

In the early stages of planning *Border Warfare*, we were surveying the
space of the Tramway, Glasgow, just after Peter Brook's *Mahabharata* had
played there. It was a strange and eerie experience. Although the place had
received some renovations to get its public performance licence, it was still
more or less derelict. We wandered round this shadowy, empty, brick-
walled space, littered with the debris of the last audience, and forgotten
remnants from the departed company, as John reeled out scenes he
planned to write for this fast-moving epic play. In his head, he saw a series

of rolling stages, pushed by stage-hands, speedily moving the action from Scotland at one end of the space to England at the other. The space itself suggested scenes to him that he could write. The wooden rafters below the rickety leaking roof could become an ideal location for a short scene in which Oliver Cromwell appeared, so that, while the audience were all looking up at a small spotlit figure, a new larger scene could be prepared behind their backs at ground level. John was truly a site-specific writer, exploring all the possibilities a space has to offer and turning them to his own advantage.

Once he knew the shape of the scene, John felt free to create the plot and the dialogue. His discussions about design always started with a practical 'We need . . .' and never a wistful 'Wouldn't it be wonderful if . . .', so the iconography was born out of a necessity to facilitate the action of the scene. From these possibilities, he could then see how many characters he could use. John often visualized the political point he wanted to make in pictures, which had yet to find words, or he sometimes just made the point without words. No character he wrote was ever incidental, even if we sometimes thought they did not have enough words to merit a costume. One of the most graphic examples of his visual thinking was the Scottish Parliament scene in *Border Warfare* at the time of the final vote for or against the union of Scotland with England. He imagined 'a packed parliament with a huge door keeping the working people out. The people of Scotland are banging on the door and eventually break it down.' There were in fact only twelve available actors, but John, undaunted, imagined the 600 spectators would have to be the extra Members of Parliament, with the actors sitting among them. I started to think that the 'huge closed and barred door' would have to be offstage, but John wanted to write the scene showing both inside and outside the Parliament. At last I understood that, when visualizing John's words, the challenge was to take what he said literally and try to find a way of realizing it, however naïve and simple that might be. And so the populace of Edinburgh crept in at the back of a central corridor created by the seated audience, each actor holding in one hand a heavy grey plank, with heads of nails beaten into it and in the other hand an old iron cooking pot. They lined all the planks up together so they looked like a solid door, and began banging with the pans on the other side, punctuating the parliamentary speeches. When the moment came to break down the door, the actors just parted the planks and silently walked with them through the midst of the packed assembly, to place the planks at the foot of the Speaker's chair in the shape of the Scottish Saltire. John delighted in the total simplicity of the image, which put into action the scene he had imagined.

In the second of his large-scale works, *John Brown's Body*—the story of Scotland's industrial classes, created in 1990 for the Tramway in Glasgow and again produced by Wildcat Theatre—he imagined the action taking place on two-tiered seating. The aristocrats would be on an upper level with a landscape of trees and countryside and the working scenes—weaving factories, miners, fishermen and agricultural workers—would be confined to a darker, lower level. From time to time, as the workers celebrated a wedding or some other event through song, the aristos would try to peer perilously down from the upper edge, but could never really see what was going on. Walking round the Tramway at the beginning of our work on *John Brown's Body*, having just heard that yet another grant application had been turned down, John said despondently, 'Life is like a roller-coaster.' Suddenly that gave us both the idea of creating a two-tiered roller-coaster around the walls of the Tramway, with the audience standing in the middle. Later we put a small round stage in the centre of the space, which was also useful as a sitting place for tired spectators.

It never entered John's head that images he dreamed up could not be realized, because he had discovered that audiences readily accepted and enjoyed his non-naturalistic staging, and this gave him tremendous freedom. He was so happy to have a small scene with herring boats when I created a boat as a costume, worn by two people in yellow oilskins, their feet making the movement of the sea. A stage direction 'in the City of Glasgow' became a small placard showing a beautiful eighteenth-century engraving held aloft by a ragged weaver. John had seen in an old engraving the horrific conditions of the textile workers at the heavy looms and wanted to recreate that on the lower stage. The choreographer, Stuart Hopps, showed him how the actors could mime the mechanical machine movements, while making the clanking, repetitive sounds of the machines by hitting the iron pillars of the Tramway with metal spoons, and that there was no need for actual looms.

He loved to invent different ways for characters to arrive in a scene—by horse, by boat or, as in the case of Percy Gimlet in *John Brown's Body*, by helicopter, dropping from the skies to announce he is 'the composite British Tory' who has been 'sent by the Arts Council to tell the other side of the story'. All his images told powerful stories and were always in the present moment, even when they were historical. As the narrator in *John Brown's Body* says: these stories 'are not in the core curriculum, but they are what you need to know'. John had developed a highly sophisticated personal vision and always hoped he would be able to restage *Border Warfare* in the palace of Westminster, where he felt it truly belonged, but where he knew, with amusement, it would never be welcomed.

Bill Paterson

Bill Paterson's career as an actor spans theatre, television and film. His films include Hilary *and* Jackie *and* Truly, Madly, Deeply. *On television a formidable list of credits include* The Singing Detective, Traffik, Wives and Daughters *and* Doctor Zhivago.

Bill Paterson started his contribution to the conference by summing up what he felt was the most important way in which John McGrath worked collaboratively.

My last work with John in a collaborative way, rather than a personal way or a private way, was twenty-seven years ago. It actually started nearly thirty years ago at the time of *The Cheviot, the Stag and the Black, Black Oil.* The fact that it is still probably the most important collaboration in my life is a measure of its importance to me and to many of the actors and designers and collaborators that he had over the years. I was trying to think of the essence of it, apart from the personal impact of John, his charm and his charisma. I think it was, as Pamela Howard said so well, that he was a catalyst of ideas. The idea of a roller-coaster is a catalytic idea. It's quite difficult to put into practice, I'm sure, for a designer, but the notion would then be passed on. I know a lot of directors do that, but John would have done it, I think, with a very open mandate.

My first memory of 7:84 with *The Cheviot* was sitting in Dave MacLennan's[1] house where we had our first meeting. The subject of the set came up for a play, that, I think, we only had the title of, but certainly no words were written down at that point. There was a date, I think, for when it was going to be performed, but that was some terrible date four weeks in the future. Somebody said 'What will the set be?' And Liz[2] brought one of the kids', one of Danny's or Finn's, pop-up books, and said 'We've got this idea and this will pop up and we will have as many sets as we can in a book.' And we thought 'What a fantastic idea. But who is going to do it on the budget that they're probably talking about?' Well that person was found in the shape of John Byrne, a genius in many respects, not only painterly, but technically. That incredible book was achieved. That catalytic idea was there and it survives to this day. This incredible thing was so central to the success of that production because it transformed the humblest Highland hall into an event. It was visually an event and it was perfect to stick on the top of a Transit van when we moved. So that catalyst, I think, was John's, and I think too about the flexibility of that inspiration.

When we were doing *The Cheviot*, we collaborated and we contributed our ideas and John developed and worked on these and produced that script. There was going to be a character who was going to come round the Highlands in the present day part of it all, what was the present day then, the early 1970s. He was going to exploit the Highland tourist connection. John suggested basing him on a figure who had appeared in *The Ballygombeen Bequest*.[3] He was going to be a cockney wide boy. He was going to be played by me, because it was my turn to do something. That was the way it happened in that show. My cockney accent was dire and even worse then. So I said

> Well this character will be very central and very necessary, but does he have to be a cockney? Because if we're not careful, we will walk into the very area of nationalist chauvinism that we are trying to avoid in this piece, if we have a character, who, as soon as he opens his mouth, shows that he comes from outside. It may be more powerful if he was a Glaswegian or from Edinburgh or whatever. And, as I do a particularly good Glaswegian accent, I'm the man to do it!

And some people: some writers, some directors, would have said 'No, no. Oh no, not at all, because . . . I'll give you the reason and that's it. It'll stay as that.' John of course said 'What a fantastic idea. Just great. Let's get at it.' And we did it. And so was created a character, who, I think, has popped up several times, and was deeply useful at that particular juncture in the show theatrically and comedy-wise, but also very useful in the months that were to lie ahead, when we had to face quite a bit of barrage that we were treading down a nationalist chauvinist Scottish National Party sort of way. And those were the days in the early 1970s, when that was quite an issue. So John's ability to suggest, to then take back an idea, to reinvent it, to rethink it on the spur of the moment, was really, what I felt at every level of his life, seemed to be operating right up to the end. So that would be my abiding memory of the many that I have of John.

He was asked a question about the way John directed actors.
I think the Variety tradition is worth exploring in the Scottish context. I remember about twenty-five years ago, when Max Wall[4] was still with us, and began performing in straight theatre, there were a lot of excited reviews from London critics saying 'My God, this man is a wonderful actor.' But how can he not be a wonderful actor? It was Max Wall and his rhythms and his sense of his whole being were actorly and he was wonderful as a performer. This was never much looked on as a problem in Scotland, because we'd had a huge tradition of Variety turns who also did regular theatre. From Duncan Macrae[5] (I'm thinking of my generation), to Roddy Macmillan[6] and Stanley Baxter,[7] all of whom had a big regular legitimate career, playing Molière and Shakespeare and Brecht, and then would do two months of panto every year at the King's or at the Pavilion.

So this was a pretty traditional thing. And John was able to exploit that very much, because a bunch of us were more attuned to that, than maybe the more internal 'Stanislavsky' type of acting. In one scene that I did in *Little Red Hen* (1975), I had to play a character, the brother George. It was like a little soap opera that took place in the centre of this fairly out-front show with a lot of out-front material. I recall that John rehearsed that scene just as carefully and just as internally, as you would do if you were doing it as a play at the Cottesloe (Theatre). I remember being aware every night of trying to play it at that level. It wasn't jumping across the footlights and mugging it to the fourth row, it was 'let's play this man, a slightly shy and retired man in his own house, playing with his little toys'. So John had a very good sense, even within the 7:84 context of variety, of rehearsing quite carefully and internally.

He had a good eye too for spotting the phoney, there's no doubt about it. I'm thinking of these scenes quite strongly on that one. There was no question but that I would get a note if it didn't feel very real, or it wasn't very good, or it was a bit slow. The eye was definitely on it all the time.

After the Conference Bill Paterson gave an additional interview.

BP: We came as three of us. John Bett, Alex Norton and I were all members of the Theatre For Youth at the Citizens' Theatre in Glasgow. We probably did one hundred and fifty performances together before we did *The Welly Boot Show*, perhaps even more.

SC: *How did* The Welly Boot Show *come about?*

BP: *The Welly Boot Show* was a bizarre event. In 1971 they had this Clyde Fair International. It was a forerunner to the Mayfest,[8] which came later. It was an attempt to lift Glasgow out of its terrible doldrums of the early 1970s. It was legendary in its ineptitude. Shows would go on and you'd be lucky if three people came. They did a show called *The Great Northern Welly Boot Show*, which was based on the Upper Clyde Shipbuilders' (UCS) work-in, when Jimmy Reid[9] and the guys took over the UCS. It was a huge, probably the biggest, industrial event of the 1970s in Scotland. So Billy Connolly and Tom Buchan[10] had written a sort of parody of it. Instead of being set in the shipyard, it was set in a welly boot works, where Billy is a leading shop steward, the Jimmy Reid character, fighting for everybody's right to carry on making wellies, when they wanted to close the welly boot works down. John Byrne designed it. It was an amazing event. It opened in Glasgow. It was a chaotic production, but there was a kind of spirit in it. Billy, of course, was just beginning to be a very big name. A year later, Kenny Ireland[11] and a few people said 'We've got to do this again. We should do this at the Edinburgh Festival.' So out went the people who were not interested, who were just doing it as a job for three weeks; and we did it as a genuine cooperative, the bottom line of cooperatives. From Billy Connolly, right through to the programme sellers, everybody got paid the same money. We took over the Waverley Market in Edinburgh, which was lying empty, and it couldn't have been a better location. It was the smash hit of the 1972 Edinburgh Festival. It just knocked everybody sideways. You couldn't get tickets for love nor money, and it launched Billy really, in a way. John McGrath saw it and said 'We're setting up *The Cheviot* and we'll have some of these guys.'

SC: *Did doing that show make you decide to join forces with John?*

BP: Alex, John Bett and I had always thought of trying to keep together and maybe form a company.

SC: *John Bett tells this story of how you and Alex were invited into the company, but he was more or less put through the mill.*

BP: I think he might be right. John didn't come across as being the horny-handed son of toil. He was the classic bohemian actor laddie. He was a wonderful man. I mean I loved him and to this day I love him in every way, but I think to John and Liz he was a bit sort of . . . 'He's not terribly kind of working class', whereas Alex and I seemed to convince them in that way.

SC: *How heavily political was it?*

BP: There wasn't any *party* political thing. You didn't have to be a card-carrying member of any leftist party. In fact, it seemed to me, the less aligned you were to any group, the happier John and Liz would be. They certainly didn't want any people from what was then the Socialist Labour League, which then became the WRP.[12] I mean that was definitely out. I suppose we were what would nowadays be called 'old Labour'.

One of the guys in *The Cheviot*, who wasn't an actor, but he played Queen Victoria when she pops up, he was a roadie-cum-fixer, an unusual kind of guy. He was quite political and we had this one night on the road, when we had a terrible row over something or other. It was one of the inevitable things you would have in any company. It was the night of the long knives, where the whole kind of tour imploded. In the midst of this, I remember him saying 'It's nothing but a Fabian wank.' And that really hurt, you know, because I think there was a sort of Fabian quality about it. A sort of do-gooding, all purpose intention, because it wasn't aligned to any cutting edge political grouping. It was a general one and that was its strength. That's why it wasn't just a piece of propaganda for one thing. It was a Socialist perspective on a bit of history, in the case of *The Cheviot*. Sure, you were being given it in an agit-prop way, but it wasn't saying 'And the answer is the Communist party and it will be solved' or 'Join IMG'[13] or 'Why don't you buy the Newsline?'[14] What it was saying was 'These big things are happening to us and the control of it is out of our hands. So you'd better find the ways to pull back from that.' I never felt at any point any awkwardness about that politically.

SC: *It must have been quite a hard life out there on the road?*

BP: Put it this way. In early 1973 I don't think John had a queue of people wanting to do that first tour of *The Cheviot*! Touring *The Cheviot* was fine, but later on we started touring shows like *Little Red Hen*. We were actually carrying a band's gear instead of what we had on *The Cheviot*, which was Allan Ross's little amplifier, which he used to sit on, with his fiddle and an amp for the mikes, and one set of lights and that pop up hook and a hamper of costumes. You could get that in to a hall, and with half a dozen of us, we could do it in twenty minutes or half an hour.

But later on the shows got heavier and heavier. There were lighting rigs. We were doing it all with a crew of hardly any more than the performing company itself. I think it was wrong. I think we pushed that too far. We never had proper stage management numbers. It was exhausting to do a show and then do that. I remember Alex saying 'I'm the guitar player here. I've got weak wrists. I'm hauling boxes and pulling things round. If I injure my wrists, we've got no show.'

SC: *Obviously this arose because of the chronic underfunding, but were there also other motives?*

BP: Oh I think so, yes. I mean there was that feeling that we all should do it. And I think that in *The Cheviot* it was fine. *The Cheviot* was very compact. That was part of it. And then we would do the dance afterwards. Quite honestly, that was good fun.

SC: *That was part of it, right from the start?*

BP: Generally we would do the dances more towards the end of the week, because people just didn't fancy being out till one o'clock in the morning on a Monday or a Tuesday. Also, people would come to the next place, if it was only forty or fifty miles away, to the dance. They might have seen the show and then we'd say, 'Well come to the dance at Dornie on Friday.'

SC: *It must have been an extraordinary experience, playing to an entirely new audience?*

BP: It was great and nobody had ever seen anything like this. Even sophisticated theatrical type audiences in Edinburgh and Glasgow hadn't seen shows that were specifically about events happening around them, but it was completely unknown in the Western Isles and the little Highland villages. I think we did two tours of *The Cheviot* and we could have probably done years of them. But, by the time we'd done *The Game's a Bogey* and gone

12a. Bill Paterson and John Bett as Mungo and Lavinia McBungle in *The Games's A Bogey*. 7:84 tour. 1972
(Photo: Barry Jones)

12b. Bill Paterson as John MacLean in *The Game's A Bogey*. 7:84 tour. 1972
(Photo: Barry Jones)

on to other shows, we were becoming like a band on tour with a bit of acting at the front of it. And it was not long after that that the company split into 7:84 and Wildcat,[15] because they concentrated on music theatre.

SC: *Was it difficult leaving?*

BP: No, because I never thought of it as *leaving*. I did *The Cheviot* and then I did *The Game's a Bogey*. These were back to back. I didn't do the next Highland show. But there was always the feeling that you'd do another show; and I did *Little Red Hen* in 1975 and then that was it.

SC: *Sometimes, in reading John's books, you get the impression that people were either with him or not. It was quite polarized.*

BP: I never felt that. John was very good with me. I was on the board of 7:84 for a while. What I found difficult with it, because it just didn't suit me, is that the whole thing needed a lot of fundraising. There was a lot of ducking and diving about, applying for this and doing that. That's what you *had* to do. The Arts Council weren't going to come up with enough. I found that completely wearing, you know, to have to sit there, and you'd have to balance this against that. And in my kind of puritanical way, I would say 'Well can we not . . . ?' We were doing a one-woman show at one point and there was all this trouble. Who's going to fund it and who's going to . . . ? Well we just did *The Welly Boot Show* for nothing. We did *Writer's Cramp*, John Byrne's first play. Just four of us rented the hall and launched it, for nothing. So I kept thinking 'Why has there always got to be battles with funding?' I know the scale of a big tour, of course, is different. But it always seemed to me that they slightly relished these battles, but I never did.

SC: *Didn't John believe though that the state should support the arts?*

BP: Absolutely and quite rightly. John was right. They're handing out money to the ballet companies and the opera companies and what would have been thought of as the 'bourgeois' end of the theatre market, and we're having to fight for everything to go round the Highland halls. But he had a real appetite for these tussles that I would never have been able to emulate.

SC: *At the time of* The Cheviot, *was it seen as odd that this had been done by someone who was not Scottish?*

BP: It never ever arose with John McGrath. Usually Scots are pretty hard about people coming in and doing things. It never even raised its head with John. I never even thought about it. That John was an interloper, coming to use something or to exploit some kind of loophole that had appeared, some money to spend? No, I think nobody felt that for a second about John. Also of course, with Liz, her background being in Glasgow and Rogart in Sutherland. There was never ever a sense of John being an incomer at all. I think the Irish Liverpool background was part of that picture. That was a great help.

SC: *How collective was the work?*

BP: The shape of *The Cheviot* was completely John's. I mean the form of it, where the scenes would be. But within that there was an awful lot of collaboration. He took it and shaped it and none

of us would have done any of it, had it not been for John. For me
the important thing is that the biggest part of the foundation of
whatever career I've had as an actor, was built on the grounds of
what John McGrath did with 7:84. I owe him so much.

Troy Kennedy Martin

Troy Kennedy Martin, film and television screenwriter, created Z-Cars *and
went on to write for* The Sweeney *as well as the award winning* Edge of
Darkness *and* Reilly Ace of Spies. *His work in film includes* The Italian Job,
Kelly's Heroes, Hostile Waters *and* Red Heat.

*Troy Kennedy Martin spoke at the conference about his collaboration with
John McGrath on* Z-Cars *and* Diary of A Young Man.

We met very early on. The first thing we were involved with was *Z-Cars*.[16]
I must confess I think I was slightly surprised, not knowing much about his
theatre work, that Elwyn Jones[17] had chosen him to construct this huge
series. But of course he brought a huge amount of experience to it.

He had this little black book, which I always slightly laughed at, in which
went various technicians, camera people, sound people, actors that he
knew. And now here was *Z-Cars* and the black book was suddenly
extremely important. Apart from his relationship with me and the scripts,
he put together an absolutely cast-iron cast, mainly out of the Royal Court,
which was to last ten years. I mean it really was a Clyde-built ship, in
terms of the casting of it, and that was incredibly important. And he cast
them because they were good actors, not simply because their faces looked
right.

He also brought a kind of authority, which was incredibly good, particularly when dealing with the BBC controllers and people in charge who
scrutinized the scripts. His technique with scripts was remarkable. I'd
already been working at the BBC for two or three years and I always
remember that what would happen with directors was that we'd get to
page seven, then we'd have a huge row and the script was never read right
through, at least by me and the director, after that. But John was very
good. He'd start with line one, then go to line two and so on. I remember
the Head of Documentaries, *Z-Cars* fell under a documentary aegis at the
time, had a lot of notes, because, amongst other things, he really resented
any idea of character being given to anyone who was wearing a hat. A
policeman's hat *was* something and you couldn't demean the police as long
as that hat was on his head. In *Z-Cars* there were lots of personal events
going on. There was the usual sort of knockabout stuff of drama and the
wives didn't have their hair permed and one of them got punched by her
husband. Well that sort of stuff had really never been seen, in the

documentary department at any rate, where people with police hats or lifeboatman's hats were being shown. So John had this kind of very quiet way of diffusing the old objections that were coming, and sort of tiring them, so that by page seven *they'd* be tired and not me. So, with very few exceptions, we didn't have any problem with the people on the fifth floor. Also BBC2 was coming on stream and *Z-Cars* kind of slipped through the net.

The other thing I remember was that he informed the piece with a kind of political structure. I'd really hewn out the stories and I guess it was the shock of going to the North for the first time. In hotels, the colour of the curtains, the carpet, the shades on the lamps, the duvet and everything else which completely clashed with everything else. There were people outside drinking till three in the morning and then driving their Jaguars away. The police never seemed to wake up before ten at night and insisted on touring you round clubs that had closed. The shock of all that had given the scripts quite an edge. But what he did was two things: 1) he was from Liverpool or from nearby and so he knew that whole area and was comfortable with it; 2) he was able to sort of inform it with this political side.

We did an interview, I think several months after *Z-Cars* started, which really was our honest approach as to what we'd put into it and what we were doing, which was received at the BBC with complete shock. I mean they thought suddenly, 'here are these two left wing agitators who've got control of this series'.

Apart from the politics, which, as I said, he sort of created, without in any way laying down any laws about it or having to persuade me in any way, it was just that somehow, things would veer his way. I would suggest scenes or rewrite scenes, not because he said 'this is what it's like' but simply because he would enthuse about some part of the scene which I had perhaps neglected to develop. He had this great sense of humour, not so much sense of humour, but a real thriving on humour. This, despite the fact that he had the huge responsibilities of trying to put all these things together. These were live shows, often with twenty or thirty sets with unbelievable things happening on the set during the day. I mean there was a fight in the bar on one of the Wednesday nights and there was a huge fight in the studio. So that sort of thing had to be controlled. He never turned down a scene because it was going to be too difficult, but mainly he loved the humour. So there was a whole feeling of underlying humour running through those early *Z-Cars* scripts which the series pretty quickly lost. I think another thing about the humour is that, particularly mordant humour or graveyard humour or policeman's humour, really adds a sense of realism to what's going on. So the darker the scene, the funnier the remarks, the more realistic it appears. So he was really good at pushing that particular aspect of *Z-Cars*.

13a. John McGrath on location in North Wales directing episode 6 of *Z-Cars*,
which was written by him. 1962

The other thing is that we worked very hard on it. One night about two
in the morning, we went out. We were both living in Earl's Court, both
living out of each other's pockets, both with girlfriends and we were
both going to get married pretty soon. We'd both been in the army. We
felt competent about doing what we were doing. We got arrested one night
about two in the morning, because it was just that awful thing of not
wanting to go back and finish this bloody script, which was meant to be in
rehearsal at nine. So we were loitering, but *not* with intent, and we got
picked up for loitering *with* intent and the police lied their heads off in
order to say that we were really trying to steal cars. But we got off. Then I
wrote a really fishy script, which John egged me on to do, about the
Metropolitan Police. We had a metropolitan policeman come up to
Lancashire who is as bent as a corkscrew and we got it to the first read
through stage, cast and everything. Elwyn Jones hadn't read it and he was
the supremo at the time. He came down, he went apeshit and cancelled the
whole production and put another script in its place. So occasionally we
did go over the edge, as far as the BBC was concerned. But it was a sort of
almost seamless kind of cooperation. We never really disagreed about
anything.

13b. Frank Windsor and Brian Blessed being directed by John McGrath in
Z-Cars episode 6. 1962

When it came to *Diary of A Young Man* (1964) which was a different
sort of kettle of fish really, we were both probably wrongly involved in
trying to create some theory in our different ways for television drama. We
were really just kind of recreating film practice. We didn't know that much
about film, we were on about things that film people had known about for
hundreds of years and we were putting this down as a new kind of theory.
So *Diary of A Young Man* was an attempt to sort of put these ideas into
practice. But it opens with a poem which goes 'When I was only 24 . . .' I
wrote that piece, but it could well have been John. So we were really in
each other's heads in a kind of way. And *Diary of A Young Man* was an
example of that.

*In an interview after the conference Troy Kennedy Martin was asked to talk
further about the theory that lay behind* Diary of A Young Man.

    TKM: Well what happened is that I had these ideas, which were
             essentially a bit like Brecht's alienation. I felt at the time that the
             camera definition, the focus, was not very strong in television. So
             when you got into a close-up, which people tended to do,

14. Troy Kennedy Martin, John McGrath and Elizabeth MacLennan outside the court after the case was dismissed. 1962
(Photo: Mirror Pic)

because they were imitating the sort of 1940s, 1950s black-and-white close-ups you get in cinema, you got that square picture, which you use in times of emotion. You know, when someone is saying goodbye or it's love or something like that, you get that picture. But on television, it doesn't have the same effect. All you see is the pimple on the nose. So the way to create emotion on television was to do exactly the opposite. It had this alienating effect, because you had to do what I decided to do—you cut between the two. It's the cut between the two pictures that gives you emotion. For example the marathon. Usually they just cut to the winners. But for some reason once they lost them in a fog, so you had these hundreds of people all desperately trying to get to twenty miles and meeting the wall. They just read out a list of the competitors, how many priests or nurses or doctors or teachers there were. They had some music in the background which was really good. You suddenly got overwhelmed by this feeling of humanity and it was so moving that I had to brush away tears, because you could see them desperately trying to run the race. This very cold mechanical list actually turned it into something much more emotional than it was if you were just looking at it ordinarily. So that was the basis,

one of the bases of the kind of theory that I had which is in 'Nats
Go Home'.[18]

SC: *And John shared these theories?*

TKM: John agreed with them and then later he politicized it. Because
then that took me to the whole business about what's important
in television. It should not be dialogue, it should be the actual
visual things. It's the visual element that actually makes it. This
therefore led me to believe that the writer wasn't really the most
important element in it. And when this thing came out, I was in
America. They held this meeting at the Writers' Guild in order
to lynch me and to say 'How dare I undermine the cause of
writing in this country, giving it all to the directors?' So then
what John did was to say that the reason why people won't move
forward on this one is because they want to maintain the word as
being the dominant means of constructing meaning in television,
because that could be actually censored. So he took the political
view. I was saying dialogue and all the rest of it should be
subordinate to that. He was saying they want to keep the
dialogue because that is where they can censor it. Once you get
into moving pictures and all the rest of it, the director then
becomes more important and you can't really nobble the director
in the same way as you can nobble the word on the page. So the
whole business of people reading scripts and blue-pencilling
them, that was where they saw the control being. So that was
very good and that was a major part of his first Edinburgh
Lecture.[19] So we did agree, but I'm not really sure that he did
take the alienation thing in, because alienation in theatre and
alienation in television were two different things. So his theatre
stuff always had alienation in it, because that agit-prop thing, the
Brecht thing is: 'We don't want them to enjoy this as some sort
of romance or a fiction, we've got to sort keep breaking them
back, saying this is reality.' So John had that element of
alienation in his writing, but once you try and impose that on
television, you've got two kinds of alienation then. You've got
the alienation of the theatre and you've got the alienation of the
box. And I think they collided in *The Cheviot*, where you're
trying to show a theatrical alienation in a medium which already
had alienation. So we didn't really ever have discussions about it.
He'd say 'That's great' or 'That's grand'. And I'd say 'Yeah' or 'I
agree'. And I would say the same thing to him.

*At the conference, Troy Kennedy Martin was asked why John and he stopped
working on* Z-Cars *as soon as they did and whether it was a mutual decision.*

TKM: Well I resigned and I think John had still got some work to
do directing some of the episodes. Things got very difficult,

particularly after the episode when the metropolitan policeman came up from the smoke. And things were changing. There had been a lot of pressure put on the programme to conform. While we know that the BBC top brass had said that everything was hunky dory, in fact the sort of things that we'd been told by the police in Lancashire were 'Don't have all the villains caught, because we don't catch any of them really. Make sure that the swearing is proper swearing and not this sort of fancy sort of stuff.' We kind of wanted a lot more realism and what the Chief Constable wanted and what the BBC agreed to in the end, was to tone it down. And they did that with me by just asking for more and more rewrites and there comes a point where you just can't do any more. They don't actually say 'Look, I think you ought to resign' or 'Perhaps you'd find some work, that's the way it is.' So I realized I had to stop and got out. I think John still had a couple of months work to do and then I think he went off to do other things too. The other thing was that both of us were more interested at this point in *Diary Of A Young Man*, which we were trying to put together, rather than *Z-Cars*. We did see *Z-Cars*, although it had these opportunities, as a kind of naturalistic series and just more of what was happening. What was interesting about it was that it had this new Northern dimension, people using Lancashire accents in mainstream drama. That caused quite a fuss but we weren't really affected by the publicity that was going on around it. We were much more interested in some kind of experiment, than staying on this bandwagon.

Jack Gold

Jack Gold's distinguished career as a director spans both films and television. In television his work has included the award winning The Naked Civil Servant *and* Catholics. *His films include* Man Friday, Sakharov *and* The Bofors Gun. *He spoke about John's work for the cinema.*

I made three short stories for the Arts Department of the BBC and as a result of that Tony Garnett offered me a film. This was in 1963/1964. I did *The Lump*, Jim Allen's first full-length drama. It was seen by Otto Plaschkes, who produced *Georgie Girl* and was looking for new projects. I'd met him and he sent me a book which I didn't particularly want to do, because I knew that your first feature is an important step. If you screw that up, you are in danger of blowing your future career. Then he offered me *Bofors Gun* which I thought terrific. Now I'd seen John, around the bar probably, at the BBC. We were never close friends or anything like that, it was more a nodding acquaintance and the odd chat.

John wrote many screenplays during his career, most notably, perhaps,

Man's Fate for Fred Zinnemann and *Voss* for Ken Russell, which, unfortunately were never made. And *The Billion Dollar Brain* which *was* made, directed by Ken Russell, with Michael Caine. These scripts were adaptations of others' work, but *The Bofors Gun*, which I directed in 1968, was all his own, based on his own stage play, which Ron Eyre[20] had directed at the Hampstead Theatre. Universal, which is a major Hollywood studio, had a very enterprising branch in London, which, in the 1960s, took enormous chances on the projects they made. They made films with Truffaut, Peter Watkins, Karel Reisz, and they took a chance on this unlikely project about a group of soldiers at night in a hut in Germany in winter. The actors were for the most part unknown in commercial film terms and they were talking to each other non-stop. There was no sex and no action. Anyway, they made it.

In an interview after the conference, Jack continued his discussion about the cinema.

SC: *How much did you collaborate with John?*

JG: On the script? Oh virtually nothing, as far as I remember. I was also, as a novice director, not really aware, it may sound dumb, that one could interfere with the script too much. That was the writer's job. You either liked it or you could perhaps say 'Would it be a good idea if maybe . . . ?' My attitude was probably different than if I'd come from the theatre, say, where the collaboration of director and writer is quite deep and strong during the development of the play. I had no experience of that. I had experience of working with reporters, suggesting how we might shoot something in relation to what they were going to say etc. etc. I could visualize the script, but I didn't really have any deeper understanding of shaping a script, or saying 'This bit's missing' or 'We need more of that'.

SC: *What about the casting? It was pretty spectacular.*

JG: I think John had suggested Nicol Williamson, who was hot after *Inadmissible Evidence* at that point. John had written the play originally apparently for him, but he couldn't do it on the stage at Hampstead Theatre Club. I think David Warner too was a given. Several of the cast we took straight from the stage play: Barry Jackson and Donald Gee. And then we cast the others. There wasn't a casting director. Otto knew casting directors and agents, so people were wheeled in for me to meet, or we'd discuss people I knew. But I was again very innocent in the whole casting world, but I knew enough about who I liked and had seen in the theatre. We were extremely lucky in getting this cast. David Warner was the well-known actor amongst them, because he'd done *Morgan*,[21] Nicol was a well-known stage actor with a terrifying reputation. People said 'Who's in it?' And I said 'Nicol Williamson' and they looked at me and made the sign of the cross over me. Ian Holm, I'd seen in the theatre at the RSC. And the others were sort of unknown. It was a very cheap film. It cost about £400,000. Nicol played O'Rourke, who challenges bourgeois values and in particular the desperate desire of Private Evans, played by David Warner, to gain promotion. In order to get that, this particular night of guard duty must be as peaceful as possible for Evans. It is, however, the eve of O'Rourke's thirtieth birthday and he is equally as desperate as Evans; in his case for some basic human understanding, having already attempted suicide once before. John deploys a wonderful group of characters in the film, individual of speech and of behaviour. The setting is claustrophobic, there are long developing scenes, presumably reflecting the stage play that it came from, and the span of time ticks away like an unexploded bomb.

SC: *In some ways, at that time, John was known more for his directing than writing. Was that difficult?*

JG: No, not in any sense whatsoever. He came along, we had two weeks' rehearsal, and he made the odd suggestion. I think he suggested John Thaw for instance, who was actually sharing a flat with Nicol at that time. We rehearsed in a drill hall in the back of St John's Wood somewhere. Part of the time was spent in learning army discipline and movements and platoons and how to stand to attention and a lot of drilling was going on. The film had a very short schedule, it was a very cheap film. So I had to plan everything, virtually every set up throughout the film, before we got to rehearsal, it's the way I worked. John was certainly at the read-through and he may have popped in after that, but I don't remember any interference from him at all. I don't remember him looking over my shoulder and I was really grateful. John was out on a limb. The producer buys the property and John was writing the screenplay and then they plucked me out of the air, although John must have seen some of the work I'd done at the BBC.

SC: *How was the film received?*

JG: It had the most amazing reviews. 'Milestone in British cinema' and so on. 'Scorching performances.' Wonderful reviews. But it had a lot of resistance from the Rank Organization. Apparently, I don't know how true it is, there was a lot of resentment about the scene where one of the soldiers is accused of 'having a crafty J. Arthur'. I think they ended up by cutting it or fading it out or changing it in some way. It was put back in a later version. But I can't imagine it was top of the bill for John Davis, who was running Rank. So it opened at the St Martin's Lane Odeon, which had only just opened, so nobody knew where the cinema was and it got no distribution at all, a few little art houses dotted round the country. Wonderful reviews, particularly for Nicol, who is, I think, devastating. When I look at it now I think everyone was terrific.

SC: *How did it lead on to* The Reckoning? *Was it soon after?*

JG: Very close, a year later. John had been writing *The Reckoning*, an adaptation of a novel *The Harp that Once*[22] for an American producer called Ronnie Schedlo for Columbia and they had a director, a very well known English director called J. Lee Thompson. He dropped out. I think he went off to do *Guns of Navarone*. There was more money and this was an altogether plusher project with better-known actors. Nicol had already been cast. It had sex and action and a flash of violence. There are, however, common elements to both films. John brought to them a critical intelligence and a ruthless pursuit of truth and honesty. He had a profound understanding of people, a great ear: for dialogue, from the scatological to the poetic; for humour; for music and for song. In both the films there's a protagonist. The word hero gives a wrong impression, unless it's, as someone said at the time, a hero of our time. Nicol Williamson played both these parts in both films. In both he is working class, Irish, Catholic, passionate, articulate, challenging to the point of destruction, both of himself and of others.

SC: *What stage was the film at, when you were asked to get involved?*

JG: I don't think the script was in its final draft, because John had a lot of voice-over in the script. And they had no director and I'd just had this success with *Bofors* and Nicol and John. Maybe it was John that suggested me, I don't know. Anyway, they asked me if I would take over the film? Sure. A second feature so soon after the first one and an interesting subject and Nicol and a much bigger budget etc. etc. So I did, and Columbia made John take out all the voice-overs. They said voice-over doesn't work. That was the myth at the time. So John said 'Mmm', because he liked voice-over. He did it in *Diary of A Young Man*. He was a great fan of it and why not?

SC: *It's a non-naturalistic device.*

JG: Absolutely. It's Brechtian. It's also a short way of giving you information and it drives things on. Anyway, they made him take it all out. And so we ended up with a script. Again, I can't remember whether I made any real contribution to it, though thinking back (it would be interesting to see if it was in the drafts of the script) the various little montages in the film might have been my idea. There's one when he goes to Liverpool and walks round Liverpool, with the singing voice of the father over it. There's another when he walks round his house in Surrey, a montage of all the things he hates about that bourgeois life: little kids in crocodiles and uniforms, the pheasants hanging in the window and women playing golf.

SC: *Maybe, in some ways, they were replacements for the voice-overs?*

JG: Could be. I think I was very conscious at the time of montage, coming from the cutting rooms. I used to do it a lot in documentaries. I used to love putting in little musical montages to sum up the heart of a film or at the end of a film. You know, flashy cutting and the right sort of counterpointing music etc. etc. I enjoyed all that and I suspect, although I couldn't swear to it, that those were my interpolations.

SC: *Was it a happy experience making the film?*

JG: Oh yes. It was a very good cast. It was a more upmarket cast in 'commercial' terms. There were known people like Rachel Roberts and Paul Rogers. It was an older cast, so there were names, solid British names. And Rachel was a sort of star at the time, I think. An Oscar-winning cameraman Geoff Unsworth, a wonderful cameraman and operator. A terrific crew and a longer schedule and everything.

SC: *How was the film received?*

JG: Not so well. Nicol again got good reviews.

SC: *Why do you think it wasn't well received?*

JG: I ran it at Moonstone[23] last year and I could see all sorts of defective directing moments. For some unknown reason I was using the zoom a lot. Someone at Moonstone said 'Had they given you a zoom for your birthday and were you determined to use it?' I sort of cringe when I look at it but it did drive on. It was quite interesting in the sense that here was a man who has fought his way out of the tribal working class of Catholic Liverpool to become part of a different tribe, the rich middle-class English business class. Here in the South, he's a success. He has a posh marriage; he's climbed ruthlessly up the corporate ladder. He's cunning, violent, atavistic. When he hears of his father's death in Liverpool, he returns and is expected to take personal revenge. His behaviour in Liverpool and London becomes totally enmeshed. He protests both sets of values, but also adheres to both. And gets away with it both ends. This is the interesting thing. There is no retribution in this film. Fate doesn't step in to punish Marler. He succeeds and John said, recently, that this film anticipated Thatcherism by ten years.

SC: *In a sense then, the film is immoral?*

JG: I don't know whether that had an effect. I honestly don't know why it didn't take off. It came out about the same time, I think, as *Get Carter*,[24] which was a better received film and a more popular film. Michael Caine was a star compared with Nicol and it was a gangster film, so, again, it's more accessible. I actually think Nicol, although he's a stunning actor, doesn't woo the audience, if you compare him to Mike Caine, who's sexier, and, maybe, that's the answer. Maybe Nicol isn't sexy in the general sense. Women don't necessarily find him sexy. I may be wrong, but I don't think they do compared to more obvious people like Albert Finney and Caine. Nicol would be totally uncompromising. He wouldn't seduce an audience. If anything he'd work against it. There wouldn't be any tricks with Nicol, no little charming moments. So it may have had something to do with why the film didn't take off. John was happy with the film. What he wanted was on the screen. I may not have been as pure with the filmmaking as maybe he'd have liked, or maybe even now, I'd have liked, if I'd had more control over myself. But it does drive along and did have a very good sense of story and pace and character. I mean he had all those strengths, John, but he was uncompromising with an audience too. I don't think he'd try and seduce an audience. He'd be 'This is what it is. This is how it is and we are not going to go pussyfooting round here. This is raw.' Maybe too there is a little tendency to caricature or stereotype, which I possibly reinforced in his look at the bourgeois class. But somehow, maybe it was me too. I was more sympathetic to the Liverpool end than to the Surrey end. So maybe we reinforced our attitudes too much, too unrealistically. I don't know. It didn't take off commercially. It didn't do badly but it didn't woof up into the stratosphere.

SC: *At the end of his life, he came back to the film industry, but perhaps at that time, there was a bit of 'If you dine with the devil, take a long spoon'.*

JG: Yes and knowing that he had politically more important work to do for which one can only admire him. I mean he could have taken the money and turned out scripts, because he was good, he could do a film script along with the best of them. And you can always get money developing scripts, you don't have to have them made. So he could have made a good living, I'd have thought. But he did want to experiment and he did want to propagate his political ideas and he did like theatre being able to do that without any of the crap that goes on in putting a film together.

John Bett

Actor John Bett is a founder member of 7:84 Scotland and has since enjoyed an international career in theatre, films and television. He also writes and directs. He had a creative relationship with John McGrath for nearly thirty years and considered him both a mentor and friend.

At the conference John Bett talked about John McGrath's approach to Scottish acting, the importance of music in his work and the way he tackled challenges.

I want to say something about John McGrath's approach to acting and most of these remarks will be about Scottish acting, because that was the context in which I worked with John—most of the time. So this is a personal statement about Scottish acting and, like all generalizations, contains some truth and some chaff. I think that Scottish acting is different from English acting in that it is kind of bold and big and honest. I think that English acting tends to be a little more restrained and refined. I'm not quite sure why Scottish acting is like that. It may be something to do with the Celtic spirit or it may be to do with a long history of Variety in Scotland. But I think that it is a general truism: that Scottish acting has this performance 'out' aspect to it. And John was thrilled with that. He loved that and he encouraged his actors to be brave and to be bold and to be big and command the arena, to get out there and fight the lions. That's one aspect.

I think too, that if there is a fault in Scottish acting (and I am sure it has many shortcomings), then that fault would be a tendency to give gravitas and meaning to everything, to 'milk the moment', as it were. And John couldn't be doing with that. He wanted everything to go with speed and alacrity. Instead of the actors sitting on the text and indulging themselves in the proclaiming of it, he wanted the actors to have confidence in the text, to trust it, to believe that in the simple act of speaking it, the rhythms of the text would come out and the music of the text would carry the piece.

And one can't talk about John without talking about the songs in his work. Music was a very important element in all the plays with which I was involved with John. I think too that music influenced his writing and his way of writing. I think he thought of his writing in terms of a piece of music with a kind of main melody with comic counterpoints and a lot of adagio, allegro, a bucket full of con brio and after a few cadenzas we'd generally come to a triumphant conclusion. I think that music was very important to him.

The other thing I'd like to say about working with John was that the challenges he gave his actors he took on himself as a writer, and he was always looking for new ways to say things. When we did *The Silver Darlings*[25] at the Citizens' Theatre, the tour was booked and the actors were booked and we still hadn't found a way of staging the play, because two thirds of the action takes place in a rowing boat at sea and we didn't know how we were going to realize this. John was convinced that a way would be found and indeed a way was found, largely through the genius of our designer Wendy Shea, who constructed a boat that had wheels. You couldn't see the wheels and the actors moved the boat with their feet. I used to kid people along that there were magnets underneath the stage. But that was John. He refused to accept that a way would not be found. John always set these challenges for himself.

The conference was followed later by an interview with John Bett.

SC: *How did you meet John?*

JB: John had come up to Scotland and wanted to set up a Scottish company and looked around and saw *The Great Northern Welly Boot Show* and saw us in it and through that made contact with us. And that's how I got involved, although I did have to submit to an interview, a grilling at David MacLennan's house with Dave and Liz and John.

SC: *Was it a collective decision then?*

JB: Yes. I think Alex and Billy (Paterson) met them in a pub. They got in, they were all right. I don't know. I was kind of . . .

SC: *Was it a class thing?*

JB: I don't know whether it was that. It might have been that. Because of my accent—sounding posh. In fact my mother is from the Isle of Skye, so I spent a lot of my childhood there. As a result of that, living on a croft with relatives who kept sheep and worked the land, I knew about the Highlands. At Dundee I had written and performed in a play called *The Cruel Wind*, which was about the Highland clearances. So our first meeting quickly established we were on the same wavelength. In fact I was a wee bit suspicious, you know, and kind of standing up for my Highland ancestors, about this man from Liverpool coming up to write about them.

The first show was *The Cheviot.* There was a magazine just started—*Scottish International* it was called—which dealt with Scottish affairs and they were going to have a conference— 'What Kind of Scotland?' All these things were springing up just then. I mean Bill Bryden[26] had had his season at the Lyceum where there had been Scots plays put on. There was quite an excitement, a kind of flowering of theatrical and cultural enterprise. So John announced that we were going to do a reading of this play at the conference, whatever state this play was in. He explained that in the play he wished us to make a connection between the exploitation of the Highlanders at the time of the clearances and the introduction of profitable sheep, and the subsequent (then-present) situation with the oil. So it wouldn't be just a historical document.

He came with a structure. Then we were sent away to research various bits and pieces. Billy, I think, did military history. I, because I'd spent a lot of my childhood on an island and I'd sat under these terrible ministers, I researched that. I actually wrote the Minister speech from personal experience, because every Sunday I suffered. We were dragged to the Wee Free Church, walked three or four miles, to sit under this terrible kind of hell fire and lament.

Working methods? In an upstairs room in the Odeon cinema, we all sat round with John in a circle and he went round trying this sentence or that and when he thought it was good, he wrote it down. He always wrote longhand. Then in the evening, he would go and tidy it all up and sometimes he would come in the next day with a whole new bit. Or sometimes he would come in with an idea for a song and we'd work on lines together or improvise and throw ideas around. We all got on terribly well and we found the same kinds of things funny. We laughed at one another, we appreciated one another's work. It was a very easy working relationship and very soon that coalesced within the group.

SC: *Was the politics in the group very overt? How politically conscious were you at the time?*

JB: I knew whose side I was on and I think that's one of the things I'm eternally grateful to John for, for reinforcing for me whose side I was on. So that wasn't a problem. Having read Prebble's book, which had come out not long before, *The Highland Clearances*, it wasn't problematic for me. I mean it's very easy to see who the bad guys were in these circumstances and not fall into the trap that it was English people. It was Lowland Scots against Highland Scots. It didn't fall into nationalistic lines.

SC: *What happened when you were uneasy about anything? Would John pronounce and say 'I'm still going to do it'?*

JB: More or less like that. I mean I remember discussing the role of a director with John. John said that he believed that really, in all honesty, a director was a benevolent dictator. And that in theatre that was how it had to be, you know. I think we did make mistakes trying to operate completely as a group. It's famous, I think, the story about the drumming; the fact that John thought he could be a drummer in the band. Everyone, he felt, should be able to use their talents across the board and therefore he could drum. So he was rather put out when he was voted out of the band!

So we went to the 'What Kind of Scotland?' conference, and, as far as I recall now, we mostly read with text at microphones, but there were a couple of little bits and pieces that we acted out. Dolina[27] sang her Gaelic songs and there was fiddle music and gags and laughter. There was a standing ovation; they wouldn't let us leave the hall. I mean it was a riot. It was a wonderful, wonderful evening. Lots of people came forward with ideas and information and strong contacts were made and alliances formed which lasted over the years, and John got a hell of a lot of feedback from people about the land leaguers, about historical things we didn't know about, which were then fed into the show.

15. 7:84 Scotland Company outside the church in Bowmore, Islay, during the
tour of *The Cheviot, The Stag and The Black, Black Oil.* 1974
(Photo: Barry Jones)

And we had another two weeks to go, so we then knew that we had something that was going to be astonishing.

SC: *Did you realize how tough touring was going to be?*

JB: You need to be young and fit really. I couldn't do it now and in fact it put me off for life really. I mean whenever my agent says there's a tour, I put the phone down. It was very tough and because it had never been done before, the vagaries of booking these halls were such that we tended to make the most incredible kind of leaps, going from Thurso to Oban to Islay to Fraserburgh—that sort of crazy geography. We were dotting back and forwards. And with the dancing, of course, the show went on till one o'clock in the morning. So then you had to pack up the van, travel back to your digs and then you were off somewhere else the next day, often quite early. And then on arrival at the new venue, there would be the setting up with the rostra and lights and everything else. And of course a lot of these halls weren't really equipped for this kind of thing. They'd never had theatre.

SC: *So everybody participated in every aspect? The driving, the setting up?*

JB: Yes, and we carried, because a lot of these halls didn't have black-out facilities, bin liners and plastic bags and lots of sticky tape. But the halls themselves, I'd never seen anything like it. I mean the whole village turned up, kids and all. These people in the Highlands were hearing their own history and some of it in their own language with Dolly singing the songs. We were talking about the oil, which was on their doorstep, so it was a very powerful emotive evening for them.

SC: *Did it change your view of theatre?*

JB: I guess I hadn't realized the possibility of that kind of response. The immediacy and pertinence to people's lives. Also, in lots of ways they were an unsophisticated audience who didn't know about the rules of theatre, the etiquette of sitting quietly etc. They didn't behave 'properly'. They shouted out, joined in the songs, roared their approval or disapproval of what was being said on stage. John would add local relevance by finding out, wherever we went, who the local landlord was. Then he would write a new verse for the song 'We are the men', which Billy and I did. So quite frequently we had one or two verses to learn before going on that evening. The response was wonderful, because people realized it was written for them. It was about their back yard. It was about their landlord, it was about something that they knew about. They'd get up and cheer or boo. That was fantastic.

And it changed. The show changed. It had a kind of slightly 'living newspaper' quality to it—in that whatever happened, because there were extraordinary developments happening with the oil politically day by day, then that was inserted into the show. The most famous was when Lord Polwarth was made Minister of Oil. John wrote a scene in which Alex as the Oil Supremo became a puppet and Billy and I worked him as if he had strings. And he had a song Lord of the Oil to the same tune as Lord of the Dance.[28]

Having gone through the Highland hall experience, we then came to the Lowlands and had a similar experience in the Citizens' in Glasgow and in the Lyceum in Edinburgh. In the Lyceum, I think they had to open the gallery for the first time in years. Queues round the block and a whole lot of interest by young people. I think that's why John then wanted in the next play to talk about industrial society and John MacLean.[29]

SC: *What was the experience like of making the television version? For most people, that is all they saw.*

JB: I know that it happened very quickly. Somebody had dropped out, a play had been cancelled and there was a gap in the schedule. They came to Cumbernauld to see the show, the producer and John Mackenzie,[30] and thought it was wonderful. I remember McGrath talking about how he wanted to do it, and the film *Cabaret*[31] being mentioned as a rough model. John was very keen that we should be seen performing *in situ*, that our work should show the relationship we had with the audience, in these Highland halls.

SC: *Where did you make it?*

JB: In Dornie. It's about ten miles east of Kyle of Lochalsh on the road to the Isles, where Eilean Donan castle is, so it's very scenic. John wanted to have the live show placed within the historical context, so we had re-enactments of the repression and the resistance. Visual images of the stuff that we could only bring to the stage in terms of reportage, such as the brutal treatment meted out to the women who resisted the sheriff's officers. There was constant interaction between the historical reconstructions and the stage show.

SC: *I think in some ways John resented being defined by that one show, because it was the one thing everybody saw.*

JB: Yes, I guess so. It did tend to haunt us all—for all kinds of reasons and also because in terms of touring theatre in the Highlands, it was a trailblazer.

SC: *After* Cheviot, *what did you go on to do with John?*

JB: The next show we did was *The Game's A Bogey* in 1974 which was going to tour working men's clubs. So it had a bigger band with proper musicians. I think there were certain key things that John wanted. He wanted the comic policeman and John MacLean and he wanted the story of MacLean and his ideas to be a motif in the show. He wanted to deal with education and the doctor and so on. He'd obviously decided that Billy would play MacLean, because he looks quite like him, and I would play, as I'd played before, some of the more establishment characters.

SC: *How did you feel about often playing the villains?*

JB: Well . . . often the devil gets the best tunes.

SC: *How long did you work together?*

JB: I did that show and then I came out of it.

SC: *But you rejoined later?*

JB: John came back to the Scottish company and asked me to take part in *Little Red Hen* in 1975. The hook to do that was the Maxton[32] speech, which is wonderful and straight out of Hansard. Maxton is speaking against a Tory motion to cut free milk to schools and his wife had just died two days beforehand from TB and Maxton refers to that in his speech and breaks down and loses the place and calls the Tory Home Secretary a murderer, and he refuses to withdraw this piece of un-Parliamentary language and, as a result, he is barred from the House of Commons. It was thrilling to do—that speech—and Harold Hobson, in the quirky way for which he was famous, dedicated his whole review to it in the *Sunday Times*. I thought *Little Red Hen* was a very important piece of work. And Billy was in that, being very funny.

SC: *So it was a regrouping of the original company in some ways?*

JB: Yes. Liz was the Little Red Hen and Billy was Ramsay MacDonald and Allan Ross was fiddler extraordinary, doubling as King George V. David Anderson and Billy Riddoch were others who had become regulars. I did the show when it came to the Shaw Theatre in London. I missed the Scottish tour. What happened was that, in a bout of extracurricular activity, I fell in a basement and broke my jaw, so I had to come out of the show before it opened in Scotland. I was in the rehearsal process and ended up with a wired-up jaw. And that's how I went to Amsterdam. There was an international festival going on at the Mickery Theatre and somebody dropped out. John phoned up. I was in Edinburgh at the time, and he said 'How would you like to come to Amsterdam?' And I said 'That would be great.' 'I'm writing a play for you.' 'But I'm wired up, I've got a wired-up jaw.' 'I know that. I'm writing a part for a guy with a wired-up jaw.' I said 'When do you want me to come?' ' Have you got a passport?' 'Yes.' 'This afternoon would be fine.' This was Thursday. And I said 'When do we open?' 'Monday.' 'What? In two weeks Monday?' 'Monday.' So he said 'Bring a typewriter.' John always wrote longhand. So I went there and I was staying in the same hotel as the actress Jenny Stoller. John was in another hotel, two doors down the street. I'd run up to his room and get the next two or three pages. He was lying in bed writing longhand. I'd type them, Jenny would read out the text and I'd type it . . . and then we'd learn it. John finished it on the Saturday and we rehearsed it on the Sunday and it opened on the Monday evening at the other end of Holland. It's called *Oranges and Lemons* (1975). It was the story of an entrepreneur, whom I played, who had been pushed out of the window by his girlfriend, because he was a greedy nasty capitalist swine. What is interesting in the play is that for once there is no socialist character. The socialist voice is the unspoken voice. So it was very interesting to do.

SC: *He was able to write that fast.*

JB: John was a very fast writer and often wrote work that was done rapidly for specific reasons. Many years later, with Lesley Joseph at Birmingham Rep, without a broken jaw, I did the play again. We went to see John about it and we didn't change very much, two or three lines. This play had been written in two and a half days, three days, and it stood up. It was amazing. And then interestingly enough I wanted to do it in Edinburgh and this was after the fiasco he'd had with *Women In Power* (1983), which I was not part of. I was going to do *Oranges and Lemons* with Vari Silvester, who was a long-term member of English 7:84. And John said 'no', because he felt he'd had such a bashing politically from the Arts Council and the press and he felt that the play wasn't political enough, that it wasn't right and he didn't want it done for those reasons. He didn't want to give his enemies a stick with which to beat him.

SC: *Then you worked together again?*

JB: Yes. I came back and was thrilled to come back to do *Border Warfare* in 1989. I thought the play was an amazing piece of work and I felt that John was vindicated after having had such a terrible time with the Arts Council. He just rose like a phoenix from the ashes after that previous disaster. And there was no compromise with it. He just wrote it as it was. And hell mend them. Structurally I think it was influenced by *Orlando Furioso*,[33] because I remember John years ago talking about these trucks racing in and out. He wanted that kind of sweep and *Border Warfare* certainly had that. It was very fast moving. Also I think Pamela Howard's work was very important to the success of the show. It knocked the audiences for six actually.

And then we did *John Brown's Body* in 1990, which was not a favourite show of mine really. It was an attempt to do the industrial history of the Clyde in a similar way to *Border Warfare*.

SC: *Why did you feel it didn't work?*

JB: Not enough time, I think, and the confusion about what it was saying. He had bits and pieces that he'd cannibalised from his own work, from other shows, from 7:84, old songs and things. So it was all a bit of a mess really, although some of it was fun to do.

Then I did *The Silver Darlings* for him. The show was really amazing and John told me, after we'd actually hit on a design for it, that Richard Eyre had turned it down at the National, saying it was unproduceable, because so much of the action takes place at sea. That was my great worry when I read it. We did it at the Citizens', but the set had to be adaptable because it was to tour the major theatres. It went to Aberdeen and Edinburgh as well. It was an amazingly powerful show. This was why I loved working with John. It was the discovery of things. Because it was poor theatre to begin with, you had to adapt, find ways of doing things. I have found that such a useful thing in my life, in my theatrical life—the necessity of finding new approaches.

I think that he cast very well. He spent a lot of time on casting, interviewing, auditioning and talking to actors and he cast people whom he thought were right for a range of parts and then he let them get on with it and I think that approach was very successful.

SC: *What was it like being directed by him?*

JB: He didn't do all that much. I mean he encouraged people to be as bold as possible. It was a different style of theatre for a lot of actors. Not so much for Billy, Alex and myself, because we'd done it. We knew about that contact with an audience, almost like Variety. But for some actors, it was not their style. It was difficult for them. In terms of actual directing, I don't know that John was all that hands-on. He expected you to get on with the acting. His concern was the text.

SC: *Was he too concerned about it?*

JB: No, I don't think he was too concerned about it. That was never a worry. What I meant was: he was concerned that the actor should reveal what was intended in the text. John made that clear. He was very good at that and it was helpful and insightful to see what the main point was. It was the clue quite often as to how to play a scene, the key to unlocking a puzzle. It seems a strange thing to say, but not all directors are keen on actors. Some of them feel that actors get in the way of realising their vision. John loved actors, admired their craft and was genuinely interested in the processes which lead to performance. He was a wonderful audience in rehearsal. No matter how many times a comedy scene had to be run through, John would always laugh. It was hugely reassuring.

Jenny Tiramani

Jenny Tiramani trained at the Central School of Art and Trent Polytechnic, Nottingham, where she was tutored by John McGrath while studying Theatre Design. She designed for Dundee Rep. and the Theatre Royal, Stratford East, before joining 7:84 England. Jenny continued to design many productions for both the Scottish and English 7:84 companies until 1985. In 2002 she designed John McGrath's HyperLynx, *the last play he wrote. Since 1997 Jenny has been Director of Theatre Design at Shakespeare's Globe.*

Jenny spoke at the conference about working with John and this was later expanded in an interview.

Most of the work that I've done with both 7:84 theatre companies England and Scotland, and with John McGrath and Elizabeth MacLennan since then, has been of a smaller scale; so I'm talking about a different kind of work to the large-scale projects described by Pamela Howard. I started working first with 7:84 England in 1978/79 when I did a production of *Vandaleur's Folly*[34] by John Arden. Then I went up to Scotland to start working with the Scottish company. The first thing I want to say is that sometimes in the theatre what you do doesn't seem to matter that much. I mean there are many different sorts of theatre and as a freelance designer, sometimes, unfortunately, one's involved in things that don't occupy your whole heart, mind, spirit, everything, every bit of you. Always, working with John McGrath, I felt what I did mattered as a collaborator. I felt that from the beginning, which was usually listening to an idea for a play from him. Mostly there wasn't a script straight away, because it's new work, and sometimes there wasn't a script until quite late on in the process. But all the way through to actually taking it to an audience and revisiting it with different audiences, I always felt that the work I did designing material both for the stage and costumes was vital and I still do.

What John Bett said about the Scottish style of acting being big and bold rang a bell for me, because I think my style of design has usually been quite big and bold. I always felt that I had that in common with John McGrath, and in producing the 7:84 work, I was always being encouraged to make as rich a statement as possible, as the person who provides, if you like, the matter for the evening, the physical matter on stage: both in terms of whatever the setting, environment, scene was, the way we staged it and what the actors wore and the style of design that hopefully related to the style of performance. So I think that that is something which isn't always associated, unfortunately, with political theatre now: that it should be such a rich telling of a story in every way, particularly in my terms, in terms of texture and colour.

Nowadays I quite enjoy subtle as well, but the first play I did for 7:84,

16a. John McGrath and Jenny Tiramani on the set of *Reading Rigoberta*. Theatre Workshop Edinburgh. 1994

Vandaleur's Folly, the design was described by Michael Billington as 'twopenny coloured rather than penny plain'. And of course that refers to black-and-white prints being penny plains, and the ones that are coloured in costing twopence. He meant it as an insult, and I didn't mind, because colour is something, to me, which our world should be about. Indeed it is what our world is about, and I've always resented too much theatre being monochrome, which it often is. It is very much easier to design something with very little colour. You do a black and white palette or maybe a cream palette. It's good taste, or it was, at the end of the twentieth century, what was considered good taste. But I don't consider full colour to be bad taste. It's just very much harder to handle.

Allied to that is the area of print, which in 7:84 was always associated with John Byrne's[35] incredibly drawn posters for 7:84 Scotland as well as his theatre design work. John McGrath was always absolutely adamant that every single thing that we produced had to have a quality to it and had to be done with great thought and contain an image that was related to the play. We needed big poster campaigns, a bit like a travelling circus, that people would see. We had a logo, which 7:84 already had before I joined, but it had always been done in a certain style and stencilled. I think one of the things that I developed was a relationship with X3 Posters whom I

16b. The Company 'crossing the Minch' in *The Catch*. Set by Jenny Tiramani.
7:84 Scotland. 1981
(Photo: Barry Jones)

already knew, and I felt their style would be very appropriate for 7:84.
They were silkscreen printers and produced beautiful handmade posters,
which you don't find now in anything like that style. John and I
collaborated with them on the posters. Very vivid images. Simple, if you
like, but bold images. Also the craft of it was very important, the message
was very important and the visual impact of it was very important. And
vivid colours. It was very much part of our work and then we'd take that
through in to the programme design. It was of a quality and an originality
of style, which really, I think, in John's mind, came from things that he'd
seen in East Germany and in Poland.

Those were the lessons I started to learn with 7:84. It was a sort of
learning curve really, that shouldn't ever stop, but that started for me with
visits, particularly to the Highlands, working on both *The Catch* (1981)
and *Blood Red Roses* (1980–1). We went up to Stornoway and the Western
Isles, because we were going to be taking a play back there, which was
directly connected to people's lives there. So we'd always go first and talk
to people, meet people, understand the situation, look at places, so that we

were never interpreting things as an outsider. I think particularly for a designer, although I guess for an actor too, that's a terribly important point. It doesn't mean that what you produce on stage is television naturalism. I don't mean that at all. I don't mean a sort of truthfulness that means you have to copy the world that you see or reproduce exactly, in what we would call a naturalistic way, a situation or an environment. But it does mean being truthful. And design often lies. Design in the theatre and in film often creates all sorts of myths about the past and the present which are very seductive. 7:84 taught me very early on that design is to do with making that particular work, that live work, directly connected with that audience. It's something that's led me to now really want to understand why somebody wears a turban, what it's made of and why it's that colour. It can inform everything and I think, particularly today, that's important to me in the world.

Respect for the people you are taking the play to is also, I think, terribly important, especially when you represent places. I mentioned Stornoway. Even though John and I went up to Harris and Lewis and Ullapool to look and to talk to fishermen and to people affected by the changing circumstances, for the play *The Catch* it turned out not to be enough. We got back and he wrote the play, having done the research and looked at places. Then he wrote a scene in Stornoway Airport, which was one place we'd not been to, and these are not places you find in coffee-table books or photographs. So we sent my husband at the time, Alastair Blotchie, who was up in Scotland as our scenic artist, on a day trip to Stornoway Airport. The poor thing, he didn't get outside the airport, but he spent something like five hours in there and it's only a small portakabin, prefab-type building, or it was at the time, to photograph it and to make sure we got it right.

The other thing about working with John and with both 7:84 companies was learning not to be a control freak about design. There is a way of approaching touring theatre which says 'This is my thing that I created and it has to be exactly like this everywhere. I'm going to put it into this situation and then I'm going to take it to another theatre and that's my work.' Well in this sort of theatre, making plays that are going to go to both theatre venues and non-theatre venues, that's not really what you're doing. You're actually taking it into situations and you're adapting it to that situation. In other words you're letting it react properly with the place it's in and how it can be presented in that place. That flexibility is a very difficult thing for a designer to take on board, because, unfortunately, of the way we are trained as visual artists in art schools, separated from actors, separated from directors and writers. I don't really hold with that sort of separation. And 7:84 has always been a company where I felt I was working with the actors, not just Elizabeth MacLennan, because we've worked together a lot, but all the actors. John was never the kind of controlling guru, who often exists in a theatre situation, who keeps the designer separated from the actors.

The other thing I want to say is, that if the audience taught me a lot of lessons about design and its place in this sort of theatre, so did the actors. When you haven't got a big team behind you, you must remember that your beautiful set has to go in the back of a small van, a Luton van usually. It has to be unloaded without too much damage by two crew and the actors and then it has to go back in quickly, leaving time for people to have a drink in the pub afterwards and not make their lives miserable, or make them get too tired or suffer injury. So this is a responsibility to bear, and two occasions come to mind. One when I'd done something really dreadful. I'd designed some metal trees for the tour of *Rejoice!* (1982), which, at the time, seemed a good way of making them. But they were heavy steel trees that were really unpleasant and all the weight was on one side, so you needed three people to lift them. And I remember one of the actors, Angela Bruce, trying to struggle with one of these into the van on the last night in Liverpool. And I remember us throwing them away, her saying 'I hate these trees. Why did you make them like this?', And me thinking 'Because I didn't think about it enough.' And actually they weren't very beautiful either; they didn't deserve to be in that show. But the opposite example was a show we did called *Big Square Fields* (1979), which we opened somewhere out of town, but it was coming to London, to the Albany Empire in Deptford and I came a few hours early before the performance for the fit-up, to see how everything was and see if I could help. In the Albany the first thing I saw was an actor on his hands and knees with one of the small backcloths on the floor, ironing the backcloth. It was Colum Meaney, the Irish actor. He wasn't a showy sort of person. And all the actors were putting the set together with great care. And I thought, 'Well it must be helping the performance, because everybody's looking after it, making sure that it doesn't get crumpled.' And that was great. Those were lessons really, in design that's working and not.

Elizabeth MacLennan

Elizabeth MacLennan started her career as an actress by performing in London's West End, playing leads in BBC television plays and acting in films. She originated 7:84 together with her husband John McGrath and her brother David MacLennan in 1971. In 1973, she was a founder of 7:84 Scotland, and she went back to live and work in Scotland with her family. She was closely involved with both companies, blazing a trail of popular political theatre across England and Scotland throughout the 1970s and 1980s. During the last fifteen years she has toured extensively with one-woman shows written by John

McGrath and has also written and performed her own play Wild Raspberries. *Her book* The Moon Belongs to Everyone[36] *describes the achievements and working methods of 7:84.*

She talked at the conference about the relationship between theatre and politics.

During the time of Pericles in Greece, the great period of classical theatre when Aeschylus was writing the *Oresteia*, and later, when Euripides and Aristophanes were at their height, the Greek word for actor was HYPOCRITIS. It meant somebody whose job is to scrutinize society, from the Greek verb 'to respond, to put under scrutiny'. Greek tragedies are about a whole society, not merely the individual, so the writers will raise public questions, and their representatives, the actors, will enact the choices of the protagonists, using ritual, music, some mockery, direct address and passing on information about what the larger forces at work are doing to the society, of which the collective audience is a responsible part.

This interaction between politics and performance was at the core of McGrath's writing and direction, particularly in the 'epic' plays—both small and large. A striking example is *Border Warfare*. It was done in 1989 when there was a growing awareness in Scotland that the Tories would

17. The Scottish Parliament of 1707 reconvenes in *Border Warfare*. Freeway Films/Wildcat Production. 1989

never restore the Scottish Parliament and that this must be addressed. *Border Warfare* was a huge epic performance in the Tramway Theatre in Glasgow, which showed the history of Scotland and the relations between Scotland and England, from the time of the Picts till Margaret Thatcher.

At one point, in the second act, the Scottish Parliament of 1707 was reconvened. It was a promenade production, performed in a huge space. Most of the time the audiences were walking around and stages came in on wheels. Enormous events were re-enacted in the play. England was at one end of the space, Scotland at the other. The audience is in the middle, taking part in the contestation. But, at the point at which the parliament was reconvened, many speeches were given from the floor by actors in full wigs, like the Duke of Argyll and the Duke of Hamilton and other figures who were there in 1707. You'd be sitting next to them in the audience. At the end of the sequence, an actor says 'And that is how the Scottish Parliament and nation abolished itself.' The audience were then asked: 'How would you have voted if you had been there that day? There will be now be an interval. Those who are voting for the Union, go through this door, and those who are voting against, go through that door, and there will be no abstentions.'

When we opened the show, I was in the audience, and I stood with my brother David, who was producing it, and John, who'd written and directed it, crouching in one corner of this vast shed, wondering 'What's going to happen?' Like a tidal wave, the audience moved towards the door which represented 'Against the Union.' A few stragglers, rather timid, went through the other door. This became a nightly event, which was, very soon thereafter, reported in the newspapers every day. As the event became known to the then Scottish MPs, because we didn't have our own parliament at that point, they started to sneak in and see what was going on. Of course everybody knew what they looked like, so when this point in the show came, the entire audience started looking. 'Here's Jimmy Maxton's nephew, John Maxton. Which way is he going to go?' Some Scottish MPs of that period, including Donald Dewar, who subsequently became the first Minister of the new Scottish Parliament, sat through the whole interval, too frightened to commit. That process has to be continued.

In a conference session, Elizabeth MacLennan was interviewed by Laura Cicognani.

LC: *I would like to start by asking you about the role of music and songs in McGrath's work?*

EM: When we were getting the material together for John's book *Naked Thoughts*,[37] I made a list of all the plays, that, as far as I know, exist, for the bibliography. You will find, that after he wrote the pop musical *Soft or a Girl?* (1971),[38] almost every play has music in it. So, instead of putting 'first performed at the Royal Court Theatre' or wherever, I've made a point of this. They are described as, for example: a play with music; a ceilidh play; a variety show; a musical play; a rock musical; a play with songs; a play with music; a musical show. Music is always there. It was central to him. Somebody yesterday remarked that McGrath was first and foremost a poet and lyricist, and that it is something that he never stopped being. The songs just go on and on and on. His last, as yet unperformed show, is a musical about the young Walter Scott, *Greenbreeks*. The styles of music and the use of music, whether it be rock music or folk music or *a capella* music or parody or satirical use of well known songs, it's an essential part of his theatrical vocabulary. Hopefully there will be a book of poems and songs coming very soon.

LC: *I want to ask you about the collaborative nature of the work. From ideas to discussions and then to writing.*

EM: This was particularly strong during the period when we had a permanent company, which was the first two years of 7:84 and the first five years of the two companies that followed. These were collective companies and things were discussed: ideas; politics; structure of the company; wages; which bar? Which hotel? Who stole the ashtrays? Everything. The subject matter was also discussed: the style; the type of music; in different ways with different shows. But, as people got to know each other better, they would be much more honest and it was easier to talk about the things that we were dealing with.

The way in which John wrote *The Cheviot* has been documented quite a lot and he researched it for years. During the writing process, there were ideas thrown in, but he always held the pen and the directorial reins. It was his show, but he encouraged everybody—technicians, musicians, actors—to find out about things and play with ideas and share them. Then, after he had written the play and directed it, they still felt responsible, not only as theatre-makers, but as people.

When the company developed as a slightly more sophisticated group, for example, we researched the question of drink and the Scottish psyche for the play *Out of Our Heads*. We actually had a paid week of discussion, which was a big luxury in those days. We couldn't afford to do previews or anything like that. We rehearsed for about three weeks and then we opened to the world's snarling press. That was the situation. So to pay people for a whole week to come and talk about a play they might not even be in, was the height of luxury! We talked about the subject of drink, the 'licence' it gives to certain types of behaviour. And it was hilarious, it was enormous fun. Some actors felt they didn't want to work like this and didn't take part.

It was an exchange of all our dreadful adolescent moments, which was very funny, which actually fed directly into the first five minutes of the second half of the play, when the group of children the play dealt with arrive in a pub for the first time. All under-age and all determined to strut their stuff in the bar, in that way that everybody has, at some point or other, done. There were about three or four minutes of complete hilarity with very few words, very little dialogue, but choreographed in detail by John, in which this adolescent relationship with drink was re-enacted with an audience. Sometimes in a mirror situation, because we played in a lot of places with bars and tables and people drinking. So that was an interesting example of how we arrived at things through discussion. It was tightly scored and written, but it was, if you like, initially 'devised' by the group. Improvisation was merely one of a range of rehearsal techniques.

He wrote *The Baby and the Bathwater* in 1984. John decided to do a play about political paranoia, because everyone at that time was getting very paranoid on the left and on the right and in the centre. And it *was* 1984. There were a lot of shifts in the language, with the right wing appropriating the language of radicalism and we wanted to deal with that. We started off wanting to write a play about Central America, which was at the time being hammered by the Contras etc. So we had a workshop, in which we acted, talked and exchanged ideas and music about stereotypes about Latin America and about Central America. Stereotypes about dictators and cigars and rolling cigars, all the visual clichés you could possibly imagine in that territory. It moved on into a discussion about the issues and so on, and how we would put the piece together theatrically. So styles were discussed and again music. At the same time, the company was doing a very different play, called *The Albannach* (which is Gaelic for 'The Scot'), an adaptation by John of a Highland story by Fionn McColla. The money was very tight and mostly taken up with *Albannach*. So we ended up with a very small company indeed doing *The Baby and the Bathwater*, and many of the people who had discussed it weren't even there. There was myself and Carlos Arredondo, who is Chilean and who didn't really need to have a big workshop, since he'd grown up and worked in Santiago and left in 1973 with half of his guitar and nothing else.

LC: *To come to the more recent work. We talked about* The Road to Mandalay.

EM: Two years ago, John was commissioned by a combined group of comprehensive schools in England and Wales to write a play

18a. Elizabeth MacLennan as Chuck Eagleburger in *The Baby and the Bathwater*.
1984

specifically for schools. It wasn't a local authority initiative. It
was people led. A couple of very imaginative head teachers got
together and e-mailed a bunch of other head teachers and said
'Do you want a proper writer to do a proper play for now?' They
asked John 'What would you like to do?' And he said 'It's the
anniversary of the Declaration of Human Rights. Let's do
something about that. Let's go and find out what the kids are

18b. Elizabeth MacLennan as George Orwell in *The Baby and the Bathwater*. 1984

interested in.' Everybody is always saying that kids under eighteen don't care about anything. That's not been my experience whatsoever.

So John and I led about thirteen workshops around the schools with fifty copies of the Declaration of Human Rights. We got groups of children together, between thirteen and seventeen, and we talked to them and said 'What do you think of this thing? Can you understand it? Can you read it?' We read bits out. We all read the fifty-two articles. It was very interesting to identify the things that they cared about. There were certain things they really cared about in there, and there were certain things they were surprised to find were in there. The ones they really cared about were: ageism; racism; sexism to an extent; slavery; child labour—all of which are prohibited by the Declaration of Human Rights. So once we'd got that going, we worked with and on examining stories about these things that they cared about. Some of them were stories that were in newspapers and I'd produce pictures out of newspapers, articles, programmes on the television: things they'd seen; things that had happened in their street and supermarket stabbings.

They started to tell us stories. They were different in every school, but there was a common pattern of their interests. There were certain characters they identified with. They identified with Lumumba[39] very much, who appeared in the play as head of the United Nations. They also identified very strongly with Martin Luther King. In one of their strongest improvisations, a group of Asian kids acted out their memory, their recollection of the 'I have a dream' speech in which the child who was playing Martin Luther King was surrounded and heckled by the National Front white kids of today. In other words they were transposing this story into their own experience. They acted out a racial incident springing from that speech, in which nobody acted black American, nobody acted West Indian. They acted Asian and National Front. They just lifted the bit of their history that they thought was important. It was quite a lesson.

We also found that the Asian girls were perhaps the most articulate group, which was quite a contrast to fifteen years before, when our boys were in a London comprehensive for a while and we had felt that the Asian girls were the most submissive quiet group among their friends. Now they had found their voice. In the group, I would say 'This is your article, your newspaper. Make a scene about this and show it to the others.' For example, I had a story about street children in Brazil and we'd find that often an Asian girl would take the lead, would be the spokesperson. We learned a lot. It really was a two-way process. Then John went away and wrote the play. Partly because the children were very shocked to hear about slave child labour in Burma today, he called it *The Road to Mandalay*. He used that song in the play, but he put new words to it about what they're up to there now. So he called it that and wrote it and sent it back to them. Then we came and did another series of workshops with the same schools about style and fun and theatricality and music and ways of doing the piece. It was a very reinforcing thing for us as much as for them. They were very engaged and funny and we found it very moving.

We found drama provision is very, very important in schools at the moment. We went to one quite impoverished school in Yorkshire where many of the dads were unemployed miners. They had five drama teachers. They used drama for history, for school plays, for social education and for fun. They used it for everything. But they didn't come out with easy solutions. There was no 'acting' going on. They came out with 7:84 type solutions, because community theatre has been influenced by our methods all over the country and their drama teachers were suggesting ways of doing things. For example: a scene between a judge and a criminal. The children would take two chairs and put them back-to-back. The judge would speak his verdict this way, the criminal would speak his story that way. They would divide up the audience. It was pure 7:84. It was a very nice feeling.

LC: *We've talked about the practice of naming the names and the responsibilities.*

EM: Information on the stage is important. John talked about it in *A Good Night Out*. People love to get the nitty gritty, they love to get the dirt. It's a very theatrical thing. You are allowed to have somebody get up and say 'This shit happened and these are the people who did it.' It's a marvellously coherent thing to do in the theatre and people love it. Often that role came to me and other people have done it as well. In *The Cheviot*, for example, we named the names of companies who were involved in the oil development and rip-offs at the time. 'And these are the people in our country who are doing it.' It's a very important part of John's writing in many of his plays, right up to *HyperLynx*, which I'm working on now. Naming names. *HyperLynx* deals with anti globalization, terrorism and the imminent threat of a US led war. It includes his own independent research, but it also uses shamelessly other sources like John Humphrys' book *The Great Food Gamble*, which names the companies that are controlling our water and our food. They're named. They can take it of course. But political activism on the stage is important and he believed it very strongly. It's important to say 'These are the culprits.' But it doesn't have to be solemn, not at all.

We did a play called *Boom* (1974) in the Highlands, and as we went through each county, we would get the figures of the 7:84 relationship in land ownership in that county. So we would say 'Here in Easter Ross, 2% of the population own 98% of the land. And do we know who they are?' Usually we could say exactly who they were. Nowadays they are trusts in the Cayman Islands and that you need to say too.

LC: *The last question is about John's involvement in the creation of the whole event, not just the writing.*

EM: It was a passionate belief with John that theatre is not just about the text on the page. I think he said in *A Good Night Out* that the dramatic text is what's left behind when the theatre's moved on—'the trail of the snail'—and that was a really difficult thing for somebody to say who believed passionately in words. It's a real hard thought-out thing. He believed that the whole experience is reliant intensely on all kinds of interaction. It's about the way people happen to be feeling. Whether the sun is still shining outside, or because they've had a terribly difficult journey to get there, or whether they've got a babysitter they can rely on at home, and whether they would rather have gone to the pictures or watched their regular series on the television. All these things affect people when they decide to come in to this place, pay their money and watch a play. They really are entitled to 'A Good Night Out'. It's a tough thing to commit to that activity and I think the striking thing about John's approach was a generosity towards that audience, a sense that they were not just punters, they were not what the theatre establishment calls 'bums on seats.' They're not. They're other people, they matter. So their event matters. And the price of their tickets, the place it is in and will we have music? What kind of music? The whole event is a huge adventure. He wanted to deal with the important things that happen in people's lives; whether it be births, wars, deaths, famine, recession and the current oppression from multi-national corporations. All the things that we deal with. Then the theatre really matters. And that is what I do it for, what I will continue to do it for and what *he* did it for. Literally to give people a good night out in all those senses of that word. To enrich their lives, their imaginative lives, their intellectual lives and their empowerment as active democratic children, old people, young people, people who can't manage the stairs, dancers, people who are written of as not possible for education, people who have problems. All of them. That is what it is for.

WORKS BY JOHN McGRATH

This listing of the works of John McGrath is taken from a fuller biblio-graphy that originally appeared in the *International Journal of Scottish Theatre (IJOST)*, vol. 2 no. 1 (June 2001). It was compiled by Ksenija Horvat and John McGrath. *IJOST* is a publication of the School of Drama and Creative Industries of Queen Margaret University College, Edinburgh.

Stage Productions

A Man Has Two Fathers, Oxford, Oxford University Dramatic Society, June 1958; Oxford Playhouse, July 1958

The Invasion, adapted from Arthur Adamov's play by John McGrath and Barbara Cannings, Oxford, August 1958

The Tent, London, Royal Court Theatre, 19 October 1958; London, BBC 3, 10 March 1960

Why the Chicken, Edinburgh, Oxford Theatre Group, 26 August 1959; English Tour, January–March 1960

Tell Me, Tell Me, London, Live New Departures, Institute of Con-temporary Arts Theatre, October 1960, tour

Take It, London, Live New Departures, Institute of Contemporary Arts, October 1960, tour

The Seagull, adaptation of Chekhov's play, Dundee, Dundee Repertory Theatre, 31 July 1961

Basement in Bangkok, music and songs by Dudley Moore, Bristol, a student group, 1963

Events While Guarding the Bofors Guns, London, Hampstead Theatre Club, 12 April 1966

Bakke's Night of Fame, adaptation of William Butler's novel *A Danish Gambit*, London, Hampstead Theatre Club, January 1968; London, Shaw Theatre, 2 October 1972

Comrade Jacob, adaptation of David Caute's novel, Falmer, Sussex University, Gardner Arts Centre Theatre, 24 November 1969

Sharpeville Crackers, London, Lyceum Theatre, April 1970

Random Happenings in the Hebrides, or, The Social Democrat and the Stormy Sea, Edinburgh, Lyceum Theatre, 7 September 1970

Prisoners of the War, adapted from the play by Peter Terson, Liverpool, Everyman Theatre, Everyman Theatre Company, 20 January 1971

Angel of the Morning, Plugged in to History, They're Knocking Down the Pie Shop, Out of Sight, My First Interview, five short plays produced as *Unruly Elements*, Liverpool, Everyman Theatre, 10 March 1971

Hover Through the Fog produced as part of Everyman's Festival of New Plays, Liverpool, Everyman Theatre, 19 May 1971; London, Bush Theatre, 25 July 1972 (with three plays); *Out of Sight*, London, King's Head Theatre, 13 January 1973

Trees in the Wind, Edinburgh, 7:84 Theatre Company at Cranston Street Hall, 25 August 1971; Liverpool, Everyman Theatre, 8 November 1971; Exeter, Northcott Theatre, 17 February 1975; 7:84 Theatre Company (England) on tour, 1979–80 including London, Royal Court Theatre, 22 January 1980

Soft or a Girl?, a rock comedy, Liverpool, Everyman Theatre, 24 November 1971; revised version *My Pal and Me*, Glasgow, Citizens Theatre, 1 April 1975 and tour by 7:84 Theatre Company (England); adapted by Stephen Lowe, Nottingham, Nottingham Playhouse, October 1974; adapted by Billy Colville, London, Half Moon Theatre, 29 May 1975

The Caucasian Chalk Circle, adapted from the play by Brecht, Liverpool, Everyman Theatre, date unknown, 1972

Underneath, Liverpool, Everyman Theatre, 7:84 Theatre Company (England) date unknown, 1972

Serjeant Musgrave Dances On, adapted from John Arden's play, Stirling, MacRobert Arts Centre, 7:84 Theatre Company (Scotland), Royal Lyceum Theatre, 22 September 1972

Fish in the Sea, music by Norman Smeddles, Liverpool, Everyman Theatre, 29 December 1972; revised version, London, 7:84 Theatre Company (England), music by Mark Brown, Half Moon Theatre, 11 February 1975 and tour

The Cheviot, the Stag, and the Black, Black Oil, Edinburgh, 7:84 Theatre Company (Scotland), 7 April 1973, Edinburgh, George Square Theatre, as part of 'What Kind of Scotland' conference (first public airing), tour; revised version, Edinburgh, Wildcat at Edinburgh Festival Theatre, 9 August 1991

The Game's a Bogey, Aberdeen, 7:84 Theatre Company (Scotland), January 1974 and tour, including Stirling, Macrobert Arts Centre, spring 1974; radio version, Radio Scotland, autumn 1979; Edinburgh, Netherbow Arts Centre, Scottish Youth Theatre, 9 August 1985

Boom, Golspie, Sutherland, 7:84 Theatre Company (Scotland), April 1974 and tour; revised version, Aberdeen, 7:84 Theatre Company (Scotland) at His Majesty's Theatre, October–December 1974 and tour

Lay Off, music by Mark Brown, Lancaster, 7:84 Theatre Company (England) at Lancaster University, 22 May 1975 and tour, including Bangor, Theatr Gwynedd, 9 June 1975, Liverpool, Everyman Theatre, 1 July 1975 and London, Unity Theatre, 10 July 1975

Little Red Hen, St Andrews, St Andrews Festival, February 1975; Edinburgh, 7:84 Theatre Company (Scotland) at Royal Lyceum Theatre, 15 September 1975 and tour; London, Shaw Theatre, 31 May 1976

Oranges and Lemons, Amsterdam, Mickery Theatre and tour of Holland, 1975; Birmingham, Birmingham Repertory Theatre Studio, 1 February 1977

Yobbo Nowt, York, 7:84 Theatre Company (England) at York Arts Centre, 1975 and tour, including London, Shaw Theatre, 8 December 1975, as *Mum's the Word*, Liverpool, Edge Hill College, 10 February 1977; as *Left Out Lady*, New York, Labor Theatre, 1981

The Rat Trap, music by Mark Brown, Amsterdam, 7:84 Theatre Company (England), 1976; London, Royal Festival Hall, 1976

Out of Our Heads, music by Mark Brown, Aberdeen, 7:84 Theatre Company (Scotland) at the Arts Centre, 1976 and tour, including London, Royal Court Theatre, 12 April 1977

Trembling Giant, English version, Lancaster, 7:84 Theatre Company (England) at Lancaster University, May 1977 and tour; Scottish Version, Dundee, 7:84 Theatre Company (Scotland) Dundee Repertory Theatre, 30 May 1977 and tour, including London, Royal Court Theatre, 20 December 1977

The Life and Times of Joe of England, Basildon, Essex, 7:84 Theatre Company (England), November 1977 and tour, including Holland and Belgium; adapted as *The Adventures of Frank*, in two parts, 'Play for Today', BBC TV, 4 and 11 November 1980

Big Square Fields, music by Mark Brown, Bradford, 7:84 Theatre Company (England), April 1979 and tour

Joe's Drum, Aberdeen, 7:84 Theatre Company (Scotland) at Arts Centre, 21 May 1979 and tour

Bitter Apples, Liverpool, 7:84 Theatre Company (England) at Everyman Theatre, 19 September 1979 and tour

If You Want to Know the Time, London, Royal Court Theatre, date unknown, 1979

Swings and Roundabouts, Aberdeen, 7:84 Theatre Company (Scotland) at Arts Centre, 26 February 1980 and tour

Blood Red Roses, Edinburgh, 7:84 Theatre Company (Scotland) at Church Hill Theatre, 18 August 1980, Edinburgh, George Square Theatre, 1 September 1980 and tour, including London, Stratford East, Theatre Royal; screenplay in three parts for Channel 4 TV, August–October 1985

Nightclass, music by Rick Lloyd, Edinburgh, 7:84 Theatre Company (England), George Square Theatre, April 1980; Glasgow, Third Eye Theatre, April 1980; Corby, Northamptonshire, March 1981 and tour, including London, Battersea Arts Centre

The Catch, or, Red Herrings in the Minch, music by Mark Brown, Edinburgh, 7:84 Theatre Company (Scotland) at Moray House Theatre, 15 August 1981 and tour

Rejoice!, music by Mark Brown, Edinburgh, 7:84 Theatre Company (Scotland) at Heriot Watt Union, 23 August 1982 and tour, including London, Battersea Arts Centre, date unknown

On the Pig's Back, with David MacLennan, Kilmarnock, Ayrshire, 7:84 Theatre Company (Scotland) and Wildcat Theatre, at People's March for Jobs, 1 May 1983 and tour, including London, Alexandra Palace

The Women of the Dunes, Ijmuiden, Holland, Regiotheater and tour, June 1983

Women in Power, or, Up the Acropolis, adaptation of Aristophanes' *Assembly of Women*, music by Thanos Mikroutsikos, Edinburgh, 7:84 Theatre Company (Scotland), Music Hall, 28 August 1983

Six Men of Dorset, adaptation of Miles Malleson's play, music by John Tams, Sheffield, 7:84 Theatre Company (England) at Crucible Theatre, 4 September 1984 and tour, including London, Shaw Theatre, 9 October 1984

The Baby and the Bathwater: The Imperial Policeman, Dunbartonshire, 7:84 Theatre Company (Scotland), Cumbernauld Theatre, September 1984 and tour; revised version, Edinburgh, 7:84 Theatre Company (Scotland), St Columba-by-the-Castle, 12 August 1985

The Albannach, version of Fionn MacColla's novel, Edinburgh, 7:84 Theatre Company (Scotland), Lyceum Studio, 3 March 1985; and tour in the Highlands including Merkinch, Community Centre, 5 March 1985; Dingwall, Town Hall, 6 March 1985 Invergordon, Royal British Legion, 7 March 1985 Bonar, Bridge Hall, 8 March 1985; Rogart, Rogart Hall, 9 March 1985

Behold the Sun, libretto by John McGrath and Alexander Goehr, Duisberg, West Germany, Oper-am-Rhein, 19 April 1985

All the Fun of the Fair, by John McGrath and others, London, Half Moon Theatre, 26 March 1986

Mairi Mhor: Woman of Skye, Edinburgh, August 1987, and tour

Border Warfare, Glasgow, Wildcat Theatre and Freeway Films, Old Museum of Transport, 23 February 1989

John Brown's Body, Glasgow, Wildcat Theatre and Freeway Films, Tramway Theatre, 20 March 1990

Watching for Dolphins, Edinburgh, Freeway Films, Theatre Workshop, June 1991

The Wicked Old Man, Leeds, West Yorkshire Playhouse, 1992

The Silver Darlings, adaptation of Neil Gunn's novel, Glasgow, Wildcat Theatre Company, Citizens Theatre, 17 August 1994; Dundee, Wildcat Theatre Company, Dundee Repertory Theatre, 17 October 1994

Reading Rigoberta, Edinburgh, Freeway Stage, Theatre Workshop, 19 August 1994

Half the Picture, by John McGrath and Richard Norton Taylor, London, Tricycle Theatre, 15 June 1994, later televised for BBC 2 transmission

The Last of the MacEachans, Edinburgh, Freeway Stage, Theatre Workshop, August 1996

Ane Satire of the Four Estates, adaptation of Sir David Lindsay's play, Edinburgh, Wildcat Theatre Company, International Conference Centre, 16 August 1996

Worksong, Scottish schools, TAG, 1 October 1997 and tour

HyperLynx, a rehearsed reading by Elizabeth MacLennan, Edinburgh, The Scotsman Assembly, Assembly Rooms, 15 August 2001. Extended by a second act, it was presented by Floodtide between May and September 2002 in Glasgow, Edinburgh and the Tricycle Theatre, London

Radio and Television

The Tent, radio, BBC 3, 10 March 1960

Bookstand, writer and director on arts series, television, BBC, 1961

People's Property, writer of *Z-Cars* episode, directed many other episodes, television, BBC 1, April 1962

Tempo, director of arts series, television, ABC, 1963

Diary of a Young Man, series with Troy Kennedy Martin, television, BBC, 1964

The Entertainers, writer and director of documentary, television, Granada, 1964

The Day of Ragnarok, television, BBC, January 1965

Mo, writer and director of documentary, television, BBC, 1965

Shotgun, with Christopher Williams, television, BBC 2, 1966

Diary of a Nobody, with Ken Russell, after George and Weedon Grossmith's novel, television, BBC 2, 1966

Ende der Vorstellung 24 Uhr, television, West Germany, 6 May 1970

Orkney, adaptation of George McKay Brown's stories, 'Play for Today', television, BBC 1, 13 May 1971

Bouncing Boy, 'Play for Today', television, BBC 1, 11 December 1972 and 25 April 1974

Plugged in to History, television, BBC 2, 13 January 1973

The Cheviot, the Stag and the Black, Black Oil, 'Play for Today', television, BBC 1, 1974

Once upon a Union, television, BBC 2, 12 March 1977

The Adventures of Frank, adaptation of *The Life and Times of Joe England*, 'Play for Today', television, BBC 1, 4 and 11 November 1980

Sweetwater Memories, writer and director of documentary, television, Channel 4, October 1984

Blood Red Roses, adaptation of the play, television, Channel 4, November 1985

There is a Happy Land, television, Freeway/Channel 4, 1987

Border Warfare, three part version of play, television, Freeway/Channel 4, 1990

John Brown's Body, three part version of play, television, Channel 4, 1990

Robin Hood, 20th Century Fox, screenplay by John McGrath and Mark Allen Smith, 1991

The Long Roads, television, BBC 2, 1992

Mairi Mhor, television, BBC 2, 1995

Half the Picture, television, BBC 2, 1995

Film

Billion Dollar Brain, screenplay by John McGrath and Len Deighton, from Len Deighton's novel, United Artists, 1967

The Bofors Gun, screenplay by John McGrath from his play *Events while Guarding the Bofors Gun*, Copefilms/Everglades/Universal, 1968

The Virgin Soldiers, screenplay by John McGrath, Ian La Fresnais and John Hopkins, from Leslie Thomas's novel, Columbia/Highroad/Open Road, 1969

The Reckoning, screenplay by John McGrath from Patrick Hall's novel, *The Harp That Once*, Columbia Pictures, 1970

Blood Red Roses, Other Cinema, 1986

The Dressmaker, screenplay by John McGrath from Beryl Bainbridge's novel, British Screen/Channel Four Films/Freeway/Sheldo, 1989

Mairi Mhor, Edinburgh, premièred at the Filmhouse, Edinburgh Film Festival, 20 August 1994

Carrington, producer, Polygram/Freeway Films, premièred at Palais des Festivals, Cannes, 21 May 1995; Edinburgh, Drambuie Edinburgh Film Festival, August 1995

Ma Vie en Rose, co-producer, CAB/CNC/Freeway/Haut et Court/Le Sept Cinema/Le Studio Canal/RTBF/TFI/WFE, 1997

Aberdeen, Freeway/Norsk Film, world première at Carlovy Vary International Film Festival, 2000, Audience Award at Hamptons International Film Festival, 2000, Young European Jury Award (Moland), Best Actress (Lena Headey) at Brussels International Film Festival, 2001

Books

A Good Night Out: Popular Theatre: Audience, Class and Form (London: Eyre Methuen, 1981; rev. edn 1984 and London: Nick Hern Books, 1996)

The Bone Won't Break: on theatre and hope in hard times (London: Methuen, 1990)

Naked Thoughts That Roam About, edited by Nadine Holdsworth (London: Nick Hern Books, 2002)

Published Playscripts

Tell Me, Tell Me in *New Departures* (London: 1960)

Events While Guarding the Bofors Guns (London: Methuen, 1966)

Jean Renoir, The Rules of the Game: a Film, translated by John McGrath and Maureen Teitelbaum (London: Lorrimer Publishing Ltd, 1970)

Angel of the Morning, Plugged in to History, They're Knocking Down the Pie Shop as *Plugged in* in *Plays and Players*, November 1972

Random Happenings in the Hebrides; or, *The Social Democrat and the Stormy Sea* (London: Davis-Poynter, 1972)

Bakke's Night of Fame (London: Davis-Poynter, 1973)

The Cheviot, the Stag and the Black, Black Oil (Skye: West Highland Publishing, 1974; rev. edn and London: Methuen, 1981)

Fish in the Sea, in *Plays and Players*, vol. 22, no. 7, April 1975 and vol. 22, no. 8, May 1975, also London: Pluto Press, 1977

The Game's a Bogey: 7:84's John MacLean Show (Edinburgh: Edinburgh University Student Publications Board, 1975)

Boom in 'New Edinburgh Review', 30, August 1975, pp. 11–30, with introduction by John McGrath

Little Red Hen (London: Pluto Press, 1977)

Yobbo Nowt (London: Pluto Press, 1978)

Joe's Drum (Aberdeen: Aberdeen People's Press, 1979)

Two Plays for the Eighties: Blood Red Roses, Swings and Roundabouts (Aberdeen: Aberdeen People's Press, 1981)

Jean Renoir, *The Rules of the Game: a Film*, translated by John McGrath and Maureen Teitelbaum (London: Lorrimer Publishing Ltd, 1990)

Six-Pack: the Scottish Plays (Edinburgh: Polygon, 1996)

HyperLynx (London: Oberon Books, 2002)

John McGrath—Plays for England, selected and introduced by Nadine Holdsworth (Exeter: University of Exeter Press, 2004)

NOTES

Chapter One

1. David Edgar, 'Festivals of the Oppressed', *The Second Time as Farce: Reflections on the Drama of Mean Times* (London: Lawrence and Wishart, 1988), p. 226.
2. E.P. Thompson, *The Poverty of Theory & Other Essays* (New York: Monthly Review Press, 1978), p. 8.
3. The most recently published collection, Nadine Holdsworth (ed.), *Naked Thoughts That Roam About: Reflections on Theatre* (London: Nick Hern Books, 2002), provides a wide range of examples of McGrath's critical essays, journalistic writings and introductions to his plays over a forty-year period. Some of these selections are relevant to this discussion, but my concern is with the earlier books, which both originated as lecture series at Cambridge University.
4. I include here John Arden's *To Present the Pretence: Essays on the Theatre and its Public* (London: Eyre-Methuen, 1977), David Edgar's numerous articles for *New Theatre Quarterly* and *The Second Time as Farce: Reflections on the Drama of Mean Times* (London: Lawrence and Wishart, 1988), and Steve Gooch's *All Together Now: An Alternative View of Theatre and Community* (London: Methuen, 1984). Joan Littlewood's *Joan's Book: Joan's Littlewood's Peculiar History As She Tells It* (London: Minerva, 1994) is more clearly an autobiography, but I would argue that her self-conscious strategies in the early work with Ewan MacColl in the 1930s, and later Theatre Workshop, were influential and encouraged many to articulate their own experiments.
5. John McGrath, 'TV Drama: The Case Against Naturalism', *Sight and Sound* 46 (1977), p. 105.
6. John McGrath, *A Good Night Out: Popular Theatre: Audience, Class and Form* (London: Methuen, 1981), p. 2.
7. ibid., p. 9.
8. ibid., p. 7.
9. ibid., p.18.
10. ibid., p. 36.
11. ibid., p. 21.
12. ibid., p. 92.
13. It may seem an idiosyncratic detail to note, but McGrath and Bourdieu died within a day of one another in January 2002. Because I had been thinking about the relationship between McGrath's ideas in *A Good Night Out* and Bourdieu's concerns in *Distinction*—and the hierarchical nature of artistic/activist and theoretical/academic discourses—the tributes to them seemed to

me markers of how constituencies identify and even measure the contributions
of major figures.

14. Pierre Bourdieu, *Distinction: A Social Critique of the Judgement of Taste*, translated by Richard Nice (Cambridge, Mass: Harvard University Press, 1984), p. 7.

15. ibid., p. 32.

16. ibid., p. 5.

17. ibid., p. 395.

18. McGrath, *A Good Night Out*, pp. 33–4. Note also David Edgar's reflections on this specific issue in his tribute to McGrath in *New Theatre Quarterly* 72 (2002), p. 306.

19. ibid., p. 97.

20. A large number of publications emerged in these years, including studies such as: John Clarke, Chas Critcher and Richard Johnson (eds) *Working-Class Culture: studies in history and theory* (London: Hutchinson, 1979), Jay Winter (ed.) *The Working Class in Modern British History* (Cambridge: Cambridge University Press, 1983), Tony Bennett, Colin Mercer and Janet Woollacott (eds) *Popular Culture and Social Relations* (Milton Keynes: Open University Press, 1986).

21. Examples include: Chris Rawlence's chapter 'Political Theatre and the Working Class' in Carl Gardner (ed.), *Media, Politics and Culture: A Socialist View* (London: Macmillan, 1979); Colin Chambers' 'Socialist Theatre and the Ghetto Mentality' in *Marxism Today* (August 1978); and Raymond Williams' 'Building a Socialist Culture' in *Leveller* (March 1979).

22. Raymond Williams, Foreword in John McGrath, *A Good Night Out*, p. x.

23. Nicholas Garnham and Raymond Williams, 'Pierre Bourdieu and the sociology of culture: an introduction', *Media, Culture and Society* Vol. 2, No. 3 (1980), p. 222.

24. Philip Corrigan and Paul Willis, 'Cultural forms and class mediations' *Media, Culture and Society* Vol. 2, No. 3 (1980), pp. 297, 310.

25. Coincidentally, Williams and Garnham note that intellectuals (specialized producers of symbolic goods) in their struggle with economic capital 'will always struggle to maximize the autonomy of the cultural field and to raise the social value of the specific competences involved in part by constantly trying to raise the scarcity of those competences. It is for this reason that while intellectuals may mobilize wider concepts of political democracy or economic equality in their struggle against economic capital they will always resist as a body moves towards cultural democracy' ('Pierre Bourdieu', 1980, p. 220).

26. McGrath, *A Good Night Out*, p. 1.

27. ibid., p. 85.

28. John McGrath, *The Bone Won't Break: On Theatre and Hope in Hard Times* (London: Methuen, 1990), p. 145.

29. ibid., p. 99.

30. ibid., p. ix.

31. ibid., p. 3.

32. ibid., p. 29.

33. I took up some of these issues in the afterword to *The Politics of Alternative Theatre, 1968–1990: the Case of 7:84 (Scotland)* (Cambridge: Cambridge University Press, 1996).

34. See chapters by Guy Van Gyes, as well as Mike Savage, Guy Van Gyes, Hans de Witte and Patrick Pasture (eds) in *Can Class Still Unite? The differentiated work force, class solidarity and trade unions* (Aldershot: Ashgate, 2001).

35. Ulrich Beck and Elisabeth Beck-Gernsheim, *Individualization: Institutionalized Individualism and its Social and Political Consequences* (London: Sage Publications, 2002), p. 30.

36. Ulrich Beck, 'Interview with Ulrich Beck', *Journal of Consumer Culture* Vol. 1, No. 2 (2001), p. 276.

37. Beck, *Individualization*, p. 31.

38. Beck defines individualization as 'a concept which describes a structural, sociological transformation of social institutions and the relationship of the individual to society' and makes it very clear it is not to be confused with the neo-liberal notion 'individualism' as an ideology. He notes 'it has nothing to do with the market egoism of Thatcherism or Bushism . . . always a potential misunderstanding in Britain and the US' ('Interview', p. 276).

39. Beck and Beck-Gernsheim position their ideas in relation to familiar models and maintain that 'new ways of living reveal dynamic possibilities for a reorganization of social relations, which cannot be adequately comprehended by following either Marx or Weber' (*Individualization*, p. 36). If it is not obvious already, it is worth noting that Beck distinguishes himself very clearly from postmodern thinking which he sees as an 'a-political, a-critical, end-of-everything attitude and perspective' ('Interview', p. 262).

40. The essay is reproduced in McGrath, Holdsworth (ed.), *Naked Thoughts*, pp. 228–39.

41. McGrath, *A Good Night Out*, p. 91.

Chapter Two

1. Arnold Wesker, *Chips with Everything* in *Wesker Plays: Volume 3* (Harmondsworth: Penguin, 1980), p. 42.

2. ibid., p. 40.

3. ibid., p. 34.

4. ibid., p. 62.

5. The interview with Itzin was originally published in *Theatre Quarterly* 19 (1975), the section on *Bofors Gun* is reproduced in Nadine Holdsworth (ed.), *Naked Thoughts that Roam About* (London: Nick Hern Books, 2002), p. 20.

6. John McGrath, *Events While Guarding the Bofors Gun* (London: Methuen, 1966), p. 8.

7. The submerged quotation is from Tennyson's *In Memoriam* (section I, stanza 1).

8. McGrath, *Bofors Gun*, p. 57.

9. McGrath, Holdsworth (ed.), *Naked Thoughts*, p. 20.

10. McGrath, *Bofors Gun*, p. 42.

11. ibid., p. 19.
12. ibid., p. 72.
13. McGrath, Holdsworth (ed.), *Naked Thoughts*, p. 182.
14. McGrath, *Bofors Gun*, p. 37.

Chapter Three

1. John McGrath, introduction to *Fish in the Sea* (London: Pluto Press, 1977).
2. Later performed by 7:84 with new title *Plugged In*.
3. John McGrath was actually born in Birkenhead, 'over the water' from the city of Liverpool.
4. George Rowell and Anthony Jackson, *The Repertory Movement* (Cambridge: Cambridge University Press, 1984), p. 157
5. Doreen Tanner, *Everyman: The First Ten Years* (Merseyside Everyman Company, 1975), n.p.
6. John McGrath, *A Good Night Out* , p. 51.
7. Michael Coveney, 'Everyman in Good Humour', *Plays and Players*, August 1975, p. 11.
8. John McGrath, *Birkenhead News*, 14 May 1971.
9. Maurice Weaver, *Daily Telegraph*, 22 October 1970.
10. Michael Billington, *The Times*, 22 October 1970.
11. McGrath, *A Good Night Out*, p. 50. It's worth noting that *The Braddocks Time* was not the first (nor by any means the last) musical documentary attempted at the Everyman. Stephen Fagan's *The Mersey Funnel* was created to mark the opening of Liverpool's Roman Catholic cathedral in 1967 (discussed above) and the Braddocks were followed by Enoch Powell (Chris Bond's *Tarzan's Last Stand*, 1973), the Fisher-Bendix occupation (Bond's *Under New Management*, 1975) and, of course, the Beatles (Willy Russell's *John, Paul, George, Ringo . . . and Bert* 1974 and Bob Eaton's *Lennon*, 1981)—amongst others.
12. John McGrath, 'Better a Bad Night in Bootle . . .' *Theatre Quarterly* Vol. 5, No. 19 (1975), p. 48.
13. The five plays which made up the original version of *Unruly Elements* were: *My First Interview; They're Knocking Down the Pie Shop; Angel of the Morning; Out of Sight; Plugged in to History* (although they were not necessarily performed in that order). Three of the plays were revived by 7:84 in 1972 and along with *Hover Through the Fog*, written for the Everyman in 1971, they were performed under the collective title of *Plugged In*. These three plays were published in *Plays and Players* (November 1972). *Plugged in to History* (directed by Alan Dossor) was also televised on BBC2's Full House on 13 January 1973. In this version the plays were directed by Alan Dossor, designed by Peter Ling and the cast included Gillian Hanna, Angela Phillips, Gavin Richards and Roger Sloman.
14. McGrath, *Plays and Players* (Nov. 1972), p. xiii.
15. ibid., *They're Knocking Down the Pie Shop*, p. xii.
16. ibid.
17. ibid., *Plugged in to History*, p. viii–ix.

18. ibid., *Angel of the Morning*, p. v.
19. ibid., *They're Knocking Down the Pie Shop*, p. ix.
20. ibid., A*ngel of the Morning*, p. iii.
21. ibid., p. v.
22. Alan Dossor, quoted in *Liverpool Echo*, 5 May 1971.
23. McGrath, *A Good Night Out*, p. 51–2.
24. Robin Thornber, *Guardian*, 20 May 1971. The other writers included John Arden, Stephen Fagan, John Hale, Charles Wood and Roy Minton. The evening as a whole was called *Everyman 71*, opening on 19 May 1971.
25. McGrath, *A Good Night Out*, p. 52.
26. McGrath, 'Better a Bad Night in Bootle. . . .' p. 48.
27. Ken Whitmore 'The Limelight Flashes on Our Side of the River', *Birkenhead News*, 19 November 1971.
28. McGrath, *A Good Night Out*, p. 52.
29. John McGrath *Soft or a Girl?* (manuscript) pp. 27–28. The play was once again directed by Dossor and designed by Peter Ling. The cast included Roger Sloman, David Goodland, Martin Fisk, Jean Hastings, Angela Phillips and Alison Steadman. Music was composed and performed by Petticoat and Vine (comprising Norman Smeddles, Syd Maddocks, Leslie Deegan, Colin Wightman and Val Coughlin).
30. ibid., p. 19.
31. ibid., pp. 34 and 61.
32. McGrath, *A Good Night Out*, p. 53. Scenes from the play were also taken to the local Fisher-Bendix factory and played during their occupation.
33. Martin Walser. Quoted in the programme for *The Caucasian Chalk Circle;* Everyman Theatre Archives, Cuttings 1971–72, Liverpool John Moores University.
34. Quoted in *Birkenhead News*, 10 May 1972; *Guardian* 3 June 1972. *Prisoners of War* was directed by Richard Eyre and the cast included Jonathan Pryce and Anthony Sher.
35. Doreen Tanner, 'Soft or Real Life?', an interview with Alan Dossor, *Liverpool Daily Post*, 28 April 1972.
36. John McGrath quoted in *Liverpool Daily Post*, 19 February 1971.
37. McGrath, 'Better a Bad Night in Bootle . . .', p. 48.
38. McGrath, *A Good Night Out*, p. 53. It's worth noting that Alan Dossor's final production at the Everyman in June 1975 was Chris Bond's play about the Fisher-Bendix occupation, *Under New Management*. This was followed by a visit by 7:84 in July with *Lay Off*.

Chapter Four

1. Elizabeth MacLennan, *The Moon Belongs to Everyone: Making Theatre with 7:84* (London: Methuen, 1990), p. 10.
2. On this see John McGrath, 'Better a Bad Night in Bootle . . .', pp. 48–49.
3. John Bull, *New British Political Dramatists* (London: Macmillan, 1984), p. 20. For a fuller analysis of the changes in the play see pp. 19–23.

4. MacLennan, *The Moon Belongs to Everyone*, p. 11.

5. From an unpublished interview with Clive Barker (1974).

6. ibid.

7. ibid.

8. Richards left immediately after to take over the running of Ken Campbell's Roadshow, and then on to Belts and Braces.

9. J. Hainsworth, 'John Arden and the Absurd', *Review of English Literature*, Vol. 7 (1966), p. 43.

10. John Arden, 'Introduction to *Serjeant Musgrave's Dance*', *Arden: Plays I* (London: Methuen, 1977), p. 13.

11. ibid.

12. Arden, 'Introduction to *Serjeant Musgrave's Dance*', p. 11.

13. Author's Preface, in *Arden: Plays I*, p. 5.

14. It is also very characteristic of Arden's own use of Music-Hall stereotypical humour, as Frances Gray points out, with specific reference to *The Ballygombeen Bequest*, in her *John Arden* (London: Macmillan, 1982), pp. 40–1. It is worth recalling in this context that the satirized figure of the property developer in *The Cheviot*, McChuckemup, first appeared in McGrath's *Trees in the Wind*.

15. Although the Bargee is not so obviously a figure of authority, in Arden's play he is active in preventing Musgrave from carrying out his revenge, and claims '*I* caught him, *I* caught him, *I* used me strategy'. (Act 3, Scene 1).

16. This borrowing from Arden's play of a recruiting meeting as a cover for the planned revenge has particular relevance at the time in which McGrath is writing, because in a period of rising unemployment recruitment into the Army can be made to seem an attractive alternative.

17. My stress.

18. Howard Brenton, 'Petrol Bombs Through the Proscenium Arch', *Theatre Quarterly*, Vol. 5, No. 17 (1975), p. 20.

19. See MacLennan, *The Moon Belongs to Everyone*, pp. 38–42.

20. From an unpublished interview with Howard Brenton by John Bull, quoted in Bull, *New British Political Dramatists*, p. 51.

21. Howard Brenton, *Marxism Today* (December 1988): quoted in Richard Boon, *Brenton the Playwright* (London: Methuen, 1991), p. 94

22. See Bull, *New British Political Dramatists*, pp. 46–9.

23. Howard Brenton, 'Messages First', *Gambit*, Vol. 1, No. 23 (1974).

24. On this, see John Arden, *To Present the Pretence: Essays on the Theatre and its Public* (London: Eyre-Methuen, 1977), p. 83; Gray, *John Arden*, pp. 89–90; MacLennan, *The Moon Belongs to Everyone*, p. 38.

Chapter Five

1. See Randall Stevenson's chapter in this book, p. 73.

2. McGrath, Holdsworth (ed.), *Naked Thoughts*, p. 92.

3. MacLennan, *The Moon Belongs to Everyone*, p. 71.

4. Letter dated 8 July 1975, 7:84 England Archive, Cambridge University Library (CUL).

5. Letter dated 8 July 1975, 7:84 England Archive, CUL.

6. Press release for 7:84 England's tour of *Fish in the Sea*, 7:84 England Archive, CUL.

7. Letter dated 22 October 1974, 7:84 England Archive, CUL.

8. Joanna Mack, 'Wit, Depth and Fun in Brilliant Play', *Western Mail*, 7 March 1975.

9. John McGrath preface to *Fish in the Sea* (London: Pluto Press, 1977).

10. ibid.

11. ibid., p. 72.

12. Sandy Craig, (ed.) *Dreams and Deconstructions* (Ambergate, Derbyshire: Amber Lane Press, 1980), p. 45.

13. McGrath, *Fish in the Sea*, pp. 32–3.

14. Janelle Reinelt, *After Brecht: British Epic Theater* (Michigan: The University of Michigan Press, 1994), p. 192.

15. McGrath, *Fish in the Sea*, p. 57.

16. Reinelt, *After Brecht*, p. 193.

17. Programme note for *Fish in the Sea*, 7:84 England Archive, CUL.

18. McGrath, *Fish in the Sea*, p. 82.

19. John McGrath, *Lay Off*, in Holdsworth (ed.), *John McGrath: Plays for England* (Exeter: University of Exeter Press, 2005), p. 262.

20. Naomi Klein, *No Logo* (London: Flamingo, 2000).

21. McGrath, *Lay Off*, in Holdsworth (ed.), *John McGrath: Plays for England*, p. 279.

22. ibid., p. 278.

23. ibid., p. 243.

24. McGrath, *A Good Night Out*, p. 96.

25. Letter dated 28 June 1975, 7:84 England Archive, CUL.

26. Beata Lipman, 'Cardiff', *Sunday Times*, 15 June 1975.

27. Anne McFerran, 'Monopoly Bop', *Time Out*, 11–17 July 1975.

28. John McGrath, preface to *Yobbo Nowt*, (London: Pluto Press, 1978).

29. ibid.

30. Michael Billington, 'Yobbo Nowt', *Guardian*, 9 December 1975.

31. Harriet Walter, 'The Heroine, the Harpy and the Human Being', *New Theatre Quarterly*, Vol. 9, No. 34, p. 111.

32. McGrath, Holdsworth (ed.), *Naked Thoughts*, p. 91.

33. Unknown author, 'Talented and Provocative Theatre Group', *Whitehaven News*, 26 June 1975.

34. McGrath, *Yobbo Nowt*, preface.

35. ibid., p. 3.

36. ibid., p. 2.

37. ibid., p. 18.

38. ibid., p. 15.

39. ibid., p. 57.

40. Michelene Wandor, *Carry On, Understudies: Theatre and Sexual Politics* (London: Routledge, 1986), p. 152.

41. John McGrath, 'Letters', *Time Out*, 29 April–5 May 1977.

42. McGrath, *Yobbo Nowt*, p. 61.

43. Billington, 9 December 1975.

44. Desmond Pratt, 'Theatres', *Yorkshire Post*, 7 November 1975.

45. Letter dated 2 June 1975, 7:84 England Archive, CUL.

Chapter Six

1. G. Gregory Smith, *Scottish Literature: Character and Influence* (London: Macmillan, 1919), p. 105; George Munro, 'The Adventures of a Playwright', unpublished typescript, Mitchell Library, Glasgow, p. 5; Christopher Small, Foreword to David Hutchison, *The Modern Scottish Theatre* (Glasgow: Molendinar Press, 1977), p. iii.

2. Femi Folorunso, 'Scottish Drama and the Popular Tradition' in Randall Stevenson and Gavin Wallace (eds), *Scottish Theatre since the Seventies* (Edinburgh: Edinburgh University Press, 1996), p. 177; Frank Bruce, *Scottish Showbusiness: Music Hall, Variety and Pantomime* (Edinburgh: National Museums of Scotland, 2000), p. 132. As Folorunso explains, music-hall and variety shows 'declined more slowly in Scotland than anywhere else in the United Kingdom': they were still widely at work in the 1960s.

3. Stewart Conn, *Play Donkey*, reprinted in *A Decade's Drama* (Todmorden, Lancs: Woodhouse Books, 1980), p. 128; Tom Gallacher, 'To Succeed at Home', *Chapman 43–4: On Scottish Theatre* (Spring 1986), p. 89.

4. Hugh MacDiarmid, 'R.F. Pollock and the Art of the Theatre', *Contemporary Scottish Studies* (1926; reprinted Manchester: Carcanet, 1995), p. 181.

5. Hector MacMillan, *The Rising*, reprinted in Bill Findlay (ed.), *Scots Plays of the Seventies: An Anthology* (Dalkeith: Scottish Cultural Press, 2001), pp. 82, 127.

6. John McGrath, *The Cheviot, the Stag and the Black, Black Oil* (London: Methuen, 1981), pp. xxvii, 77, 66.

7. 'From Cheviots to Silver Darlings: John McGrath interviewed by Olga Taxidou' in Stevenson and Wallace, *Scottish Theatre since the Seventies*, p. 154.

8. John McGrath, *Joe's Drum*, reprinted in *Six-Pack: Plays for Scotland* (Edinburgh: Polygon, 1996), p. 293; *Border Warfare*, in *Six-Pack*, p. 8; *Little Red Hen* (London: Pluto Press, 1977), pp. 2–3.

9. 'From Cheviots to Silver Darlings', *Scottish Theatre*, p. 151.

10. MacLennan, *The Moon Belongs to Everyone*, p. 43.

11. *Clydebuilt Souvenir Programme* (Edinburgh: 7:84, 1972), p. 3.

12. Hutchison, *The Modern Scottish Theatre* p. 106.

13. Critics have sometimes identified still further ancestors, and further connections of McGrath's work with a Scottish tradition. Barbara Bell suggests particular analogies with the Scottish National Drama of the early nineteenth century, largely based around adaptations of Sir Walter Scott's fiction, and dependent, she considers, on 'the very popular theatre forms McGrath identifies as forming the basis for his work' (p. 4). See Barbara Bell, 'From

Murray to McGrath' in Alasdair Cameron and Adrienne Scullion (eds), *Scottish Popular Theatre and Entertainment* (Glasgow; Glasgow University Library, 1996), pp. 1–11.

14. Gerry Mulgrew, 'The Poor Mouth' in *Chapman: On Scottish Theatre*, pp. 64–5.

15. McGrath comments of work included in *Six-Pack: Plays for Scotland* 'although these plays are written for Scotland, I am not ethnically Scots, being an itinerant Liverpool-Irish person of Welsh upbringing, Oxford and London training, and Scottish only by marriage, domicile and commitment' (p. ix).

16. Quoted in Bull, *New British Political Dramatists*, p. 29.

17. ibid., p. 16.

18. John McGrath, 'Is the Dream Over?' in the programme for *John Brown's Body*.

19. MacLennan, *The Moon Belongs to Everyone*, p. 148.

20. Only *apparently* unanimously, of course: McGrath's theatre could never assume that it was preaching to the converted, and never did, as he explains in 'The Year of the Cheviot', included as a preface in the Methuen edition of the play. See also Maria DiCenzo, *The Politics of Alternative Theatre in Britain, 1968–1990: The Case of 7:84 (Scotland)* (Cambridge: Cambridge University Press, 1996), pp. 180–1, 207–8, 218.

21. John McGrath, *Blood Red Roses*, reprinted in *Six-Pack* (note 8), pp. 223–4.

22. Sandy Craig, 'Unmasking the Lie: Political Theatre', in Sandy Craig (ed.) *Dreams and Deconstructions: Alternative Theatre in Britain* (Ambergate, Derbyshire: Amber Lane Press, 1980), p. 44.

23. See Baz Kershaw, *The Politics of Performance: Radical Theatre as Cultural Intervention* (London: Routledge, 1992), pp. 164, 161.

24. 'From Cheviots to Silver Darlings', *Scottish Theatre*, p. 157.

25. Hugh MacDiarmid, *A Drunk Man Looks at the Thistle* (1926); reprinted in Michael Grieve and Alexander Scott (eds), *The Hugh MacDiarmid Anthology: Poems in Scots and English* (London: Routledge and Kegan Paul, 1975), p. 97; preface to *Six-Pack*, p. viii.

Chapter Seven

1. John McGrath, *The Bone Won't Break*, p. 54.

2. John McGrath, 'The Year of the Cheviot' in *The Cheviot, the Stag and the Black, Black Oil*, p. vi.

3. Elizabeth MacLennan, *The Moon Belongs to Everyone*, p. 44.

4. ibid., p. 43.

5. John McGrath, 'Unpublished interview with Clive Barker, 1974' in Holdsworth (ed.) *Naked Thoughts*, p. 54.

6. Michael Lynch, *Scotland: a new history* (London: Pimlico, 1992).

7. Thomas Owen Clancy and Barbara E. Crawford, 'The Formation of the Scottish Kingdom' in R.A Houston and W.W.J. Knox (eds), *The New Penguin History of Scotland* (London: Allen Lane The Penguin Press, 2001), p. 28.

8. John McGrath, 'Introduction', *Six-Pack* (Edinburgh: Polygon, 1996), p. vii.

9. Bill Findlay, 'Beginnings to 1700', in Bill Findlay (ed.), *A History of Scottish Theatre* (Edinburgh: Polygon, 1998), pp. 23–24. See also, *passim*, Bill Findlay, 'Robert Garioch's *Jephthah and The Baptist*, Why he considered it "my favourite work"', *Scottish Literary Journal*, Vol. 25, No. 2, 1998, pp. 45–66.

10. See for instance his comments on the Royal Court Theatre in McGrath, *A Good Night Out*.

11. See Ian Brown, 'Gateways: from the past to the future' in Ian Brown (ed.) *Journey's beginning; the Gateway Theatre building and company, 1884–1965*, (Bristol: Intellect Press, 2004) for a more detailed argument that this repressive phase was effectively ended by the performance of John Home's *Douglas* in 1756 as a result of a conscious cultural *coup* by major Enlightenment and Kirk figures.

12. Barbara Bell, 'Murray to McGrath' in Alasdair Cameron and Adrienne Scullion (eds), *Scottish Popular Theatre and Entertainment* (Glasgow: Glasgow University Library Studies, 1996), pp. 3–4.

13. Donald Campbell, *Playing for Scotland: A history of the Scottish stage 1715-1965* (Edinburgh: The Mercat Press, 1996).

14. *A History of Scottish Theatre.*

15. Bill Findlay, 'Scots Language and Popular Entertainment in Victorian Scotland: the Case of James Houston' in Cameron and Scullion, *Scottish Popular Theatre and Entertainment*, p. 17.

16. ibid.

17. John McGrath, 'The Year of the Cheviot' in *The Cheviot*, p. viii.

18. Bill Findlay, 'Introduction', *Scots Plays of the Seventies* (Dalkeith: Scottish Cultural Press, 2001), p. xiii.

19. John McGrath, 'The Year of the Cheviot' in *The Cheviot*, p. xi.

20. Alasdair Cameron and Adrienne Scullion, 'W.F. Frame and the Scottish Popular Theatre Tradition' in Cameron and Scullion, *Scottish Popular Theatre and Entertainment*, p. 45.

21. ibid.

22. ibid., p. 46.

23. Cairns Craig and Randall Stevenson (eds), *Twentieth Century Scottish Drama* (Edinburgh: Canongate Classics, 2001), p. ix.

24. Maria DiCenzo, *The Politics of Alternative Theatre in Britain*, p. 87.

25. Femi Folorunso, 'Scottish Drama and the Popular Tradition', in Stevenson and Wallace (eds), *Scottish Theatre since the Seventies*, p. 176.

26. ibid., p. 177.

27. ibid., p. 183.

28. ibid., p. 182. In this passage Folorunso includes the following endnote with regard to what we 'now know': 'Cf. Robb Lawson, *The Story of the Scots Stage* (Paisley: Alexander Gardner, 1917) and James Dibdin, *Annals of the Edinburgh Stage* (Edinburgh: 1871). Although these books are very useful, especially as general introduction, they both lack detailed analysis. The best work I have come across in that direction is Sarah Carpenter's 'Drama and Politics: Scotland in the 1530's', Meg Twycross *et al.* (eds), *Medieval English Theatre*, Vol. 10, No. 2 (1988).'

29. Maria DiCenzo, *The Politics of Alternative Theatre in Britain*, p. 85.
30. McGrath, Holdsworth (ed.), *Naked Thoughts*, p. xvii.
31. John McGrath, *A Good Night Out*, p. 56.
32. ibid., p. 34.
33. Craig and Stevenson, *Twentieth Century Scottish Drama*, p. x.
34. John McGrath, 'Unpublished interview with Nadine Holdsworth, 23 May 1999' in Holdsworth, p. 221.
35. Maria DiCenzo, *The Politics of Alternative Theatre in Britain*, p. 86.
36. I am indebted to Bill Findlay for this insight, drawing on the work of Christopher Harvie in *No Gods and Precious Few Heroes; Scotland 1914–1980* (London: Edward Arnold, 1981). I am most grateful to Dr Findlay for his helpful comments and advice on drafts of this chapter.
37. John McGrath, 'Scotland: the Writing on the Wall', *The Weekend Guardian*, 1–2 April 1989, pp. 2–3, in Holdsworth (ed.), *Naked Thoughts*, p. 188.
38. Tom Nairn, *The Break-up of Britain* (London: Verso, 1981) p. 162, cited in Cairns Craig, 'Constituting Scotland', *The Irish Review*, No. 28, Winter 2001, p. 5.
39. ibid.
40. McGrath, Holdsworth (ed.), *Naked Thoughts*, p. xiv.
41. John McGrath, 'Scotland: the Writing on the Wall', *The Weekend Guardian*, 1–2 April, 1989, pp. 2–3, in Holdsworth (ed.), *Naked Thoughts*, p. 189.
42. Katja Lenz, *Die schottische Sprache im modernen Drama* (Heidelberg: Universitätsverlag C. Winter, 1999), p. 352.
43. Fiona M. Douglas, 'The Role of Scots Lexis in Scottish Newspapers', *Scottish Language*, No. 21 (2002) p. 2.
44. John McGrath, 'Scotland: the Writing on the Wall', *The Weekend Guardian*, 1–2 April, 1989, pp. 2–3, in Holdsworth (ed.), *Naked Thoughts*, p. 189.
45. John McGrath, Holdsworth (ed.), *Naked Thoughts*, p. xviii.
46. ibid., p. xvii.
47. Scottish Society of Playwrights, *Playwrights Register: Directory of Scottish Playwrights* (Edinburgh: Scottish Society of Playwrights, 2001).
48. John McGrath, 'Introduction', *Six-Pack*, p. ix.

Chapter Nine

1. *Wigan Evening Post & Chronicle*, 18 April 1975.
2. The whereabouts of shooting scripts and related papers for *TV Cheviot* remained unclear. With the help of Elizabeth MacLennan of 7:84 and Sally Harrower at the National Library of Scotland (NLS), however, significant documents have been located and I am able in this chapter to flesh out and share the story. In addition, I am grateful to BBC Written Archives Centre, Caversham Park, for permission to use archive and other BBC copywright material. Finally, I thank my colleague, Lez Cooke, who furnished me with the transcript of the interview cited here which he conducted with McGrath in April 2000.
3. Lez Cooke, unpublished interview with John McGrath, 27 April 2000.

4. From 1960, McGrath worked for five years in the BBC, writing and directing a range of programmes, including *Z-Cars*, which he initiated with Troy Kennedy Martin in 1962.

5. McGrath cited in Cooke, April 2000.

6. For information on Mackenzie's initiation and work on the *TV Cheviot*, I am indebted to a telephone interview I conducted with John Mackenzie on 21 January 2002.

7. The postponed project emerged subsequently as a Peter McDougall film, *Just Another Saturday*.

8. McGrath in Cooke, April 2000.

9. ibid.

10. ibid.

11. Internal BBC memorandum, 26 February 1974.

12. *The Cheviot, the Stag and the Black, Black Oil* including introduction, 'The Year of the Cheviot', p. vi.

13. A letter to McGrath, dated 7 June 1974, from John Prebble suggests that McGrath was mistaken in his belief that the speaking of Gaelic was actually banned by law. Prebble points out that, '*the speaking* of Gaelic was never banned *by law* [his emphases] although the work of the SPCK to eradicate it, and the fact that schools established by the Commission of Forfeited estates did not teach it, amounted to the same thing'. An ambiguity about the legal status of Gaelic appears to have run through history. I am grateful to Professor William Gillies of the Department of Celtic and Scottish Studies at the University of Edinburgh for confirming that, even at the time of writing of *The Cheviot*, resistance to the use of Gaelic remained in the upper echelons of the Civil Service, though there was no law actually debarring anybody from speaking it. A Gaelic Language Bill, sponsored by the late Donald Stewart MP, which sought to give legal status to the language was, however, talked out (*c.* 1975).

14. McGrath, *The Cheviot*, p. xxvi.

15. ibid.

16. ibid., p. xviii.

17. Marx, Karl and F. Engels, *Manifesto of the Communist Party* (Peking: Foreign Language Press, 1972), pp. 34–5.

18. Internal BBC memorandum, 26 February 1974.

19. McGrath's recollective reconstruction in Cooke, April 2000.

20. Sound transcript 2245, BBC Written Archive: 1, 1974, Reading.

21. ibid., 5, 1974, Reading.

22. ibid., 8–9, 1974, Reading.

23. ibid.

24. Cooke, April 2000.

25. ibid.

26. *Radio Times*, 30 May 1974, p. 10.

27. *Daily Telegraph*, 7 June 1974.

28. *Guardian*, 7 June 1974.

29. BBC Audience Research Report (1974), VR/74/347, p. 1 (BBC written Archive, Reading).
30. ibid., p.2.
31. All letters cited are held in the John McGrath archive, National Library of Scotland. So long after the transmission and the writing of these letters, it has not been possible to seek permissions to print extracts from them, but I hereby acknowledge the correspondents.
32. Letter to McGrath, dated 15 July 1974 in McGrath archive, National Library of Scotland.
33. For a discussion of the 1970s debate as it pertained to TV Drama, see T. Bennett, *et al.*, (eds), *Popular Television and Film* (London: British Film Institute/Open University, 1981), with reference to *Days of Hope*.
34. Internal BBC memorandum, 26 February 1974.

Chapter Ten

1. Bertolt Brecht, 'The Popular and the Realistic' in J. Willett (ed.) *Brecht on Theatre* (London: Eyre Methuen, 1964), p. 109.
2. ibid., p. 110.
3. ibid., pp. 107–8.
4. John McGrath, 'Introductory Notes', Two Plays for the Eighties: *Blood Red Roses* & *Swings and Roundabouts* (Aberdeen: Aberdeen People's Press, 1981), p. 5.
5. Quoted in interview by Lizzie Francke, in 'Bessie', *City Limits*, 16–23 October 1986, p. 32.
6. John McGrath, 'Blood Red Roses', *Sight and Sound*, November 1986, p. 361.
7. Georg Lukács, 'Narrate or Describe?', *Writer and Critic* (London: Merlin, 1978), p. 111.
8. John McGrath, quoted in Christopher Kenworthy, 'When battling Bessie took on the giants', *TV Times*, 5 December 1986.
9. Georg Lukács, 'Narrate or Describe?', p. 142.
10. Jennifer Selway 'The bark of a British mongrel', *Observer*, 31 January 1993.
11. John McGrath, Selway interview.
12. Raymond Williams, 'A Defence of Realism', *What I Came to Say* (London: Hutchinson Radius, 1990).
13. Raymond Williams, *Politics and Letters: Interviews with 'New Left Review'* (London: New Left Books, 1979), p. 221.
14. Judith Williamson, 'Permanent Revolution', *New Society* , 17 October 1986.
15. ibid.

Chapter Eleven

1. From *To an Island Princess*, in Robert Louis Stevenson's *Songs of Travel*, published in Janet Adam Smith (ed.), *Collected Poems* (Edinburgh: 1971).
2. A helpful list of books, book chapters, refereed journals and a selected number of newspaper articles can be found in the appendix to Ksenija Horvat, 'John

McGrath: An Updated Checklist and Bibliography', *International Journal of Scottish Theatre* Vol. 2, No. 1 (June 2001). The final reference, not included in Horvat's selection, is the title of an article in the *Daily Telegraph*, (Saturday 30 January 1993, TV & Radio section, p. 6) previewing *The Long Roads*.

3. This applies as much to formal lectures such as *A Good Night Out* (London: Methuen, 1981) as it does to brief introductions to his plays, such as the preface to *Six-Pack* (Edinburgh: Polygon, 1996).

4. In *Scottish International*, October 1971, pp. 10–15, reproduced in John McGrath, *Naked Thoughts that Roam About* (London: Nick Hern Books, 2002), p. 29.

5. Targets included the bourgeois theatre, of course, in all its manifestations and the straight political fight with the Conservative government from 1979–97. But there was also the prevailing ideology of such establishment but non-governmental organizations as the BBC and the Arts Council of Great Britain, metropolitanism, Naturalism (both on stage and on screen), American cultural imperialism, Scottish nationalism, English colonization of Scotland and a whole host of more specific battles over details within these bigger campaigns.

6. I have suggested elsewhere (in an obituary notice in the *Sunday Herald*, 27 January 2002) that when McGrath married Elizabeth MacLennan, whom he met as a student at Oxford, in 1962, he married Scotland too. In both cases, it was a marriage made in heaven which lasted all his life. McGrath without Scotland, and indeed vice versa, would have been a very different story. Widely differing types of people felt able to confide personal stories, not just about the Clearances, but about a whole range of history, folklore, song and story, which led directly to work running from *Random Happenings in the Hebrides* (1970, published in *Six-Pack*, 1996) through to *A Satire of the Four Estaites* (1996).

7. As far as I am aware, there is only one other work in this category, a BBC Play for Today called *Bouncing Boy* (1972), which was a comedy with feminist overtones. Everything else was an adaptation or reworking of existing material, either his own, originally written for the stage, or other people's. Some were notably original in other ways. In *State of the Union* (1977), another Play for Today, twentieth-century journalists door-stepped the leading figures in eighteenth-century Edinburgh over the events leading up to the Union of Scottish and English Parliaments. Much of the text, however, was taken from the historical record.

8. In the collection of Elizabeth MacLennan. I am very grateful to her for drawing it to my attention and for other generous assistance with this chapter, in particular details of the McGrath family history. The views expressed remain my own.

9. McGrath was a staunch supporter of his friend Troy Kennedy Martin's campaign to break out of the natural/realist school of television drama which had sprung up in the 1960s. He and McGrath put theory into practice at different times, working together on *Diary of a Young Man* (1964). McGrath was still making 'The Case Against Naturalism' in 1977 (*Sight and Sound*,

Spring 1977, pp. 100–5) and wrote and directed the highly experimental *Adventures of Frank* (1980).

10. In the *Daily Telegraph* interview quoted in note 2.

11. Best Writer, BAFTA Scotland, 1993. McGrath received a number of lifetime achievement awards but apart from a *Scotsman* 'Fringe First' at the Edinburgh Festival Fringe, nothing else for any specific work.

12. In *Keep Right On: Twenty Years of 7:84*, an *Ex-S* documentary for BBC Scotland, broadcast in 1993. Further unbroadcast parts of this interview, which was conducted by me, are included in McGrath (ed. N. Holdsworth), *Naked Thoughts that Roam About* (London: Nick Hern Books, 2002), pp. 163–5.

13. For a toe-curling account of McGrath trying to get an original play produced at this time, see McGrath, Holdsworth (ed.), *Naked Thoughts*, p. 197. *The Wicked Old Man* was eventually staged by Jude Kelly at the West Yorkshire Playhouse in 1992 where it promptly died from terminal indifference.

14. J. Caughie, *Television drama; realism, modernism and British culture*, (Oxford: Oxford University Press, 2000), p. 179 et seq.

15. *Theatre Quarterly*, Vol. V, No. 19, 1975, pp. 39–54.

16. The Broadcasting Act, 1980 (London: HMSO, 1980). J. Caughie, *Television drama*, p. 190, describes it as 'a licence to break the hidden rules of broadcasting'.

17. David Rose, McGrath's long-term collaborator, was replaced at Channel 4 as Head of Drama by David Aukin in 1990. Aukin had until then been chiefly associated with the National Theatre, not an organization McGrath had much time for and, understandably, had his own production slate. McGrath used to joke that after Aukin joined the board of Channel 4 in 1989, he, McGrath, never got another commission from it.

18. According to Tristram Powell, who directed the film, the official audience was 3.4 million. Interview with author, December 2002.

19. *Robin Hood* was for 20th Century Fox. *The Dressmaker* was a Film on Four, produced by Freeway.

20. Interview with the author, December 2002.

21. Powell confirms that, while McGrath very properly took no part in directing the actors or framing individual shots, he was heavily involved in every aspect of the production.

22. Apparently, these soirees were quite regular events. Powell had been among the guests on this occasion, which is partly why McGrath chose him to direct *The Long Roads*, though his experience with older actors in directing a three-part adaptation of Kingsley Amis's novel, *The Old Devils* (1991), not long before, was also a factor.

23. 'The Bark of a British Mongrel', *Observer*, 31 January 1993.

24. Recalled by Elizabeth MacLennan during an event at the Edinburgh International Book Festival in 2002 in the *Scotsman*, 23 August 2002, p. 6.

25. S. Frith, *Performing Rites* (Cambridge, Mass.: Harvard University Press, 1996, which makes the connection between critical analysis and the way most people actually talk about art, in his case music.

26. J. Caughie, *Television drama*, chapter 8.
27. All reviews quoted were published in editions either on the day of transmission or the day after.
28. I have not been able to establish with any certainty why he chose the title, apart from the obvious metaphorical reference to the journey of life and the distances we place between one another. He certainly knew the Stevenson poem quoted in the epigraph, which is the earliest reference I have discovered.
29. Sir William Burrell was a Glasgow shipping magnate who amassed a vast fortune in the first half of the twentieth century and spent a lot of it, with a discerning eye, on a substantial collection of fine and decorative arts. On his death, he bequeathed the entire collection to his native city. The City commissioned an award-winning building specifically for the collection.
30. Duncan Petrie, *Screening Scotland* (London: British Film Institute, 2000).
31. Colin McArthur (ed.), *Scotch Reels: Scotland in Cinema and Television* (London: British Film Institute, 1982).
32. In George Brandt (ed.), *British Television Drama in the 1980s* (Cambridge: Cambridge University Press, 1993), chapter 10.
33. The fictional island of Alexander McEndrick's classic Ealing comedy *Whisky Galore!* (1949).
34. This line is not in the original script. Edith MacArthur, who kindly lent me her copy of the shooting script to prepare this chapter, recalls that it was a suggestion by Robert Urquhart during filming which McGrath enthusiastically embraced.
35. See note 34. *Machair,* a Gaelic word which has been appropriated into English, is a unique habitat found on the sandy parts of the west coast of Scotland, especially the Western Isles, an extraordinarily lush carpet of flowers at the edge of the sea fertilized by deposits of seaweed and minerals from countless shells. As it turned out, the Highland weather declined to co-operate during the filming in July 1992 and the scene as filmed shows Peter in rough pasture in a blustery wind against a lowering sky. It is still beautiful, though, in a harsher way, a harshness which somehow makes the line all the more moving.
36. This is not to ignore the one-person plays McGrath wrote in the 1990s culminating in *HyperLynx* (2002), where the ideas were every bit as big although the resources were, perforce, small. But work on a large scale, which involves winning consent, including major funding, from others rightly commands more attention.

Chapter Twelve

1. 'Plugged in to History', *Plays and Players*, November 1972, p. viii.
2. John McGrath, *Watching for Dolphins* in Holdsworth (ed.), *John McGrath: Plays for England* (Exeter: University of Exeter Press, 2005), p. 331.
3. ibid., p. 326.
4. ibid., p. 340.
5. ibid., p. 337.

6. McGrath, Holdsworth (ed.), *Naked Thoughts that Roam About*, pp. 231–2.
7. Castoriades, quoted from McGrath's notebooks, quoted in Holdsworth (ed.), *Naked Thoughts that Roam About*, p. 234.
8. Cornelius Castoriades, *The Imaginary Institution of Society: Creativity and Autonomy in the Social-Historical World*, (Cambridge: Polity Press, 1997).
9. McGrath, Holdsworth (ed.), *Naked Thoughts*, p. 239.
10. John McGrath, *HyperLynx*, (London: Oberon Books, 2002), p. 32.
11. ibid., p. 44.
12. Drew Milne, 'Cheerful History: the Political Theatre of John McGrath', *New Theatre Quarterly*, 72 (2002), pp. 313–24.
13. John McGrath, *A Good Night Out*, p. 110.
14. John Caughie, in T. Bennett, S. Boyd-Bowman, C. Mercer and J. Woollacott (eds), *Popular Television and Film* (London: British Film Institute/Open University, 1981), p. 349.
15. McGrath, *Watching For Dolphins* in Holdsworth (ed.), *John McGrath: Plays for England*, p. 331.
16. McGrath, *HyperLynx*. p. 4.
17. John McGrath, *The Last of the MacEachans*, unpublished typescript, 1996, p. 16.
18. ibid., p. 16.
19. ibid., p. 17.

Chapter Thirteen

1. David MacLennan. John McGrath's brother-in-law. Writer and director. Co-founder of 7:84 and later Wildcat, of which he was Artistic Director.
2. Elizabeth MacLennan, John McGrath's wife. Danny and Finn are John McGrath's sons.
3. Play by John Arden and Margaretta D'Arcy. Performed by 7:84 in 1972.
4. Max Wall 1908–90. English music hall star who, late in life, also played in straight theatre.
5. Duncan Macrae 1905–67. Music hall star and actor.
6. Roddy Macmillan. 1923–79. Actor and writer.
7. Stanley Baxter b.1926. Comedian and actor.
8. Annual Glasgow Arts Festival.
9. In 1971 the Tory government decided not to keep the Upper Clyde Ship-builders afloat. A fourteen-month work-in ensued and saved the jobs of 8,500 people. Jimmy Reid was one of the leaders of the work-in.
10. b.1931. Scottish poet.
11. Theatre Director. Since 1993 Artistic Director of the Royal Lyceum Theatre Company, Edinburgh.
12. Workers' Revolutionary Party. Originally led by Gerry Healy.
13. International Marxist Group.
14. Workers' Revolutionary Party newspaper.
15. David MacLennan founded Wildcat in 1978. It specialized in musical theatre.
16. 1962.

17. 1923–82. Producer and writer. Became BBC Head of Series.
18. *Encore*, London, 1964.
19. James MacTaggart memorial lecture, Edinburgh International Television Festival, 1976.
20. Theatre and television director.
21. Feature film directed by Karel Reisz and written by David Mercer.
22. Patrick Hall (London: Heinemann, 1967).
23. Moonstone (an offshoot of the Sundance Institute) workshops founded by John McGrath for writers and directors.
24. 1970. Feature film directed by Mike Hodges.
25. John McGrath's adaptation of the novel by Neil M. Gunn, which he directed in 1994.
26. Scottish director and writer.
27. Dolina MacLennan, actress and singer.
28. Sydney Carter's hymn, written in 1963.
29. John MacLean 1879–1923. Founding father of Scottish Republican Socialism.
30. John Mackenzie directed the television version of *The Cheviot, the Stag and the Black, Black Oil*.
31. 1972. Directed by Bob Fosse.
32. James Maxton. 1885–1946. Leading figure in the Independent Labour Party in Scotland. Elected MP for Bridgetown, Glasgow in 1922. Pacifist.
33. *Orlando Furioso*. Play based on the work of Ludovico Ariosto (1474–1532). Directed by Luca Ronconi at the Spoleto Festival in 1969.
34. *Vandaleur's Folly: An Anglo-Irish Melodrama*, written by John Arden with Margaretta D'Arcy (also co-director:) produced 1978.
35. Playwright and designer.
36. Methuen, London 1990.
37. McGrath, Holdsworth (ed.), *Naked Thoughts That Roam About*.
38. Liverpool Everyman, 1971.
39. Patrice Lumumba 1925–61. African nationalist leader. First Prime Minister of the Democratic Republic of the Congo. Assassinated.

INDEX